T...
POOR...
FUGITIVES

D0715840

Brian Maidment

THE
POORHOUSE
FUGITIVES

*Self-taught poets and poetry
in Victorian Britain*

CARCANET

For Kathy and Caroline

First published in Great Britain in 1987 by
Carcanet Press Limited
208-212 Corn Exchange Buildings
Manchester M4 3BQ

This Fyfield edition published in 1992.

A CIP catalogue record for this book is
available from the British Library.
ISBN 0 85635 970 X

The publisher acknowledges financial assistance
from the Arts Council of Great Britain

Set in 10pt Bembo by Paragon Photoset, Aylesbury
Printed and bound in England by SRP Ltd, Exeter

Contents

5

2   THE PARNASSIANS

6

8

Acknowledgements

It is hard to offer acknowledgements for this book without offering a detailed intellectual history of my life. Nevertheless, many people have, knowingly or unknowingly, contributed to the compilation of this volume. First among them are many librarians, especially the keepers of local collections in the Greater Manchester and Lancashire areas, and the staff of Manchester Polytechnic Library, who have given me unstinting and courteous support. Booksellers, too, have been crucial allies, notably John Worthy, Ed Tyson, and George Kelsall. Many individuals have helped merely by understanding the value of the literature I discuss in the following pages, and by their personal support for the work. The encouragement of Louis James, Phillip Collins, Kathleen Tillotson, and Alan Bellringer has meant much to me. Martha Vicinus will always deserve my thanks not just for her interest but also for *The Industrial Muse*, to which this anthology forms a belated postscript. Paul Salvesen, Ruth and Edmund Frow, and Terry Wyke have all made important suggestions and recommended texts for inclusion. The Research Committee of the Faculty of Humanities, Law, and Social Sciences at Manchester Polytechnic has been generous in its support. The work on this volume could not have been undertaken without leave of absence and travel grants. I hope the Committee will feel its good faith has been justified.

Bigger debts still are owing to many of my colleagues in the Department of English and History at Manchester Polytechnic, with whom I have worked, and from whom I have learnt, over many years. Of many friends and fellow teachers Alan Kidd, Ken Roberts, Trefor Thomas, Tony Coxon, Laurence Coupe, Margaret Beetham, Alf Louvre, and Jeff Wainwright have contributed most directly to the writing of this book, yet their contributions are only the most obvious of many that must remain anonymous here. Successive generations of students have variously enjoyed, endured, and explained some of these texts and, more warily, responded to my explications of them. They deserve thanks, for their interest has been a constant source of encouragement. Mike Freeman and Michael Schmidt have been unfailingly consistent in their particularly agreeable version of what publishers ought to be. Robyn Marsack has contributed not only to the accuracy of the text but also to the pleasures of publication.

Above all other sources of strength, I would wish to recognize the consistent presence of Ian Rogerson, a most scholarly librarian, as the tutelary spirit in this book. The sense of an artisan tradition is as real to him as it is to me, and his energy in supporting its recovery has matched his pleasure in seeing the project grow.

Writing this book would have been a much less satisfying experience without the advice and friendship of all those I came into contact with during my research. The following anthology would have been the poorer without the presence of all its contributors, although none of them is to blame for its shortcomings.

Introduction

This book is a heavily annotated anthology of writing by, or about, a large number of Victorian writers who might be collectively described under a number of terms: 'poets of humble birth', 'uneducated poets', 'industrial poets', 'regional poets', 'auto-didacts', 'artisan writers'. The most obvious term would be 'working-class writers', but in fact I prefer to call this book an anthology of work by *self-taught* artisan poets. In using a cultural, rather than a political, economic, or geographical determinant, as the primary mode of discriminating the writing which comprises this anthology, I have deliberately stressed the literariness, the linguistic and formal self-consciousness, which is characteristic of writing by self-taught working men. The writings represented here are, of course, never innocent of political and economic meaning. Many readers will doubtless see this book as an anthology of working-class writing, making educational and cultural determinants subservient to other forms of class determination by an easy or unproblematic elision. But I think that the literariness of these poems — their sense of literary tradition, their obsessive allusions to other poems from other cultural locations, their sense of formal possibility, their confusion (or often creative tension) between subject and manner — is a major source of their interest. No literature as self-conscious as this offers a direct or unmediated account of class attitudes. What we have in these poems is a complex commentary on how the British poetic tradition might be read — or rather re-read and re-interpreted — in relation to various emergent senses of class identity. There is a strong case for reading the work of self-taught writers in primarily literary terms (as they themselves often wished), for we learn from reading these poems as much about the ways in which poetry might be read as we do about working-class beliefs and attitudes. In stressing these literary elements, and the importance of tradition, there is a danger of over-emphasizing the conservatism of much artisan writing, a conservatism which is both literary and social in its vision. But the literary issues raised inevitably also raise the ideological ones: how far are literary forms themselves, however ably appropriated to the needs of fast-developing working-class writers, an aspect of an inescapable middle class cultural hegemony, which would dominate the practice of writing whatever the ideological perspective of the author? This book is an anthology, so it seeks not to resolve but rather to raise and inform such important historical issues, in the hope that more readers and scholars will attempt the more detailed critical appraisal that poetry by self-taught writers still requires.

Within the whole field of Victorian self-taught and artisan writing, I have built this anthology round the identification of three traditions of literary endeavour. The first is a tradition of Chartist and radical writing linked specifically with other forms of political activism. This is not to suggest that such poetry is inevitably explicitly political in content, but rather to link its production to writers with known political engagements at other levels. Such a definition is not entirely satisfactory, and needs to be supplemented by a sense of the formal distinctiveness of Chartist and radical writing in comparison with other forms of self-taught literary production. This formal distinctiveness is evident in a number of ways: a differing sense of readership; a differing sense of the literary occasions for poetry, many of which depend upon communal or collective occasions within the political movement; a belief that major changes in consciousness can be described poetically, especially through the medium of symbols; and a continuing attempt to popularize poetic discourse and make its purposes explicitly popular. Chartist and radical poetry is addressed generally to two audiences — upwards to the aristocracy and Government, which it seeks to challenge or threaten, and outwards to the already converted radical groups and followers, where its function is confirmation and uplift, a way of furthering group feelings of communality and common purpose.

In these senses Chartist and radical writing is entirely different from the Parnassian strand in self-taught writing, which has as its aim the demonstration of cultural achievement within the working and artisan classes. The ambitions of Parnassian poetry are very obvious in terms of form and content — much Parnassian writing uses the most complex and elaborate traditional forms within the British literary tradition, from the Spenserian stanzas of Thomas

Cooper's *Purgatory of Suicides* to the sonnets of William Billington. Much Parnassian writing used the heroic couplet, and indeed found that form highly applicable to the kind of moral indignation which underlies much of this work. Yet the Parnassian strand in self-taught writing offers more than weak copies of anachronistic great poems from within the British tradition. First of all it represents a conscious cultural attempt to join in literary discourse at the highest possible level, to have a voice, on equal terms with all others, in the cultural and philosophical debates of the time. Clearly, as this anthology shows, this equality was illusory, but none the less, the endeavour was both culturally necessary and often personally heroic. In addition, Parnassian writing did have a more distinctively topical and social focus than the abstract forms of Romantic poetry which it sought to rival. Indeed, Parnassian poetry was at its best in discussing social issues through the forms and modes of eighteenth century moral and contemplative verse rather than in the ambitious philosophical abstractions derived from Shelley or Wordsworth. The subjects of Parnassian verse — the comparison of city and country, the breakdown of moral institutions under urban pressure, social injustice, domestic suffering, and human endurance — however 'unpolitical' or 'unradical' the treatment may have been, offered self-taught poets the opportunity to display their literary accomplishments in formal verse, and the whole strand of Parnassian verse became of central importance as the focus of a debate within the middle classes over the nature and purpose of working class cultural attainments. The ambition to rival the educated classes in poetry was clearly perceived as a rivalry in broader cultural and political terms. If Parnassian writing offered a social challenge at a less threatening level than Chartist poetry, still it served a crucial purpose in articulating artisan ambitions in a newly clear and precise way.

The third tradition I have identified is that of deliberately homely rhyming, often carried out in an entirely local manner, and through the medium of dialect or the vernacular. Deliberately shunning the inspirational ambitions of the Parnassians, the homely rhymers sought to articulate common feeling within the working and artisan classes at the lowest level of cultural ambition. The most common forms used are those of simple, short lyrics, short enough and bland enough to fill the poetry corner of a provincial newspaper. The strengths of homely rhymers are largely those of the identification and expression of the commonplaces of urban and industrial experience.

Clearly, these categories and definitions are not mutually exclusive, and several writers appear in all three traditions according to the chosen mode of their work. Using such terms carries the further danger of institutionalizing artificially imposed, retrospective perceptions of literary traditions, derived from current preoccupations of historiographical description of class and its development as a concept. The divisions I have made are meant to have primarily a literary weight, which seeks to avoid classifying poems mainly through an interpretation of their ideological intention. Not all Chartist poetry is simply 'radical' in its politics, nor is all homely rhyming conservative and conciliatory in its social perspective, even if the dominant literary tendencies can be identified roughly with certain ideological stances. However the reader attempts to deal with such complex issues, it is clearly wrong to *evaluate* the quality of such poetry through reference to the quality of its political analysis alone. While an original or deeply held political vision might produce complex poetry of high quality, it is the poetry and not the shades of political opinion which this book seeks to represent. The extent to which contemporary political preoccupations have shaped historical awareness of Victorian self-taught writers can be gauged by the selectiveness of published work. With the exception of Martha Vicinus's genuinely pioneering *The Industrial Muse* (1974), the emphasis has fallen heavily on Chartist writing, on local writing, especially in dialect, and on the genre of autobiography, in fact the only literary genre other than poetry much used by self-taught writers. These are of course the genres which appear to offer historians access to most factual details of artisan life, though most historians have until the last few years been notably insensitive to the complex nature of literature as historical evidence. Until the recent work of David Vincent, Patrick Joyce, and others, there has been no sense, for example, that autobiography might be a fictive genre with literary conventions of its own, and even these recent critics find the nature of literary evidence highly problematic. Dialect writing has always had its devotees, especially in the provinces, and Chartist and radical poetry has always survived as part of the proper endeavour of the socialist movement to retain a sense of the history of oppositional cultural activity. What I have identified as Parnassian literature is the main area which has received scant attention, perhaps for obvious reasons. Parnassian poetry has little in the way of overt political interest, its literary ambitions often outstrip the abilities of its writers, much of the verse is derivative, or often obscure in its mythological, classical, or historical allusiveness. Yet I think it is wrong to ignore this mode of writing as being necessarily less interesting than the oppositional or local strands of writing by self-taught authors. In representing all these traditions in relation to each other I follow the lead of Martha Vicinus, though I have tried to avoid using the same examples, or even the same authors, as she does — luckily, the number of self-taught writers and their abundant works make such variety possible.

Yet none of these studies, the most useful of which are listed at the end of this volume, have tried to read self-taught writers in relation to a persistent middle-class interest in them as an aspect of wider political and social development — especially as an aspect of class awareness. Not surprisingly, this middle-class interest was primarily *biographical* rather than literary, though the two were, to middle-class thinking, interdependent. The lives of the self-taught poets revealed more of the cultural aspirations, to say nothing of the hardships, of early industrial working-class life, than the poetry, which was often silent on precisely those matters which were of most interest to middle-class observers, commentators, and enthusiasts. The frequent turning away from literary evaluation into political and social commentary is obvious enough from a reading of the prose commentaries contained in this anthology — though the reverse, an attempt to dismiss self-taught writers by concentration on their technical inexperience, is also readily apparent. Middle class literary interest in self-taught writers was also inevitably ideological, and there is no doubt that the frequent intervention of the middle classes into self-taught writing — expressed in the various ways illustrated in chapters four and five — represented the extremely rapid formulation of a precise middle-class ideology for describing working class cultural activity.

This book, then, is written in the belief that ordinary readers and students have not had full access to the many sources available for considering the complex and interesting subject of Victorian artisan poetry. Partly a working anthology, it is also intended to be a guide to further reading, both in the sources listed for each extract, and in the brief reading list of recent criticism. Many of the extracts here have never been reprinted since their original publication, and I have tried to avoid well-known anthology pieces and local favourites. The enormous mass of available material which has been excluded from these pages can only be hinted at by what has been included. My aim has not been to try to unearth those forgotten masterpieces which might suggest an oppressive neglect within bourgeois historiography. I have not been able to discover, either, any substantial body of work by women writers within the artisan context, though this is an area where further research might be done. This said, I believe that much of the writing represented here does offer a powerfully expressed social vision. In the absence of easily available radical or oppositional literary genres, the continuing use of eighteenth-century modes of moral indignation by ambitious self-taught writers, and the use of near-oral, communal, simple lyric forms and literary occasions by politically or communally motivated writers, both suggest regard for poetic possibility, and a clear awareness of the nature of literary form. In short, much of the writing here is an intelligent response to prevailing literary and social constraints. Nor have I tried to find, as Vicinus does, 'authentically' working class or extremely 'oppositional' points of view: to evaluate this poetry in terms of its political ideology would lead to an entirely simplified view of the nature of self-taught writers and their work.

Some poems are here because they are merely typical. Much of the prose in this anthology is as illustrative of ideological process as of literary skill. Yet, this said, I think it has proved possible to discriminate in favour of the most competent and powerfully expressed examples of those processes of literary production which I seek to describe, without losing too much in the way of typicality. If many of the poems here are exceptional in their competence or success in the use of particular literary modes, they none the less represent many less well-achieved poems which aimed to do similar things. There are a few occasions when I have deliberately chosen a poor poem for its illustrative or instructive typicality, but generally I have not felt compromised as a historian of literature by trying to discriminate in terms of literary quality and achievement. The celebratory nature of chapters 1, 2, and 3 will only be fully grasped after reading chapters 4, 5, and 6. Given the tremendous social, economic, and ideological constraints under which self-taught writers wrote, an anthology of their work not undertaken out of respect, admiration, and sympathy would be bound to fail. Neither idealization nor patronage offer a proper approach. I hope the literary nature of my endeavour, underpinned by a respect tempered but not fundamentally challenged by critical issues, will offer this literature in a way that is not only accurate and instructive, but also moving.

There are a few authors I regret leaving out of this anthology. These will doubtless be added to all those which individual readers feel should not have been ignored. Readers in the North-East and in the industrial Midlands will surely feel that their own regions have stronger claims than those acknowledged here. Ellen Johnson is not here, though she has received her due elsewhere in Julia Swindells's study *Victorian Writing and Working Women* (Polity Press, 1985). Of the Chartists and Radicals, J. B. Leno is not here, nor the vigorous rhetoric of Robert Peddie whose *Dungeon Harp* deserves hearing. Many other writers, only half available through Kovalev's and Ashraf's work, are needed to fill out the Chartist tradition. John Overs, who is important through his correspondence with Dickens, and who published much of his work in *Tait's Magazine*, is not represented. Nor is the Midlands invalid George Heath. However, I believe that this anthology will have succeeded if it arouses the partisanship of its readers. More interesting still would be a fundamental challenge to the shape and structure through which this book constructs an account of self-taught writers. In representing the past through its literary production, we inevitably remake that past. At best the following anthology is only a version of what might have been.

List of Illustrations

The initial letters used on the cover of the book are drawn from
the illustrations to W. J. Linton's *The Poorhouse Fugitive*
(London, R. Oastler, 1845) and are by Thomas Sibson.

Chapter One

CHARTISTS AND RADICALS

William Thom of Inverury

Understandably, Chartist poetry has been of much more interest to historians than to literary critics. Indeed, the definitions of what might constitute a 'Chartist' or a 'radical' poem in early Victorian Britain have depended entirely on the contextual approach which historians have brought to this literature. Chartist and radical literature has thus been defined as either works written by authors known to have been active in popular or radical politics (regardless of the particular political position of any particular poem) or to be that literature which expressed political or social attitudes which were widely held by radical groups or individuals (regardless of the particular literary problems posed by such an approach). I think it is a pity that more attention has not been paid to the ways in which radical or Chartist poetry might be defined largely by the poetic genres used, or by analysis of the very specific symbolic language widely found in the political poetry of the 1840s, or by examining the nature of the readership, audience, and occasion presupposed in such poems. Chartist poetry, while quite various in mode and form, none the less possesses a number of common characteristics: a strong sense of orality, for example, or a strong sense of communal occasion and the appropriate rhetoric, or a willingness to align the devices of popular literature — pathos, melodrama, refrains, and catchphrases — with quite sophisticated literary skills in order to convey ideas or abstractions by emotional as well as intellectual means. Clearly the use of these techniques is closely linked to the particular and unique nature of Chartism as a popular political movement, but Chartist literature has a distinctive quality apart from the political points of view it represents. The address of Chartist poetry reveals its uncertainties along with its ambitions. Many poems presume a double, perhaps ultimately a contradictory, readership: one influential but intransigently hostile, the other politically sympathetic but powerless. How could one language, one form of address unite such differing readers in concerted political action? Even the form of action presupposed by Chartist poems showed an unsettling dualism: was significant social action adequately achieved in a change of attitude, or an extension of sympathy, or was the only action of any importance physical? In short, the recurrent problems specifically addressed by Chartist poetry were those of poetic form and address, the technical difficulties of achieving significant, communal rhetoric at a time of overwhelming practical urgencies.

The three main recent accounts of Chartist literature have been built from the assumptions that Chartist poetry can be defined adequately through the biographies of its authors, and through examination of the point of view expressed in the poems. Two of these books, Y. Kovalev's *An Anthology of Chartist Literature* (Moscow, 1956) and Mary Ashraf's magnificently detailed *An Introduction to Working Class Literature in Great Britain* (2 vols., East Berlin, 1978), which is both a critical study and an anthology based on a close study of the Chartist periodical press, are textbooks written for Eastern European students of British culture. It is amazing that there has been no British equivalent of these studies, and this book, brief as it is in comparison, at least allows British students access to some of this literature. I have placed Chartist and radical writing in a context which emphasizes its literary and cultural relationships to aspects of class development in the early Victorian period beyond the purely political. The narrowly political focus of Kovalev and Ashraf, which clearly is central to their purposes as educators, seems to me to deny the importance of literary allusion and tradition, and in addition oversimplifies the complexity of literary discourse as an aspect of class formation by seeking merely to *confirm* the existence of radical dissent more usually, and clearly, identified elsewhere in working-class culture. The third major account of Chartist literature, in Martha Vicinus's wider study of industrial literature *The Industrial Muse* (London, 1974) is largely a survey of the main writers and their works within an industrial and urban historical context. Her book, despite a vast number of misprints and some theoretical naïvety, remains a major pioneering study. It is an acknowledgement of the importance of all these studies that I need to explain the differences of my own approach. Not only have I tried in most cases to avoid using texts made available by these books, but I have also tried to give a more detailed sense of literary genre as a determinant not only of Chartist literature but of the whole way of thinking exemplified widely in the Chartist movement. Poetry, perhaps unexpectedly in view of the pressing political realities of the 1840s, formed an

important site for the working out of a number of Chartist preoccupations vividly illustrated in the following poems: what would a
revolution be like? how would it feel to live in a post–revolutionary
world? how is it possible to imagine a consciousness other than one's
own? how could the domestic and the hum–drum be linked to wider
political struggle? how could a radical history of Britain be written?
All these are issues addressed by Chartist poetry, in addition to its
obviously functional uses in the oral occasions of Chartist politics,
and they all raised considerable linguistic, generic, and formal
problems. The ambitiousness of Chartist poetry is of more than
passing interest, as the formal and technical issues of public political
poetry have still not confidently been resolved in Britain.

The following poems are printed approximately in chronological
order, but the majority date from the decade of most intense
Chartist activism prior to the disasters of 1848. I have tried in the
notes to stress literary characteristics rather than re-telling the
biographies of the authors or trying to explain the political assumptions
made in, and by, the texts, and the order of the poems is as much
dictated by their formal similarities as by their date or context. On
several occasions, authors who appear here as radicals or Chartists
also appear in the next chapter as 'Parnassians'. The distinction
between radical poetry and, for example, poetry of moral indignation
like J. C. Prince's 'The Death of the Factory Child' is a fine one,
which I hope to make largely in terms of literary mode, poetic voice,
and the poem's sense of presumed audience.

My aim in this chapter is to give some sense of the ways in which
specifically political viewpoints might be formulated poetically in
the early nineteenth century by those writers without access to
formal education, but with all the complex of resources, difficulties,
and grievances which were the inheritance of self-taught writers. It
should be said that many of the Chartist poets were of less deprived
educational and social backgrounds than many of the writers represented
in Chapters 2 and 3 of this anthology — indeed, a writer like Ernest
Jones was from quite an affluent middle-class background. However,
if the term 'self-taught' is stretched occasionally in this chapter, I
have been determined to look here at the common literary problems
of articulating minority and oppositional points of view, using only
those resources from bourgeois literature which seemed appropriate
or capable of subversion to those writers without automatic access
to literary culture. The results, if not always entirely successful in

their search for confident oppositional literary modes, do at least show powerful ways in which the oral and vernacular could be brought into touch both with changed political imperatives and with conventional polite discourse.

Alexander Rodger
THE TWA WEAVERS

From *Poems and Songs, Humorous, Serious, and Satirical* (New and
Complete edition Glasgow Alexander Gardner 1901), 113–116.

It is proper that this section of the anthology should begin with a
poem about the plight of the handloom weavers in the early Industrial
Revolution, for the decline of this proudly independent group of
workmen became a dominant symbol for the effects of industrialization on traditional rural industrial culture. As Rodger's note makes
clear, despite its early date, this angry dialogue foreshadows later
events. It raises a number of formal and generic issues which are
central to the reading of self-taught poetry in early Victorian England.
The poem is an eclogue, the dramatized conversation poem which, in
its classical form, had the celebration of the countryside and rural
virtues as its main intention. While classical eclogues were not without
an element of complaint over hard times or ruined crops, here the
source has been subverted by both subject (industrialization and its
social consequences) and tone (an interesting combination of anger,
wry humour, and stoicism). Yet in addition to its classical allusion,
the poem also draws on traditional ballads both in its language and in
its formulation of class difference, in terms which go back to the
sixteenth century and such poems as 'The Kings New Serving Man'
where a sense of injustice is formulated, as here, in terms of historical
comparison between then and now. In addition, Rodger's poem takes
strength from the Scottish vernacular song tradition, with all the
complex inter-relationships of vernacular and polite which that tradition
implies. Rodger (1784-1846) was by turns a silversmith, a weaver, a
poet, a music teacher, a cloth inspector, a pawnbroker, a journalist,
and an unrepentantly radical politician who had been imprisoned for
his political views. His first volume, a small collection of miscellaneous
poems, was published by Richard Carlile in 1821, under the authorship
of 'Alexander Rodger, an Operative Weaver of Glasgow'. In putting
'The Twa Weavers' at the beginning of this anthology, it is possible to
see how traditional dissent, and the use of traditional forms and
language in fresh political and social contexts, shades into the more
precisely directed political programme of the Chartist movement.

27

Author's note:

At the time this piece was written, the condition of the handloom weavers was sufficiently deplorable; but it was nothing compared to what their sufferings have been since that period. Year after year they have been wending the downward way to misery; and if at any time a glimpse of sunshine did appear, it was so transient as only to render the darkness of their condition more visible. In fact, the tale of the 'twa Weavers' may be looked on more as a prophetic enunciation of 'things to be' than of things that then actually 'were.' Written 1819.

When War and Taxation had fleec'd us right sair,
And made us, like scaur-craws, a' ragged and bare,
Twa poor weaver bodies a'e day chanc'd to meet,
Wi' scarcely a shoe on their stockingless feet:
Their lank ribs were seen through their cleeding to shine,
And their beards might have pass'd for a hermit's lang-syne.

'Weel, Robin,' quo' Tammas, 'what way do ye fend,
And do ye aye live yet, out-by, at Woodend?'
'Live! — live! I *live* naewhere; I starve at Tollcross:
Gude, I'm owre like you, and that is our loss;
For a' things around us against us combine,
Which mak' us look back wi' regret on langsyne.

'These three weeks a 'rinnin', I've risen at *three*,
An' wrought just as lang as a body could see;
An' a' that I've made o't, in that time, I trow,
Wad scarce get *potatoes* and *draff* for a sow:
What then! — we are counted a parcel o' swine,
And laughed at whene'er we look back to langsyne.

'But what need we speak o' our ain private case,
When famine and want are portray'd on ilk face;
When thousands, whose prospects in life were once fair,
Now pine in starvation, and sigh in despair;
When toil, and disease, and chill penury join,
To blast every comfort the poor had langsyne.

'But what is the cause, man' o' a' this distress?
And is there nae method to get it made less?

'The cause! tak' my word, there are causes enow,
And causes that lang may gar poor Britain rue,
Unless she return (as I humbly opine)
To the guid hamely fashions, in days o' langsyne.

'That lang, bloddy *war*, entered into by *Pitt*,
Has burdened her sae that to move she's scarce fit; —
Has cramp'd a' her energies — dried up her sap —
And driven her poor bairns frae her fostering lap;
And under that burden she must ever pine,
Unless she just *do* — as she *whiles did* langsyne.

'And that *Paper swindle* — O curse their Bank notes!
O that they were cramm'd down the bankers' ain throats,
For had it not been for their auld rotten rags,
John Bull might still had some *wind* in his bags;
But now he's bereft o' his good yellow *coin*,
That clinket sae sweetly in days o' langsyne.

'But volumes on volumes could scarce tell the skaith
Which that paper bubble — that engine o' death —
Has wrought to the world, by its fause gilded show,
While a' has been hollow, and rotten below; —
Soon, soon, may it burst! like a powder-sprung mine,
And then we may hope for good days, like langsyne.

'And see — we submit, like a parcel o' slaves,
To be tax'd and oppress'd by a junto o' knaves,
Wha buy themselves seats in our HOUSE, *up the gate*,
There laugh at our sufferings, and ca' that debate,
Whilst at our expense, their ain pouches they line;
L____d send them a Cromwell! like Cromwell langsyne.

'And mark! a vile, profligate, sinecure band,
Devouring by wholesale the fat o' the land,
Which from our industry is wrung every day,
To feed and to fatten such reptiles as they;
Whilst they on their sofas, supinely recline,
Unlike our AULD BARONS — the pride o' langsyne.

'But look nearer hame, and ye'll see how we're crush'd,
How toss'd about, trampled on, driven, and push'd,
And see how the working man's substance is shar'd,
Amongst the Monopolist, Taxer, and Laird,
Who, by screwing, and squeezing, and pinching, combine,
To *ghostify* him who was *substance* langsyne.

'And look at machinery, the bane o' our trade,
What thousands by it hae been reft o' their bread,
Yet where is the man who would wish it destroy'd,
Were it for the good o' the public employ'd,
Instead for supporting establishments fine,
O' chiels wha were scarcely worth twopence langsyne?

'And some o' our Priesthood (Gude bless the hale pack!)
How glibly, ilk Sunday, they lay aff their crack,
And tell their gull'd hearers, that these trying times
Are solely brought on by the poor people's crimes;
And then, wi' their sanctified cant, how they whine
About passive obedience, like hirelings langsyne.

'But, true to their Order, their interest, and coat,
Wi' their *triple-taed fork*, in the *Kirk-and-State* pot,
They wale for themsel's the best bit o' the *beast*,
On which they mak' sure aye to guttle and feast,
Whilst we and our families on tears aften dine,
And silently sigh for the days o' langsyne.

'Now these are a few o' the ills which, I think,
Have driven auld Britain to misery's brink,
And made her *free sons*, once intrepid and brave,
To envy the lot o' the African *slave*;
Poor Britain! how sadly thy glories decline,
How quench'd thy proud spirit — thy fire o' langsyne.'

'Hech, man! — if what ye now hae stated be fact,
Our prospects, indeed, are most gloomy and black;
But do ye not think they may yet brighten up?'
'Indeed, to be candid, I have nae siccan hope,
Unless the BLACK BOX to the flames we consign
And begin a new score, like our *Fathers* langsyne!'

A BUNDLE OF TRUTHS — A PARODY

Written about the time of Hone's trial. From *Poems and Songs*, 235–6.

A second example of Rodger's Regency radicalism, 'A Bundle of Truths' hits at all the familiar targets of early nineteenth century political dissent, a set of targets usually summarized as 'the Old Corruption'. In drawing on vernacular song and street balladry for his verse form and language, Rodger is using the mode of Blake's *Songs of Experience* and Shelley's *Mask of Anarchy* as well as those of Hone and his political allies. The political analysis remains largely moral, the values those of Enlightenment philosophical radicalism rather than of class politics.

> GEORGE, the Regent's, chaste and wise
> Castlereagh's an honest man,
> Southey tells no fulsome lies,
> England's free — likewise Japan:
> Sidmouth's acts are all upright,
> Canning's modest as a maid;
> Darkness can be proven light,
> So can Britain's debt be paid.
>
> > Hey triangle, derry down,
> > Doctor, old bags, wig and gown,
> > O how grave a judge can tell,
> > 'Truth's a libel — false as hell.'
>
> Johnny Bull is plump and stout,
> All his sons are fat and fair;
> Spies are worthy men — no doubt;
> Taxes are as light as air.
> Ellenborough's mild and just
> Ministers no rights invade;
> Prison keys are brown with rust,
> Jailors starve for lack of trade.
>
> > Hey triangle, etc.
>
> Parsons are a liberal race,
> Noble paupers waste no cash;

Everything now thrives apace —
Paper's sterling, gold is trash.
Parliament is pure as snow —
Vile corruption hides her head:
Everybody now must know,
Dearest grain makes *cheapest bread*.

Hey triangle, etc.

Trying times are fairly past;
Want no more dare show his face;
Treason is pent up at last,
Close within a *thimble's space**
Wealth has banished discontent,
Press and People both are free,
Doctor Sadmouth — pious saint —
Grunts 'Amen: so let it be'.

Hey triangle, etc.

* When the treason hunters made a domiciliary visit to Frank Ward, an honest working tailor of Nottingham, they searched every hole and corner for the expected 'treason,' but without success. One of the faithful, more knowing than the rest, narrowly inspected all the *thimbles* in the house, lest, peradventure, he might find the treason lurking there. — *Author's note*.

William Thom
WHISPERINGS FOR THE UNWASHED

From *Rhymes and Recollections of a Hand-Loom Weaver*, ed. W. Skinner (Glasgow, Alexander Gardner, 1880). First edition 1844.

While similar in political stance and social analysis to Rodger's 'The Twa Weavers', Thom's 'Whisperings for the Unwashed' shows a considerable development in the direction of more familiar Chartist idiom in its use of melodrama, its violent diction full of traditional political associations, and above all, in its fervent, if qualified, call to action. The kind of action called for in the poem's peroration is, significantly, moral and intellectual rather than directly political; Thom believes that the central role of the self-taught writer is that of raising and rousing popular consciousness. As his title suggests, Thom speaks for, rather than from, the dispossessed weavers in this poem, and only finds himself capable of hidden, but potentially subversive 'whisperings'. His political argument begins to move beyond a simple perception of social inequality based on the greed, inhumanity, and inherited privileges of the aristocracy and the State to a sense of the particular history of more closely defined social and economic groupings than the 'rich' and 'poor'. The 'you' so confidently addressed in the poem suggests that Thom was clear about his intended audience and that he perceived it to have a distinct identity based on common interests and values. In using the town drummer as a metaphor for wider calls to social and political awareness, Thom begins to shift his vernacular directness in the direction of the more sophisticated imagistic methods which characterize much explicitly Chartist poetry.

William Thom (?1799–1848), like Rodger, was admired by Victorian critics for his lyrics rather than his more extended social poetry. A handloom weaver in Inverury for much of his working life, Thom was greatly attracted by the literary life, and he was briefly fêted in London on the publication of his *Rhymes*. His later life was 'wandering and unsettled' according to a proposed memorial tablet inscription written by George Gilfillan, and Thom's susceptibility to both drink and flattery, coupled with the vicissitudes of his literary career, made him a frequently cited archetype of the self-taught, and self-destructive, poet.

'Tyrants make not slaves — slaves make tyrants.'

SCENE — A town in the North. TIME — Six o'clock morning.
Enter TOWN DRUMMER.

RUBADUB, rubadub, row-dow-dow!
The sun is glinting on hill and knowe,
An' saft the pillow to the fat man's pow —
Sae fleecy an' warm the guid '*hame-made*',
An' cozie the happin o' the farmer's bed.
The feast o' yestreen how it oozes through,
In bell an' blab on his burly brow,
Nought recks he o' drum an' bell
The girnal's fou an' sure the 'sale';
The laird an' he can crap an keep —

33

Weel. weel may he laugh in his gowden sleep.
His dream abounds in stots, or full
Of cow an' corn, calf and bull;
Of cattle shows, of dinner speaks —
Toom, torn, and patch'd like weavers' breeks;
An' sic like meaning hae, I trow.
As rubadub, rubadub, row-dow-dow.

Rubadub, rubadub, row-dow-dow!
Hark, how he waukens the Weavers now!
Wha lie belair'd in a dreamy steep —
A mental swither 'tween death an' sleep —
Wi' hungry wame and hopeless breast,
Their food no feeding, their sleep no rest.
Arouse ye, ye sunken, unravel your rags,
No coin in your coffers, no meal in your bags;
Yet cart, barge, and waggon, with load after load,
Creak mockfully, passing your breadless abode.
The sately stalk of Ceres bears,
But not for you, the bursting ears;
In vain to you the lark's lov'd note,
For you no summer breezes float,
Grim winter through your hovel pours —
Dull, din, and healthless vapour yours.
The nobler Spider weaves alone,
And feel the little web his *own*,
His hame, his fortress, foul or fair,
Nor factory whipper swaggers there.
Should ruffian wasp, or flaunting fly
Touch his lov'd lair, 'TIS TOUCH AND DIE!
Supreme in rags, ye weave, in tears,
The shining robe your murderer wears;
Till worn, at last, to very '*waste*,'
A hole to die in, at the best;
And, dead, the session saints begrudge ye
The twa-three deals in death to lodge ye;
They grudge the grave wherein to drap ye,
An' grudge the very *muck* to hap ye.

———

Rubadub, rubadub, row-dow-dow!
The drunkard clasps his aching brow;
And there be they, in their squalor laid,
The supperless brood on loathsome bed;
Where the pallid mother croons to rest,
The withering babe at her milkless breast.
She, wakeful, views the risen day
Break gladless o'er her home's decay,
And God's blest light a ghastly glare
Of grey and deathly dimness there.
In all things near, or sight or sounds,
Sepulchral rotteness abounds;
Yet he, the sovereign filth, will prate,
In stilted terms, of Church and State,
As things that *he* would mould anew —
Could all but his brute self subdue.
Ye vilest of the crawling things,
Lo! how well the fetter clings
To recreant collar! Oh, may all
The self-twined lash unbroken fall,
Nor hold until our land is free'd
Of craven, crouching slugs, that breed
In fetid holes, and, day by day,
Yawn their unliving life away!
But die they will not, cannot — why?
They live not — therefore, cannot die.
In soul's dark deadness sead are they,
Entomb'd in thick corkswollen clay.
What tho' they yield their fulsome breath,
The change but mocks the name of death,
Existence, skulking from the sun,
In misery many, in meanness one.
When brave hearts would the fight renew,
Hope, weeping, withering points to you!

Arouse ye, but neither with bludgeon nor blow,
Let *mind* be your armour, *darkness* your foe;
'Tis not in the ramping of demagogue rage,
Nor yet in the mountebank patriot's page,
In sounding palaver, nor pageant, I ween,

In blasting of trumpet, nor vile tambourine;
For these are but mockful and treacherous things-
The thorns that 'crackle' to sharpen their stings.
When fair Science gleams over city and plain,
When Truth walks abroad all unfetter'd again,
When the breast grows to Love and the brow beams in Light —
Oh! hasten it Heaven! MAN LONGS FOR HIS RIGHT.

Chartist Lyrics

The following group of Chartist lyrics, all of them written by non-professional poets whose main interest was in political activism, illustrate clearly the complicated inter-relationship of differing purposes for literature within the wider context of the Chartist movement. The initial function of these lyrics is to create and extend group identity and political solidarity. Both the sense of occasion and the formal construction of these poems point to orality and communality. Recitation was a method of reading which alluded to long traditions of oral and collective popular poetry, but lyrics like these also attempted to make a clear link between thought and action. Political contemplation and fellow feeling might be modulated into political activism through the medium of poetry. In my view, this close connection between reading and doing was seldom properly established because the recitation of the poem often seems to have served a *cathartic* effect rather than a persuasive one, so that the social aggression in the poem was sublimated or acted out rather than developed into action beyond the poem. Reading became to some extent a substitute for action, a self-contained political act without further implications.

A further function of these relatively simple lyrics is that of threat. They are addressed outwards to 'the enemies of the people' — the aristocracy, the Church, the yeomanry and magistrates, the mill owners — as well as inwards to the collective needs of the group. It is not easy to address both mill owners and a radical work-force at the same time and in the same language. Industrial ballads, which lie outside the scope of this anthology, are in particular riven by this kind of double, even contradictory form of address. Such problems are identifiable here as well as in more formally ambitious and sophisticated poems like J. C. Prince's 'The Death of the Factory Child' (p. 111).

Yet Chartist lyrics had considerable philosophical ambitions beyond their specifically topical political purposes. The dominant literary strategy in these poems is the playing off of carefully contrived, accessible, and memorable lyric forms against quite complex *symbolic* modes of writing. These apparently simple poems set themselves no less a task than that of describing the unknown, perhaps even unknowable, nature of dramatic political change and its inevitable consequences of violent changes in individual human consciousness. Contrary to the views of many middle-class analysts of the violent language of working-class writing, the 'cursing and swearing' that was so often remarked in self-taught political poets, the descriptions of the revolutionary process both at a political and an individual level are largely carried out through fervent, often very striking, use of extended symbolism reinforced by the careful use of specific lyric verse forms which enact movement, energetic release, and celebration. The symbols draw heavily on processes of change within nature — fire, floods, earthquakes, even glaciers — to stress the 'naturalness' of the revolutionary process. These ambitious attempts to bring into being post-revolutionary consciousness in and through language seem to me a major reason for examining Chartist lyrics in more detail; they subvert lyric assumptions in just the same way, for example, as Blake subverts the nursery rhyme. The lyric energy of these poems brings together the psychological drama of Romantic lyrics with a sense of specific political endeavour.

The following brief selection of lyrics is not meant to lead readers away from the much more detailed accounts of Chartist songs contained in Kovalev's anthology and Ashraf's historical study. Both of these writers have drawn on extensive reading of the Chartist periodicals where the enormous number of these lyrics testifies to their importance in the wider development of Chartist modes of political consciousness. I do not wish to detach Chartist lyrics from their specific historical context here, but rather to see them alongside other poetic genres in which political dissent becomes evident.

Ebenezer Jones
WHEN THE WORLD IS BURNING

From *Studies of Sensation and Event* (London, Pickering, 1879). This
volume reprints Jones's poems in a re-organized form, and includes
notes on the poems by R. H. Shepherd, and accounts of Jones's life
and work by Sumner Jones and W. J. Linton. 'When the World is
 Burning' is reprinted from *Ainsworth's Magazine* (January 1845).

[Stanzas for Music]

When the world is burning
Fired within, yet turning
  Round with face unscathed;
Ere fierce flames, uprushing,
O'er all lands leap, crushing,
  Till earth fall, fire-swathed;
Up amidst the meadows,
Gently through the shadows,
  Gentle flames will glide,
Small, and blue, and golden.
Though by bard beholden,
When in calm dreams folden, —
  Calm his dreams will bide.

Where the dance is sweeping,
Through the greensward peeping,
  Shall the soft lights start;
Laughing maids, unstaying,
Deeming it trick-playing,
High their robes upswaying,
  O'er the lights shall dart;
And the woodland haunter
Shall not cease to saunter
  When, far down some glade,
Of the great world's burning
One soft flame upturning
Seems, to his discerning,
  Crocus in the shade

W. J. Linton
THE GATHERING OF THE PEOPLE

From *The English Republic* 1851, 136–7.

A Storm-song

Gather ye silently
  Even as the snow
Heapeth the avalanche:
  Gather ye so!
Gather ye so!
  In the wide glare of day,
Sternly and tranquilly,
  Melt not away!
Flake by flake gather;
  Bind ye the whole
Firmly together —
  One form and one soul!
Are ye all gathered?
  Welded in one?
Hark to the thunder shout!
  Now roll ye on!
Roll ye on steadily;
  Steadily grow;
Swifter and swifter roll!
  Who stays you now?
Leap from your hill of right;
  Burst on the plain!
Ye were born in those valleys;
  There shall ye reign.
Roll on in thunder!
  Man's buildings are there,
Lo! they mock'd at your movement
  Now hide their despair!

Roll, roll, world-whelmingly! —
  Calm in your path
Glory walks harvest ward:
  God rules your wrath.

'It is accomplished:'
            Melt we away!
The Phoenix To-morrow
            Is child of To-day.

Gather ye silently!
            Even as the show
Buildeth the avalanche,
            Gather ye, NOW!

Edward P. Mead
THE STEAM KING

From *The Northern Star*, 11 February 1843.

There is a King, and a ruthless King,
    Not a King of the poet's dream;
But a Tyrant fell, white slaves know well,
    And that ruthless King is Steam.

He hath an arm, an iron arm,
    And tho' he hath but one,
In that mighty arm there is a charm,
    That millions hath undone.

Like the ancient Moloch grim, his sire
    In Himmon's vale that stood,
His bowels are of living fire,
    And children are his food.

His priesthood are a hungry band
    Blood–thirsty, proud, and bold;
'Tis they direct his giant hand,
    In turning blood to gold.

For filthy gain, in their servile chain
    All nature's rights they bind;
They mock at lovely woman's pain,
    And to manly tears are blind.

The sighs and groans of Labour's sons
　　Are music in their ear,
And the skeleton shades, of lads and maids,
　　In the Steam King's hells appear.

Those hells upon earth, since the Steam King's birth
　　Have scatter'd around despair;
For the human mind for heav'n design'd,
　　With the body, is murdered there.

Then down with the King, the Moloch King,
　　Ye working millions all;
O chain his hand, or our native land
　　Is destin'd by him to fall.

And his Satraps abhor'd each proud Mill Lord,
　　Now gorg'd with gold and blood;
Must be put down by the nation's frown,
　　As well as their monster God.

The cheap bread crew will murder you
　　By bludgeon, ball, or brand;
Then your charter gain and the power will be vain
　　Of the Steam King's bloody band.

Then down with the King, the Moloch King,
　　And the satraps of his might:
Let right prevail, then Freedom hail!
　　When might shall stoop to right!

James Syme
LABOUR SONG

Edinburgh, 14 December 1840. Published in *The Northern Star*,
26 December 1840.

Sir — the following stanzas were suggested by the Accidental
perusal of a Whig recommendation to the sons of toil to 'sing' at
their labour, and thereby render it 'almost a pastime'.

This song was sent to the 'feelosophers,' who perhaps only retailed the idea; but as they have taken no notice of it, I make bold to send it to a journal which I constantly read, and which rears its proud front despite of all the attempts of creatures like unto these 'Chambers' to destroy its influences.

I am, Sir, yours respectfully,

James Syme

Toil, brothers, toil; sing and toil,
    From earliest dawn till dark.
What matter, though kings and priests should spoil;
    You have nothing to do but work.

Go form the richest fabrics,
    And the costliest robes of gold,
To deck the legal plunderers,
    While you're shivering with the cold.

Sing, brothers, sing, sing and toil,
    Though ragged and scant of bread;
You are honoured — the palace deigns to spoil
    From the workman's lowly shed.

Toil, brothers, toil; let the anvil ring
    With clanging blows, and strong;
Go forge the ponderous bars, and sing
    (As you pant and sweat) a song.

Then sing, brothers, sing, 'the good and great,'
    Who tenant the gay saloon,
Who 'graciously' stoop from their high estate,
    And rob you! Blissful boon!

Toil, brothers, toil, sing and toil;
    Draw not the avenger's blade,
Though perjured legislators spoil
    Your famishing children's bread.

Raise palace homes upon the land,
    Send navies ocean o'er;

The sickle wield with sturdy hand,
  The sparkling mine explore.

Toil, brothers, toil, from dawn to dark;
  Let not the heart complain,
Though you have hardly aught, save work;
  The idler all the gain.

Then toil, brothers, toil, sing and toil,
  Let not a curse be said,
Though mitred knaves, and princes, spoil
  Each comfort from your shed.

Sing, brothers, sing, I'd have you sing
  But let your ditties be
Such anthems as can only ring
  From spirits that are free.

Oppression's funeral dirge go sing,
  And peal the dying knell
Of public plunder and each courtly thing.
  Such songs would suit you well.

Ernest Jones
THE SONG OF THE LOW

Published in several forms, and set to music, the following version of
this poem is from *Notes to the People* (March 1852), vol. II, 953.

> We're low — we're low — we're very, very low,
>   As low as low can be;
> The rich are high — for we make them so —
>   And a miserable lot are we!
>   And a miserable lot are we! are we!
>   A miserable lot are we!
>
> We plough and sow — we're so very, very low,
>   That we delve in the dirty clay,

Till we bless the plain with the golden grain,
      And the vale with the fragrant hay.
Our place we know — we're so very low,
      'Tis down at the landlord's feet:
We're not too low — the bread to grow
      But too low the bread to eat.

      We're low, we're low, etc.

Down, down we go — we're so very very low,
      To the hell of the deep sunk mines.
But we gather the proudest gems that glow,
      When the crown of a despot shines;
And whenever he lacks — upon our backs
      Fresh loads he deigns to lay,
We're far too low to vote the tax
      But we're not too low to pay.

      We're low, we're low, etc.

We're low, we're low — mere rabble we know,
      But at our plastic power,
The mould at the lordling's feet will grow
      Into palace and church and tower —
Then prostrate fall — in the rich man's hall,
      And cringe at the rich man's door,
We're not too low to build the wall,
      But too low to tread the floor.

      We're low, we're low, etc.

We're low, we're low — we're very very low
      Yet from our fingers glide
The silken flow — and the robes that glow,
      Round the limbs of the sons of pride.
And what we get — and what we give,
      We know — and we know our share.
We're not too low the cloth to weave —
      But too low the cloth to wear.

      We're low, we're low, etc.

We're low, we're low, — we're very, very low,
      And yet when the trumpets ring,
The thrust of a poor man's arm will go
      Through the heart of the proudest king!
We're low, we're low — our place we know,
      We're only the rank and file,
We're not too low — to kill the foe,
      But too low to touch the spoil.

      We're low, we're low, etc.

A CHARTIST CHORUS

From *The Northern Star*, 6 June 1846.

Go! cotton lords and corn lords, go!
   Go! Ye live on loom and acre,
But let be seen — some law between
   The giver and the taker.

Go! treasure well your miser's store
   With crown, and cross, and sabre!
Despite you all — we'll break your thrall,
   And have our land and labour.

You forge no more — you fold no more
   Your cankering chains about us;
We heed you not — we need you not,
   But you can't do without us.

You've lagged too long, the tide has turned,
   Your helmsmen all were knavish;
And now we'll be — as bold and free,
   As we've been tame and slavish.

Our lives are not your sheaves to glean —
   Our rights your bales to barter:
Give all their own — from cot to throne,
   But ours shall be THE CHARTER!

A Manchester Operative
JUST INSTINCT AND BRUTE REASON

From *Howitt's Journal* (6 March 1847) vol. 1, 132.

At first glance 'Just Instinct and Brute Reason' looks very like the preceding group of Chartist lyrics. It is different, however, in its non-oral, indeed profoundly literary and allusive, mode; in its place of publication, in a magazine of popular progress aimed at artisans but produced by well-meaning metropolitan cultural entrepreneurs; and not least in its startling density and attack. To use a relatively simple lyric for complex philosophical abstractions might seem foolhardy, but the anonymous author triumphantly combined personal anger at social injustice with a literary method at once accessible and profound. The argument put forward about the 'unnaturalness' of the industrial system links this poem with many others which depend on the contrast between city and countryside as metaphors for social change. Few of the other poems manage to define this contrast with the kind of abstract precision of the 'Manchester Operative'. Certainly Howitt, while acknowledging the poem's evident quality, recognized in it an intellectual and cultural challenge far beyond that conveyed by most self-taught poets, as his timid editorial commentary suggests.

> Keen hawk, on that elm-bough gravely sitting,
>   Tearing that singing-bird with desperate skill,
> Great Nature says that what thou dost is fitting —
>   Through instinct, and for hunger, thou dost kill.
>
> Rend thou the yet warm flesh, 'tis thy vocation;
>   *Mind* thou hast none — nor dost thou torture *mind*:
> Nay thou, no doubt, art gentle in thy station,
>   And, when thou killest, art most promptly kind.
>
> On other tribes the lightning of thy pinion
>   Flashing descends — nor always on the weak:

In other Hawks, the mates of thy dominion,
   Thou dost not flesh thy talons and thy beak.

O, natural Hawk, our lords of wheels and spindles
   Gorge as it grows the liver of their kind:
Once in their clutch, both mind and body dwindles —
   For Gain to Mercy is both deaf and blind.

O, instinct there is none — nor show of reason,
   But outrage gross on God and Nature's plan,
With rarest gifts in blasphemy and treason,
   That Man, the souled, should piecemeal murder man.

[Editorial comment] Our operative is severe, but perhaps his sufferings are, and for misery we must make ample allowance. At all events, he is a *poet*, and poets 'learn in suffering.' — EDS

Ebenezer Elliott
THE BLACK HOLE OF CALCUTTA

From *Corn Law Rhymes* 1834. This text is taken from *The Poetical Works* (William Tait, Edinburgh, 1840), 108–109.

Ebenezer Elliott (1781–1849) was easily the best known 'radical' self-taught poet of the early Victorian period. Elliott was the first self-taught writer to make any impression on middle-class consciousness, but this would perhaps not have mattered much if he had not become the rhyming spokesman for the Anti-Corn-Law League, a largely middle class pressure group who sought an alliance with various artisan and working-class groupings in pursuit of their political and economic reforms. Elliott was fortunate not just in the cause he wrote for, but also in coming from Sheffield, which meant that his voice was (however falsely) regarded as precisely representative of the manufacturing industries, and especially of heavy manual labour. That many perceptions of Elliott were wrong is not to the point: he served as a focus for middle-class accounts of the cultural and industrial progress of the 'unknown England' north of Birmingham, and could not escape being regarded as, in George Gilfillan's appalled phrase, 'the self-chosen deputy to Parnassus of the entire manufacturing class'. Elliott's fame was further ensured when his work was used as the central cultural expression described in essays by Carlyle, Gilfillan, and Kingsley, as well as in W. J. Fox's seminal essay which actually dates the beginning of working-class writing to the publication of *Corn Law Rhymes* in 1834. (These essays form a central part of Chapter 4.) Elliott certainly did not deserve to be admired only for his typicality. As an occasionally successful employer of labour, an erratically radical politician, and a poet of considerable variety whose best work belongs more properly to the next chapter, Elliott is interesting more for his untypicality, and for the staggering amount of interest his life and work generated within the liberal middle classes, than for his representativeness.

There were two biographies of Elliott published soon after his death, one by John Watkins and a second by 'January Searle', the Leeds progressive G. S. Phillips, and his work has always been a major source for students of industrial culture. Of recent criticism, Asa Briggs's essay in *The Cambridge Journal* (1950), 686–695 has been augmented, but not outmoded, by K. Chandler's 1984 thesis (Sheffield Polytechnic). There is also a bibliography by Simon Brown (Leicester University, 1971).

The following two poems from *Corn Law Rhymes* provide an extended essay in the short line, breathless couplets widely used in the radical vernacular idiom, and a triumphant hymn-like poem written in celebration of the 1832 Reform Bill. Both show Elliott's assurance in the popular idioms of radical poetry, even if their content is humanitarian rather than outspoken or subversive.

> What for Saxon, Frank, and Hun,
> What hath England's bread-tax done?
> As the struggle and the groan
> For the shadow of a bone;
> Like a strife for life, for life,
> Hand to hand, and knife to knife,
>
> Hopeless trader! answer me,
> What hath bread-tax done for thee?
> Ask thy lost and owing debts;
> Ask our bankrupt-thronged Gazettes.
> Clothier, proud of Peterloo!
> Ironmaster, loyal too!
> What hath bread-tax done for you?
> Let the Yankee tariff tell,

None to buy, and all to sell;
Useless buildings, castles strong,
Hundred thousands, worth a song;
Starving workmen, warehouse full,
Saxon web, from Polish wool,
Grown where grew the wanted wheat,
Which we might not buy and eat.
Merchant, bread–tax'd trade won't pay —
Profits lessen every day!
Sell thy stock, and realize,
Let thy streeted chimneys rise;
And when bread tax'd ten are two,
Learn what bread tax'd rents can do.
Sneak! that would'st for groat a–year
Sell thy soul, and sell it dear!
Self–robb'd servile! sold, not bought,
For the shadow of a groat!
Unbrib'd Judas! what thy gain,
By sad Europe's millions slain —
By our treasure's, pour'd in blood
Over battle–field and flood!
Bread–tax'd profits, endless care,
Competition in despair.
With thy bile and with thy gear,
Wheels and shuttles gainless here,
With the remnant of thy all,
Whither, reptile, wilt thou crawl?
What hath bread–tax done for me?
Farmer, what for thine and thee?
Ask of those who toil to live,
And the price they cannot give;
Ask our hearths, our gainless marts,
Ask thy children's broken hearts,
Ask their mother, sad and gray,
Destined yet to parish pay.

Bread–tax'd weaver, all can see
What that tax hath done for thee
And thy children, vilely led,
Singing hymns for shameful bread,

Till the stones of every street
Know their little naked feet.

Building lawyer's nominee!
What hath bread-tax done for thee?
Ask thy fainting thoughts that strive
But to keep despair alive;
Ask thy list of friends betray'd,
Houses empty, rents unpaid,
Rising streets and falling rents,
Money-fights for half per cents;
Ask yon piles, all bread tax built,
Guiltless, yet the cause of guilt,
Swallowing fortunes, spreading woes,
Losing, to make others lose.
Breadtax-eating absentee,
What hath bread-tax done for thee?
Cramm'd thee, from our children's plates,
Made thee all that Nature hates,
Fill'd thy skin with untax'd wine,
Fill'd thy purse with cash of mine,
Fill'd thy breast with hellish schemes,
Fill'd thy head with fatal dreams —
Of potatoes basely sold
At the price of wheat in gold,
And of Britons sty'd to eat
Wheat pric'd roots instead of wheat.

England! what for mine and me,
What hath bread-tax done for thee?
It hath shewn what kinglings are,
Stripped thy hideous idols bare,
Sold thy greatness, stain'd thy name,
Struck thee from the rolls of fame,
Given thy fields to civil strife,
Changed thy falchion for the knife,
To th' invading knout consign'd
Basest back, and meanest mind,
Cursed thy harvests, cursed thy land,
Hunger-stung thy skill'd right hand,

Sent thy riches to thy foes,
Kick'd thy breech, and tweak'd thy nose,
And beneath the western skies
Sown the worm that never dies.

Man of Consols, hark to me!
What shall bread-tax do for thee?
Rob thee for the dead-alive,
Pawn thy thousands ten for five,
And, ere yet its work be done,
Pawn thy thousands five for one.

What shall bread-tax yet for thee,
Palaced pauper? We shall see.
It shall tame thee and thy heirs,
Beggar them and beggar their's,
Melt thy plate, for which we paid,
Buy ye breeches ready made,
Sell my lady's tax bought gown,
And the lands thou call'st thy own.
Then of courses five or more,
Grapery, horse-race, coach-and-four,
Pamper'd fox-hounds, starving men,
Whores and bastards, nine or ten,
Twenty flunkies fat and gay,
Whip and jail for holiday,
Paid informer, poacher pale,
Smoker's license, poison'd ale,
Seat in senate, seat on bench,
Pension'd lad, or wife, or wench,
Fiddling parson, Sunday card,
Pimp, and dedicating bard —
On the broad and bare highway,
Toiling there for groat a-day,
We will talk to thee and thine,
Till thy wretches envy mine,
Till thy paunch of baseness howl,
Till thou seem to have a soul.

Peer, too just, too proud to share
Millions wrung from toil and care!
Righteous peer whose father fed
England's poor with untax'd bread!
Ancient peer, whose stainless name
Ages of old have given to fame! —
What shall bread tax do for thee?
Make thee poor as mine and me:
Drive thee from thy marble halls
To some hovel's squalid walls;
Drive thee from the land of crimes,
Houseless, into foreign climes,
There to sicken, there to sigh,
Steep thy soul in tears, and die —
Like a flower from summer's glow,
Withering on the Polar snow.

Church bedew'd with martyrs' blood,
Mother of the wise and good!
Temple of our smiles and tears,
Hoary with the frost of years!
Holy church, eternal, true!
What for thee will bread tax do?
It will strip thee bare as she
Whom a despot stripp'd for thee;
Of thy surplice made a pall,
Low'r thy pride, and take thy all —
Save thy truth, establish'd well,
Which — when spire and pinnacle,
Gorgeous arch, and figured stone,
Cease to tell of glories gone —
Shall still speak of thee and Him
Whom adore the Seraphim.

Power, which, likest Heaven's might seem
Glorious once in freedom's beam;
Once by tyrants felt and fear'd,
Still as freedom's dust revered!
Throne, established by the good,
Not unstain'd with patriot blood,

Not unwatch'd by patriot fears,
Not unwept by patriot tears!
What shall bread tax do for thee,
Venerable monarchy?
Dreams of evil, spare my sight!
Let that horror rest in night.

THE PRESS

From *Poetical Works* (1840), 118.

God said — 'Let there be light!'
Grim darkness felt his might,
        And fled away;
Then startled seas and mountains cold
Shone forth, all bright in blue and gold,
        And cried — "'Tis day! 'tis day!"
'Hail, holy light,' exclaim'd
The thundrous cloud, that flam'd
        O'er daisies white;
And lo! the rose in crimson dress'd
Lean'd sweetly on the lily's breast;
        And, blushing, murmur'd — 'Light!'
Then was the skylark born;
Then rose the embattl'd corn;
        Then floods of praise
Flow'd o'er the sunny hills of noon;
And then, in stillest night, the moon
        Pour'd forth her pensive lays.
Lo, heaven's bright bow is glad!
Lo, trees and flowers all clad
        In glory, bloom!
And shall the mortal sons of God
Be senseless as the trodden clod,
        And darker than the tomb?
No, by the *mind* of man!
By the swart artisan!
        By God, our Sire!

Our souls have holy light within,
And every form of grief and sin
                    Shall see and feel its fire.
          By earth, and hell, and heav'n,
          The shroud of souls is riven!
                    Mind, mind alone
Is light, and hope, and life, and power!
Earth's deepest night, from this bless'd hour,
                    The night of minds is gone!
          'The Press!' all lands shall sing;
          The Press, the Press we bring,
                    All lands to bless:
O pallid Want! O labour stark!
Behold, we bring the second ark!
                    The Press! The Press! The Press!

Gerald Massey
THE AWAKENING OF THE PEOPLE

From *The Ballad of Babe Christabel, with other Lyrical Poems*
(London, David Bogue, 1854), 148–9.

After Ebenezer Elliott, Gerald Massey (1828–1907) was the best
known of the Victorian working-men poets, and his literary career
lasted well beyond the collapse of early Victorian radicalism. As with
Elliott, his celebrity was created more by middle-class interest than
through any particular superiority in his writing. Massey also gained
from being London based, and by becoming part of the group of
Christian Socialists centred on F. D. Maurice. An avid enthusiast for
schemes, movements, and periodicals, Massey became well-versed
in European political theory, and took to writing poetry largely as a
way of extending the audience for his optimistic views of human
potentiality. Despite his undoubted knowledge of politics, Massey
saw his poetic task as being 'above the pinnacle of party zeal', and
concerned with 'the politics of eternal truth, right, and justice'. His
work is both exhortatory and rhapsodic, and bears early traces of the
mysticism and spiritualism which obsessed his later life. Most of
Massey's poems were collected from original publication in
magazines, and his work was easily available in collected form in the
1850s and 1860s, usually with the important Preface which Massey

wrote for the third edition of his *Collected Poems* in 1854. In 1889 Massey collected his work again into a two-volume edition called *My Lyrical Life*, re-arranging and altering many poems in the process. 'The Awakening of the People' is typical enough of Massey's lyric fervour and rhapsodic diction, although his work is more varied and ambitious than the political lyrics alone would suggest.

O sweet is the fair face of Nature, when Spring
    With living flower-rainbow in glory hath spann'd
Hill and dale; and the music of birds on the wing
    Makes earth seem a beautiful faery land!
And dear is our first-love's young spirit-wed bride,
With her meek eyes just sheathing in tender eclipse,
When the sound of our voice calls her heart's ruddy tide,
    Up-rushing in beauty to melt on her lips.
But earth has no sight half so glorious to see,
As a People up-girding its might to be free.

To see men awake from the slumber of ages,
    With brows grim from labour, and hands hard and tan,
Start up living heroes, the dreamt-of by Sages!
    And smite with strong arm the oppressors of man:
To see them come dauntless forth 'mid the world's warring,
    Slaves of the midnight mine! serfs of the sod!
Show how the Eternal within them is stirring,
    And never more bend to a crowned clod:
Dear God! 'tis a sight for Immortals to see, —
A People up-girding its might to be free.

Battle on bravely, O sons of humanity!
    Dash down the cup from your lips, O ye Toilers!
Too long hath the world bled for Tyrant's insanity —
    Too long our weakness been strength to our spoilers.
For Freedom and Right, gallant hearts, wrestle ever,
    And speak ye to others the proud words that won ye:
Your rights conquer'd once, shall be wrung from you never;
    O battle on bravely; the world's eyes are on ye;
And earth hath no sight half so glorious to see,
As a People up-girding its might to be free!

Thomas Cooper
TWO CHARTIST SONGS

From *The Poetical Works of Thomas Cooper* (Second edition, London, Hodder and Stoughton, 1886), 285–8.

Thomas Cooper's career (1805–1892) offers many close parallels with that of Massey. Cooper lived on well past his close engagement in Chartist activism to become a well-known lecturer and preacher. His poetry was similarly subordinate to his political intentions, and he, like Massey, saw the role of poetry as primarily that of elevating his class rather than subverting it. Cooper's fame was widespread as a result of his imprisonment for political offences, an imprisonment which was to produce his 'prison-rhyme', the enormously ambitious *Purgatory of Suicides*, written in Spenserian stanzas, and perhaps more widely praised than read in Victorian England (see Chapter 2). The following two poems are Cooper's self-styled 'smaller prison rhymes', which fall more readily into the modes and language of conventional Chartist exhortation and group re-inforcement. Cooper's most famous work is, justly, his *Life of Thomas Cooper Written by Himself* (1872), which describes not only his Chartist days but also his disillusion with active politics and his retreat into more abstract thought.

A song for the free — the brave and the free—
     Who feareth no tyrant's frown:
Who scorneth to bow, in obeisance low,
     To mitre or to crown;
Who owneth no lord with crosier or sword,
     And bendeth to Right alone;
Where'er he may dwell, his worth men shall tell,
     When a thousand years are gone!

For Tyler of old, a heart-chorus bold
     Let Labour's children sing!
For the smith with the soul that disdain'd base control,
     Nor trembled before a king;
For the heart that was brave, though pierced by a knave
     Ere victory for Right was won —
They'll tell his fair fame, and cheer his blythe name,
     When a thousand years are gone!

For the high foe of Wrong, great Hampden, a song —
      The fearless and the sage!
Who, at king-craft's frown, the gauntlet threw down,
      And dared the tyrant's rage;
Who away the scabbard threw, when the battle blade he drew,
      And with gallant heart led on!
How bravely he fell, our children shall tell,
      When a thousand years are gone!

For the mountain child of Scotia wild —
      For noble Wallace a strain!
O'er the Border ground let the chaunt resound:
      It will not be heard in vain.
For the Scot will awake, and the theme uptake
      Of deeds by the patriot done: —
They'll hold his name dear, nor refuse it a tear,
      When a thousand years are gone.

An anthem we'll swell for bold William Tell,
      The peasant of soul so grand!
Who fearlessly broke haughty Gesler's yoke,
      And set free his fatherland:
His deeds shall be sung, with blythesome tongue,
      By maiden, sire, and son,
Where the eagles climb o'er the Alps sublime,
      When a thousand years are gone.

For our Charter a song! It tarrieth long —
      But we will not despair;
For, though Death's dark doom upon us all may come,
      Ere we the blessing share —
Our happy children they shall see the happy day
      When freedom's boon is won;
And our charter shall be the boast of the Free,
      When a thousand years are gone!

The time shall come when Wrong shall end,
When peasant to peer no more shall bend —
When the lordly Few shall lose their sway,

And the Many no more their frown obey.

> Toil, brothers, toil, till the work is done —
> Till the struggle is o'er and the Charter's won!

The time shall come when the artisan
Shall homage no more the titled man —
When the moiling men who delve the mine
By Mammon's decree no more shall pine.

> Toil, brothers, toil, till the work is done —
> Till the struggle is o'er and the Charter's won!

The time shall come when the weaver's band
Shall hunger no more, in their fatherland —
When the factory child can sleep till day,
And smile while it dreams of sport and play.

> Toil, brothers, toil, till the work is done —
> Till the struggle is o'er and the Charter's won!

The time shall come when Man shall hold
His brother more dear than sordid gold —
When the Negro's stain his freeborn mind
Shall sever no more from human kind.

> Toil, brothers, toil, till the world is free —
> Till Justice and Love hold jubilee!

The time shall come when kingly crown
And mitre for toys of the Past are shown —
When the Fierce and False alike shall fall,
And Mercy and Truth encircle all.

> Toil, brothers, toil, till the world is free!
> Till Mercy and Truth hold jubilee!

The time shall come when earth shall be
A garden of joy, from sea to sea —
When the slaughterous sword is drawn no more,
And goodness exults from shore to shore.

> Toil, brothers, toil, till the world is free —
> Till goodness shall hold high jubilee!

Melodrama, Pathos, and Narrative

Despite widespread admiration for Crabbe's poetry among self-taught writers, an admiration specifically acknowledged in Ebenezer Elliott's most ambitious poem *The Village Patriarch*, the narrative and dramatic modes were not widely used by Chartist and radical writers for political purposes, although both were widely adopted for the poems of sustained social and moral indignation illustrated in Chapter 2. Given the existence of highly melodramatic Chartist fiction, and an entire genre of factory melodrama for the theatre, such neglect of the narrative and melodramatic poetic modes is perhaps surprising. The direct emotional appeal of the particular instance of suffering or oppression is largely passed over in poetry for the more abstract psycho-dramas of poetic reflectiveness, or the symbolic analyses of the processes of social change, or description of philosophical concepts like 'justice' or 'freedom'. Poetic self-consciousness, always liable to inhibit self-taught writers, tended to lead artisan writers towards earnest and speculative verse, or else to the communal and oral modes already described. There are, however, a number of narrative poems which remain unashamed of their focus on topical cases of individualized hardship, and which use pathos as a forceful dramatic device rather than as a component of poetic or moral sensitivity. The cathartic intention of these poems is clear, particularly when they are confidently and publicly declaimed. No mere exercises in domestic sentimentality, the success of such unabashedly pathetic and melodramatic poems confirms contemporary interest in melodrama and 'sensation' as more than passing academic fashion.

The following three short examples of domestic narrative poems are drawn from prolific and well-established poets who used a variety of forms and genres in pursuit of wide appeal. The first two poems also come from sequences of related poems on similar themes, the first from Ebenezer Elliott's famous *Corn Law Rhymes* (which were, of course, anti-Corn Law rhymes) and the second from W. J. Linton's *Rhymes and Reasons Against Landlordism*. These two sequences began as unrelated single poems published in periodicals, and then were slowly accumulated into their sequence form. The third is an uncollected magazine contribution of William Thom's, which appeared in the wide-circulation, Edinburgh-based *Tait's Magazine*.

Ebenezer Elliott
SONG

From *Corn Law Rhymes*, which were first published in volume form in 1834 as part of *The Splendid Village, Corn Law Rhymes and other Poems*.

Tune — 'Robin Adair'

Child, is thy father dead?
   Father is gone!
Why did they tax his bread?
   God's will be done!
Mother has sold her bed;
Better to die than wed!
Where shall she lay her head?
   Home we have none.

Father clamm'd thrice a week —
   God's will be done!
Long for work did he seek,
   Work he found none.
Tears on his hollow cheek
Told what no tongue could speak:
Why did his master break?
   God's will be done!

Doctor said air was best —
   Food we had none;
Father with panting breast,
   Groan'd to be gone:

Now he is with the blest —
Mother says death is best!
We have no place of rest —
    Yes, ye have one!

W. J. Linton
SONG

From *The English Republic* (1851), 188.

The leaves are still; not a breath is heard:
    How bright the harvest day!
'Tis the tramp of a horse, the boughs are stirr'd
    The Agent comes this way.
Was it an old gun-muzzle peep'd
    Beyond yon crimson leaf?
A shot! — and Murder's bloody sheaf
    Is reaped.

Who sold the farm above his head?
Who drove the widow mad?
Who pull'd the dying from her bed?
Who robb'd the idiot lad?
Who sent the starv'd girl to the streets?
Who mocked grey Sorrow's smart?
Yes! Listen in thy blood. His heart
    Yet beats.

Not one has help for the dying man;
    Not one the murderer stays,
Though all might see him where he ran,
    Not even the child betrays.
    O wrong! Thou hast a fearful brood:
    What inquest can ye need,
Who know revenge but reap't the seed
    Of blood.

William Thom
THE FOOD-RIOTER BANISHED

From *Tait's Magazine* (Edinburgh 1847), 318.

> *"'Fellow, you have broken our laws!'*
> *"'Yes, your honour; but not until your laws*
>   *had broken me.'*
> *"'Sir, that's nothing to the point.'*
> *"'No, your honour — nothing whatever.'"*
>   — *Justice Made Easy*

Well, sorrow is a simple word
   All meaningless and dead
To him who hears the famish'd cry;
   'Oh, Father, give us bread!'

It scares lean Labour from its seat
   A fiercer form is there;
Now, misery waits so biddingly,
   Handmaiden to despair.

'Save well at noon,' the wise one says,
   'Ye'll better fare at night;'
And where there's anything to save,
   The wise one's very right.

Well Mary saved! Oh, many an hour
   She stole from rest and sleep,
To sew and save the o'erworn weeds
   Her skill could scarcely keep.

She saved the morsel from her lips
   To still the bairnie's din;
The Kirk seat-rent, the beadle's fees,
   She saved, for 'fear o' sin.'

She sought, and saved ilk kindly thought
   That near her bosom came;
And held it, hoarded in her heart,
   To welcome 'father' hame.

She croon'd the cradle lullaby
   Sae sorrowfully sweet,
'Tween sob and sang, 'He'll come ere lang,
   Oh, bairnies, dinna greet!'

He never came. Yon dowie law!
   If lawfu' deeds they be.
When mongers fatten at their will,
   An' puir folks left to dee.

'An maun I leave them helpless now,
   When maist my help they need?
And maun I dree a felon's doom
   Wha ne'er did felon's deed?

I dinna grudge to leave a land
   Whaurin I daurna be;
But, oh, I mourn yon drearie hame,
   Wi' a' that's dear to me.

' 'Twas there, in timorous infancy,
   My foot first touched the soil
That mair than thirty seasons saw
   My willing arm toil.

'Although I held anither's plew,
   Or sow'd anither's grain,
I gied a benison as leal
   As if they'd been my ain.

'I watched and blessed the infant briard
   In morning glory spread,
And blessed the bonny dew that set,
   Like pearls, ilka mead.

'We saw it wave in stately ranks,
   Our gowden fields aroun'
Each stem a sturdy warrior
   To battle famine doun.

'I saw it pass our breadless door,
  An' borne unto the sea,
A father's fury rieve my heart —
  How could it ither be?'

Well, patience is a silly word,
  So meaningless and dead,
To him who hears the sickening cry,
  'Oh, father, give us bread!'

Historical Narratives

The two following poems, Ernest Jones's 'Leawood Hall' and W. J. Linton's *Bob Thin — or, The Poorhouse Fugitive* seem at first glance to belong to the previous section of melodramatic narratives. But while they show much of the melodrama, pathos, and declamatory energy of more specifically Chartist narrative (especially in the latter parts of *Bob Thin*, which I have chosen not to include here because of a considerable weakening in the force of the poem as it goes on), they also both sustain a detailed historical analysis of the growth of class division and economic oppression from feudal times. It is this historical narrative which subsumes the contemporary incidents under its wide gaze. Similar ambitious accounts of the British experience are to be found in the work of self-taught writers — Elijah Ridings' *The Isles of Britain* which was widely republished in his *The Village Muse* in the 1850s provides another interesting example in a similar mode.

'Leawood Hall' is described as a 'Christmas Tale' in its sub-title, and it forms the most substantial work in the 'Plough and Loom' section of Jones's excellent collection *The Battle Day*, a section in which Jones brings to rural themes the energy of his metropolitan radical politics. The simple lyric stanzas and the constant allusions not just to ballad themes but also to the feudal world described in ballads are combined with the blatant melodrama of the narrative to make the poem consciously popular in its address. The historical sweep of the narrative, however, and the sense of the way in which present violence is the product of a long history of injustice, give the poem considerable seriousness and a sense of purpose. As in *Bob Thin*, the poet is consciously exploring ways of subverting popular dramatic poetry into a serious account of the history of British oppression of the labouring poor. 'Leawood Hall' makes an interesting comparison with Tennyson's nearly contemporary *Maud* as a study in rural alienation.

Ernest Jones
LEAWOOD HALL

From *The Battle Day and Other Poems* (London, Routledge, 1855).

In a cottage on a moor
    Famine's feeble children cried;
The frost knocked sharply at the door,
    And hunger welcom'd him inside;

In the moonlight cracked the leaves,
    As the fox across them passed,
And the ice-drops from the eaves
    Rattled to the whirling blast;

On the black hearth glowed no ember,
    On the damp floor lay the rime,
Elfin haloes of December
    For the sainted Christmas-time;

And a pale girl sat there chanting
    Mournfully to children twain,
Like some sweet house-spirit haunting
    Old men's homes with childhood's strain.

Ellen was a maiden fair
    With that beauty meek and frail,
Softened by the hand of care
    From the red rose to the pale.

But the children had no feature
    Of the blithe child's merry grace,
Still of spirit — small of stature —
    Manhood's thought on childhood's face.

And a woman, thin and eager,
   Tossed upon a litter low,
Lifting up large eyes of fever,
   With a look of angry woe.

Harsh complaints and words unkind
   To each and all in turn addressed,
For pain, with searching hand, will find
   A bitter drop in every breast.

Bearing all with passive mood
   While her sharp invective ran,
In cold and fearful calmness stood
   A silent, melancholy man.

O'er his brow the moonbeam lingered
   'Mid the lines that passion wrought,
Like an angel, glory-fingered,
   Shewing heaven the dangerous thought.

He had toiled in hope's assurance,
   Toiled when hope had changed to fear,
Toiled amid despair's endurance —
   These were sorry thanks to hear.

Yet he chid not her reproving,
   Bore it all in quiet part —
Said: It is but misery moving
   Pulses foreign to her heart.

Still in solemn silence bound,
   Scarce a sign of life he gave,
But fixed his eyes upon the ground,
   As though his look could dig his grave.

Sudden through the broken pane
   Faintly gleamed a ruddy light,
And something like a festive strain
   Came thrilling through the heart of night.

With flashing eyes that woman wan
  Rose like shade against the wall:
'Hark! hark! the festival's began!
  'The tables groan at Leawood Hall!'

'The rich man feasts — and Leawood's near —
  'What honey stores his golden hive!
'Go! bid him give those dying here,
  'One crust to save their souls alive!'

———

The night grew dark — but from a height
  Afar the lordly mansion shone,
Shone pillar white and portal bright,
  Like trellis work of fire and stone.

Along the roads, from every side
  The blazing lamps were racing all,
As fast the guests invited hied
  To share the feast at Leawood Hall.

It was a Norman castle high —
  It was a keep of ages rude,
When men named murder — *chivalry*
  And robbery was called — *a feud*.

There barons stern once housed in pride,
  And coined the labourer's heart to gold:
On field and fell the labourer died,
  While they were gay in holt and hold.

What they had lavished to replenish,
  They o'ertaxed endurance' length,
Drunk his labour down in Rhenish,
  And grew strong upon his strength.

Men of haughtiness! unthinking
  In their selfishness of caste,
'Twas his life-blood they were drinking!
  But 'twould poison them at last.

69

From the dust that they were treading
   Some stood up by force or craft,
Till, the scutcheoned peer o'erheading,
   In his face the *trader* laughed.

Then, his triumph once insuring,
   This new conqueror fiercely rose,
Smote the people's neck enduring,
   After they had crushed his foes.

And those mighty tyrant-blasters
   Settled into slaves again;
They had only changed their masters,
   And that change was worse than vain.

Since then, a sterile-thoughted man
   Had lorded it o'er Leawood fair,
Who as an errand-boy began,
   And ended as a millionaire.

And his son, by slow degrees,
   Mounted life with golden feet,
For the son knew how to please,
   And the sire knew how to cheat.

Before he rose, the people's friend,
   He feigned at all their wrongs to burn;
Now, as he bent, made others bend,
   And played the tyrant in his turn.

Patroniz'd each bible-mission;
   Gave to charities — his *name*;
No longer cared for *man's* condition,
   But carefully preserved — his *game*.

Against the Slave-trade he had voted,
   'Rights of Man' resounding still;
Now, basely turning, brazen-throated,
   Yelled against the Ten Hours' Bill.

———

Oh! Leawood Hall was gay that night;
   Shone roof and rafter, porch and door,
And proudly rolled the sheeted light
   Its glory over Leawood Moor.

Full in the glare the labourer stood;
   The music smote him like a blast,
And through the rich ancestral wood
   He heard the fat deer rushing past.

'While we are starving!' cried his love;
   'But they are watching!' said his fear.
'Twixt hell below and heaven above —
   What dost thou on the balance here?

Through the hall the beggar spurning,
   Menials drove him from the door:
Can they chide the torch for burning,
   They cast smouldering on the floor?

Say not: 'This is no fair sample,
   'This was but the menial's part!'
'Twas the master's past example,
   Filtered through the servant's heart.

'Man is born — and man must live!'
   Thus anger read its maddening creed:
'If I take what they won't give,
   Can heaven itself frown on the deed?'

———

That night a fierce and haggard man
   From Leawood Hall was seen to run; —
But ere the fearful race began
   The rifle's deadly work was done.

Ye pampered drones! pursuit is vain,
   Give o'er the godless, cruel strife!
As well o'ertake the hurricane:
   Despair and love fly there for life.

———

Long the anxious wife sat waiting,
    Fainter grew the children's cry;
E'en the wind, the desolating,
    Slept to his own lullaby.

The father came — but hot and wild
    The open door he staggered past;
His brow was knit but still he smiled,
    Like sunset over tempest cast.

'Food! food!' he cried, 'they feast tonight,
    'And I have brought our share as well;
'Wife! we were starving — 'twas our right!
    'If not — as God wills — heaven or hell!'

Then spoke his wife with inward pride
    To think her counsel proved so brave;
'I knew you could not be denied;
    'Now bless the gentle hand that gave.'

He strangely smiled in wondrous mood,
    And, with the haste of fever, quaffed
Down to the dregs a fiery flood;
    And still he smiled — and still he laughed.

He smiled to mark their spirits rise,
    And that his wife had ceased to sigh,
And how the ardour in her eyes
    Gave her the look of times gone by.

He laughed to think how small a cost
    Might brighten poverty's eclipse;
But sudden silence strangely crossed
    With blanching hand his quivering lips.

Then oft he kissed each little child,
    And looked as one who'd much to say;
But, ere he spoke, some pinion wild
    Waved the unuttered thought away.

And Ellen marvelled to behold
    Such fitful change and sudden cheer;
He had so long been stern and cold,
    This kindness seemed a thing to fear.

And fainter grew his smile and bitter,
    And his face turned cold and grey,
While slow he sank down on the litter,
    And strength's last bravery broke away.

Then they saw where, heartward glancing,
    Deep the cruel rifle smote;
While death's gurgling march advancing
    Sounded up his gasping throat.

Clung, like leaves of Autumn's serest,
    Wife and children to his side;
He turned his last look on his dearest,
    And, thus sadly gazing, died.

Courage now no more dissembled
    Broken strength and baffled will;
The wistful children stood and trembled,
    And the room grew very still.

W. J. Linton
BOB THIN OR THE POORHOUSE FUGITIVE

Illustrated by T. Sibson, W. B. Scott, E. Duncan and W. J. Linton
(London, Richard Oastler, 1845).

This extraordinary doggerel epic by Linton is a telling experiment in
genre. The original text is illustrated by Thomas Sibson's powerful
engraved woodblock capital letters which supply a running commentary to the text using the graphic idiom of Seymour and Cruickshank
— a collaboration which may have been the outcome of a jointly
projected radical history of England which Linton and Sibson had
planned in 1842 or 1843. (The project is described on p. 50 of F. B.
Smith's biography of Linton, *Radical Artisan*, Manchester 1973.)

Although Linton describes his own work as 'doggrel rhyme', the ambitions of his poem are clear enough — the linking of the history of oppression undergone by the weaver Bob Thin to the larger history of English capitalism, and even if Linton's facetiousness and occasionally forced jollity can be irritating, he none the less succeeds in using a vernacular voice to impressive effect. The poem is an interesting exercise in the kind of radical poetic rewriting of history evident in, for example, Ernest Jones's 'The Cost of Glory' or 'The Plough and Loom'. I do not believe that Linton's poem has been reprinted since its original publication.

THE LIFE AND ADVENTURE OF BOB THIN

A political — philosophical — historical — biographical — anecdotical — allegorical — parenthetical — pathetical — prophetical — poetical — logical — metrical — and moral new poor-law tale.

Men like not prosy tales: we'll try
How doggrel rhyme fits history.

Time was when every man was free
To manage his own cookery:
Whether he got it in the chase,
Or grew and eat it in same place.
This was old time, long ere the days
When 'merrie England' bask'd in the blaze —

Now, blessings on her wrizled face! —
Of royal Betty's summer glory:
Those were the days to come before ye.
And here, though it delay our story,
We must indulge our loyal pen
With a laudatory paren-

Thesis, to tell of Betty's goodness,
Trusting to be excused — our rudeness,
Bet's sire (Well, Liza's, at your pleasure)
Was one who knew no law but the measure
Of's will — a most elastic tether:

He had (and some make question whether
'Twas done of grace or despotism)

74

Taken advantage of a schism
Among the shepherds who care for souls,
To spoil some of their fishes and rolls.
That is to say, he turn'd adrift

Sundry friars, out of whose thrift —
Rogues as they might be, ne'ertheless —
The poor had succour in distress.
Beggars and monks were told to shift.
Woe to the poor! till glorious Bess
(Who wink'd not, save at manliness)

Swore by 'od's teeth, her father's oath,
(A practice to which she was not loath)
That every man had a right to live,
Even though his labour might not thrive.
Who bars the claim of one past labour

To share the abundance of his neighbour,
Denies the right of pity, sent
By Heaven to be the muniment
Of Justice, else most justly shent.
This was the law by Nature given,
When man, unbreech'd, unshod, was driven

From the untailor'd paradise —
That garden of content which lies,
According to our clearest notion,
Some leagues beyond the extremest ocean;
Or, in more measured words express'd,
Just fifteen paces to the west

Of the angel with the flaming sword:
But, quitting this, which (take our word!)
Is an insolvent speculation,
To jog along with our narration;
Let us endeavour to unravel
The tortuous track of human travel,

Out of the naked innocence,
Through the rude windings of offence,

To that sophisticated morn
Which witness'd our tale's hero born.

Well, as we said, in the olden days,
When ladies never miss'd their stays
(Because, in truth, they'd not been granted:
A cherub might as well have panted
For a dandy pair of pantaloons,
Or whale have sigh'd for table-spoons)

Days more than 'golden,' double-worth'd,
When horrible gold was all unearth'd —
The days of Natural Equal —
Ity and property for all;
There were no Poor-laws, for this good
Reason, that no man wanted food;

And none on's neighbour any ravages
Committed; till at length some savages,
A lordly, idle set of stoats,
Seiz'd peaceful husbandmen by th' throats,
And over Nature's gentlest code,
On roaring Rapine rough-shod rode.

Here is the origin of what
Is call'd the law of scot and lot.
After a time, a cunning rascal,
Almost as 'cute a chap as Pascal
Was in geometry, to invent
A plan by which to circumvent

The aristocratic testament
Set wits to work, and money made,
Merely to accommodate his trade, —
A sort of circulating medium
By which men might relieve the tedium
Of the antique clumsy bartering, —

How to swop all and every thing.
Then ships were built and cities stood

On site of many a noble wood;
And, stead of breaking lances featly,
Men learnt to bleed a pocket neatly,
Till war, defrauded of his 'sinews,'

Lay a bound Triton 'mong the minnows —
Like Gulliver at Lilliput,
Or knight head-stuck in muddy rut.
So stepp'd our world from times as Goth wild,
To the very presence of a Rothschild;
Till even 'this corner of the west'

Got shares in civilization's best.
Now, to apply the application
To the back of our own happy nation: —
We've had our scions of misrule,
Of the illegitimate Norman school,
Who've laid our husbandmen in bond —

Like eels pent up in shallow pond —
Curfewing us, and then with 'charters'
Just lighting some to adore their garters;
All this we've borne, and worse behind,
The money-men who 'sow the wind,'
And 'bills of rights' by taxes paid —

Like child by its mother overlaid —
Till, what with thief's and murderer's ration,
We've cross'd to a tarnation station —
At least a break-leg elevation.
We've told how royal Betsy swore,
That right of rights belong'd to the poor:

Of late the Solons of the nation
Out of their bag of legislation
(The bag o' the spider, not o' the bee)
Have spun a web, a twist of three,
Of such a monstrous complication —
Good meanings it is said pave hell:
There's not a doubt but they meant well —
It threats the poor with worse starvation

Than when bluff Harry kick'd the monks out:
Our tale will show you what 'tis about.
'Your introduction tires the reader:
Directly with your tale proceed!' Y'ur
Honour's will shall be obey'd.

BOB THIN a weaver was by trade . . .

In Campden-gardens, Bethnal-green,
Bob's homestead was, not over clean,
Nor in most healthy atmosphere,
Lying unfortunately near
To Lamb's-fields marsh, a stagnant pool

Of some three hundred square feet, full
Of the spawn of dire contagion, which
Dwelt rankly there and in a ditch
That skirt'd North-street, neighbourly.
The weltering ditch crawl'd filthily;
Yet with most kind, though lame, endeavour

To drain the place, which landlord never
Attempted: he could let his hovels,
Why pay for sanitory shovels?
No law sets bounds to the landlord's wealth,
Albeit his rent is his tenant's health
Transmuted. This locality

Was a Mr Christian's property;
He leased it of one General Fever,
Ground landlord of the estate of Weaver.
The fine, an occasional weaver's life
(No matter if 'twere child or wife),
Paid regularly to the thrilling

Of the owner's heart and pocket filling
Alternately: 'twas very strange,
Good tenants were so given to change.
The atmosphere, we said, was sickly,
With wretched dwellings planted thickly,
Weavers' 'and else,' all sons of toil,

Born serfs of this most loathly soil,
This drainless swamp; by landlords clogg'd,
Whose lives unholy gain so fogg'd,
No charity might enter in
To cheer the misers' wintering.
Even in this place of misery

Lived Bob in his prosperity;
In a poor-furnish'd, 'two-room'd' hole,
Undrain'd, unventilated, foul,
Mean, miserable as the soul
Of landlord Christian: yet Bob spun
From morn till 'dewy eve,' was one

Whose labour never was relax'd,
Who had been duly christen'd, tax'd,
And rated; and thus lived in the lees
Of a fat-bishop'd diocese.
But Bob's was no uncommon case:
He fared like others of his race,

Of the working Pariah caste, who meet ye
In the heart of London's wealthiest city —
London for 'charities' renown'd:
Despite the daily traces found
Of hoary Squalor's crippled feet
'Twixt Lambeth and Threadneedle-street.

Squalor resides in Bethnal-green!
And there, oftimes, our gracious Queen
Cheereth not with her lustrous face
The common dimness of the place;
Though she delighted, it is said,
To see Van Amburgh's lions fed;

God bless her Majesty's sweet features!
Lions are interesting creatures.
Yet, Lady! would it not be grander
To feed the hungry poor who wander
Through all weather, early and late,
To and fro — for they dare not wait —

Before your guarded palace-gate:
With whom even Pimlico abounds,
Worse cared for than your Graces hounds?
The very dogs lick'd Lazarus' wounds.
Good God! The court-fool stops us short: —
What! Famine introduced at Court? . . .

Back to our tale. Bob's family
Quit, as we said, most ruefully,
The home of their prosperity.
Who loves not home, however poor?

Yourself the master of the door;
There, though sore hunted, to be free: —
What wretch would choose captivity?
Bob had no choice; relief forbidden
To all but those in workhouse hidden,
Under the 'regulations.' He

Might choose to starve at liberty,
Alone, but, for his family's sake,
Must bow his honest pride to take
The felon chain and prison rations
Of the 'amendment' regulations.
Alas! he may not claim a bone

Even in the workhouse: — be it known,
Though Bethnal-green might own his sire,
That Bob was born in Monmouthshire:
And, therefore, 'twas most fit and proper
He should be deemed an interloper
In Bethnal Union, where abound

Such men as the Samaritan found,
But few Samaritans — no libel;
They're Christians and believe the Bible.
Nor may their justice tolerate
Any addition to the rate,
To burden men of wealth, whose profit

Bob spun, though he might share none of it.
'But had he no right to relief?'
None. 'Why?' We'll answer you in brief:
What claim has the beggar on his thief?
The 'Guardians' smiled their sage approval,
And duly order'd the removal

Of the strange paupers: so they sent
The wretches to their 'seetlement' —
Let no man call it punishment.
'Twas for his own convenience' sake:
When the now-slumbering trade should wake,
He'd be so handy to resume

His place at the accustom'd loom; —
So care they for the poor man's doom.
Now, as the cart of charity glode
With easy carriage on the road,
Bob thought he might as well beguile
With converse close his travel while.

Oyster — May the Lord keep you, man,
And all who read this true relation,
Out of his sphere of operation!
Here man and wife were torn asunder:
God-join'd, but to be parted under
The 'regulations': each one buried

From the other's wretchedness; both hurried
Into their lonely graves. For the rest,
Their treatment was not of the best.
One item may suffice to show
How careful of each other's woe
Are human things, albeit extremely

Zealous to wear a visage seemly
As fairest-whiten'd sepulchre: —
Look at that tomb of the labourer,
Yon profit-plaster'd villain; Sir!
Though his hoarded wealth is the charnel-dew,
Though he stole the byeword of the Jew,

Verily he will prate to you
Of the great Improvidence; nor tinge
His corpse-face, though a man should twinge
His 'soul' with the workhouse 'dietary' —
Food being ruled a necessary.
Pray you note how the profit-monger

Caters for those who can work no longer!
For breakfast — bread, not without stint:
The men have seven ounces, and a pint
And half of skilly — a thin kind
Of 'gruel,' such as you can find
Nowhere except on the hard tables

Of 'regulation' human stables.
For dinner — meat, five ounces twice
Each week; 'potato-hash'; soup; rice,
Nearly a pound; coarse bread, and cheese,
Two ounces of the latter: these
Are their alternate luxuries.

When millionaires can wring no more
Out of the earnings of the poor,
Thus does their charity atone
For their cupidity. 'Tis done
(At least, so poor-law doctors say)
For the labourers' benefit, that they

May hang upon their own resources;
Meanwhile in his plethoric courses
The master wallows. Who shall wrest
The portion of the poor opprest?
Bob, from his wife and children parted
Droops in his prison, broken-hearted.

He dreameth not of better days,
His sorrow-glazed and stolid gaze
Shutter'd with hopelessness,; and curst,
As of all criminals the worst,
He buries in his 'infamy'
The care of life, and fain would die.

Question and answer came as follows: —
Quoth Question, out of Bob's cheek-hollows,
While answer sate with arms a-kimbo, —
Pray tell me why I'm set in limbo? —
Answer — Because the Well-to-do
Can find no better use for you. —

What right have they to order me? —
Answer — The right of property. —
Question again — But how invented?
It can't be shown that I consented:
And every compact doth demand
Two parties. — You will understand,

Replies the other, your assent
Was duly given by Parliament,
Your representatives, and — Stay!
Will you be good enough to say,
How these same representers got
At the will of one who had no vote? —

Answer — My friend! you are not able
To comprehend this veritable
Fair feature of our Constitution,
Which — Favour me with a solution
Of that fine-sounding word! What is't? —
Hereupon Answer clenched his fist,

Eloquently. — Will tell me where
It may be found? — Reply, a stare
And sort of clutching at the air
After a phantom; then a frown,
Which fairly knocked the Question down:
At last came words: — It is not fit

That poor men should in judgement sit
Of this most reverend mystery.
If you examine history,
The courtly Hume's, where he relates
Of 1668's
Most Dutch and glorious 'Revolution,'

King William and his Constitution,
And the 'Convention,' you will see
How Parliament right loyally
Confirm'd the Hollander's accession,
For having ratified their session.
It follows, as a thing of course,

As good things ever must grow worse
By alteration, that the code,
Even the horse King William rode,
Which our wise ancestors approved
Should by their sons be ne'er improved
Throughout all time. — Bob heard no more

Until the party reached the door
Of Godstone Union poorhouse, where,
After the usual courtesies,
And introduction of the keys,
They were admitted to the care
Of the poorhouse king, a sort of human

His very life is lifeless torpor:
Bob Thin is changed into a Pauper. . . .

Later Radical Lyrics

For a number of reasons — the collapse of organized Chartism after 1848, the growing incorporation of self-taught writers into orthodox literary culture, the growth of local readerships interested in the work of local bards — it is much harder to identify specifically political and oppositional poetry written by self-taught writers in the latter half of the nineteenth century. Certainly specific issues like the Cotton Famine take over from the more generalized political idealism of early self-taught writers. In keeping with the general changes in the nature of poetry by self-taught writers, the more politically radical poems written between 1860 and 1900 exhibit more parochial and less ambitious forms and poetic diction. The collapse of the idealistic, symbolic, and abstract discourse undertaken by Chartists is very obvious, even though many of the ablest Chartist writers, especially Ernest Jones, W. J. Linton, and Gerald Massey, continued to write extensively in the 1860s and beyond. The poems here suggest, in two cases at least, the more localized and domestic kind of political comment found in late Victorian self-taught writers, while the third group, by the Tyneside writer Joseph Skipsey, suggests how self-taught writing could, on rare but memorable occasions, be energized and inspired by imitation of major writers within the British poetic tradition. In appropriating Blake for his poetic model, Skipsey, who had clearly learnt something besides humiliation from his acquaintance with Dante Gabriel Rossetti, shows once again how the dominant poetic tradition could be persistently re-read in a more radical and oppositional way. While imitation often collapsed into feeble and derivative verse, there were many occasions when the rigorous or even obsessive reading of self-taught writers allowed them to revalue poetic form in the light of their own experiences as working men. Skipsey's lyrics, coming at a time when few were reading Blake, let alone imitating his direct yet complex lyric method, show a powerful sense of the relevançe of Blake's visionary grasp of the disintegrative social forces released by industrialism.

Joseph Ramsbottom
PREAWD TUM'S PRAYER

From *Phases of Distress: Lancashire Rhymes* (Manchester, John Heywood, 1864). This volume, occasionally also called *Lays of the Cotton Famine*, is a reprint of a number of dialect poems which had had wide circulation as broadsides, pamphlets, or newspaper contributions throughout the Cotton Famine of 1860–1861.

> Theaw God above, alone to-day
>   Areawt i'th broad, green fields aw've come
> Aw want twothri words to say,
>   Aw shouldno like to say awhoam.
> Mi heart's too full, an' feels so sore,
>   Aw'm sure ut betther aw should be,
> If aw could tell mi sorrows o'er,
>   An' tell em on'y Lord, to thee.
>
> An' here, among o'th' whistlin' brids,
>   Among o'th' pratty posies here,
> Ther's summat i' mi breast ut bids
>   Me neaw to speak witheawt a fear.
> An' here i'th'sun's great cheerin' leet,
>   Wheer sich sweet freshness springs fro' th'sod,
> Fro carpin' men aw'm eawt o'th seet,
>   Alone wi God's things, an' wi God.
>
> No een bi Thine should rest o' me;
>   No ear bi nee, if aw mun tell
> This tale ut brings its pain to me,
>   Wi little blame for 't to mysel.
> When cares are great, an' comforts few,
>   Heaw busy folks ull pry an' stare,
> An' toot an' sper abeawt one, too,
>   Tho' bare back'd Want's an awful scare

To' th' creepin' things: they fling at th' poor
    Their praise and pity, sneers an blame,
An' little whisp'rins spread, for sure,
    Ut makes folks deawbt one's honest name.
Aw darno speak to th' good men here,
    Tho' that some gradely help met bring;
For th' buzzin' wasps are everywheer,
    An awlus use their peighsunt sting.

'Why Tom o' Joe's is gone for dow,
    For o' so hee he held his yead;
Exalt yoarsel, yo'll be browt low,
    Is what we'n awlus seen and read.'
When Bob o' Mat's his case made known,
    Wi stingin' words he'r sorely vext;
'Preawd folks mun rep sich things they'n sown;'
    They'd crush us wi a Bible text.

For men to moan an' walk abeawt,
    An' get folks' help by tales o' woe,
When they could weel mak' shift witheawt,
    Is wrong, and rascally an' o'.
When things one conno help arise,
    An' weigh us heavily to th' greawnd;
When th' wife jeighns th' childer's hongry cries
    For bread, an' o' are clemmin' reawnd; —

What is a fayther then to do
    Ut's dhrained his tother springs o' done?
We'd awlus sorrows quite enoo,
    Bo beggin' caps em every one.
Aw've sthriven hard, an' soon an' late,
    An' long aw've hid mi soory plight;
Bo th' growin' ills o' this bare state
    Han broken deawn mi sperits quite.

Mi childher'n bin mi greatest care:
    It breaks mi heart to see em clem;
Aw'd tak o' th' ills a double share,
    If Plenty would bo' play wi them;

87

For be these thrials wrong or reet,
    A mon con ill his temper keep
Ut sees his childer every neet
    So hongry sob thersels to sleep.

Aw've seven on 'em yon a whoam,
    Are clemmin', beside me an' th' wife;
We dunno see heaw help can come,
    Nor comfort con we find i' life.
Aw canno stoop to th' pauper's dole
    An' beggin's noa for folks liek me;
Do Theaw support mi sinkin soul —
    God, help me neaw, or le' me dee.

Eawr little Jimmy's wortchin' yet,
    Bo what con his two shillin' do?
Mi wife does hardly owt bo fret —
    Eawr bits o' thraps are o' run thro'.
Theaw know's what one like me ud feel,
    To see his stock o' things gwo less;
A mon ut likes his whoam so weel,
    To strip his heawse an' no redhress.

Relations' gifts, an' gifts o' friends,
    We'n sowd 'em o' with many a soik;
Bo th' sthrongest sperit awlus bends,
    When honger gnaws, an' childer skroik.
To empty stomachs toime runs slow,
    An' mis'ry gethers reawnd his yead,
Ut hongry waits till neet shall fo'.
Ut he may sell his goods for bread.

Aw've waited so, when th' day wur breet,
    Aw kept close in, an' aw could tell
Heaw oft aw've started off at neet
    To sell an' didno want to sell.
When this breet sun's bin sattl't deawn,
    An' stars bin glimm'rin o'er mi yead,
Heaw oft aw've sadly ta'en to th' teawn
    A table, cheer, or else a bed!

Aw've sthript mi heawse, left th' wife i' tears,
   I' tears aw've made mi lonely thrack,
While th' childher's cries rang on mi ears, —
   "Be sharp, neaw, daddy, win yo back!"
Wi sick'nin' heart an' faintin' feet
   Aw took, last week, eawr fither bed;
Mi wife begg'd — 'Dunno tak it t'neet,'
   An' th' choilt i' th' arm said — 'Mammy, bread!'

Mi things kept less'nin', one bi one,
   An' nowt has ta'en their places up;
Mi whoam's neaw like a barn — they're gone —
   We're left wi noather bite nor sup.
O! it wur hard eawrsels to dhraw
   Fro th' things i' th' heawse we'd aulus known;
For eawr warm beds, t' put up wi sthraw
   For every cheer, a boother stone!

O gone are th' jokes an' th' jolly play
   An' th' childher' music, th' welcome seawnd
Has dhriven oft mi cares away,
   When plenty made its daily reawnd.
Mi merry little flock oitch neet
   Ud prattlin' romp upon my knee;
Aw darno let em neaw, for th' seet
   O' their pale faces bothers me,

An' yon, before mi feighrless grate,
   On seven sep'rate stones they sit;
Th' wife shar'd among em th' last o' th' mayt,
   An' 's sobbin' while they're atin' it.
An' sadness sits i' every face,
   For th' youngest choilt i' th' heawse looks glum,
An' Wants long bwony arms embrace
   Neaw every livin' thing awhoam.

Aw'r fyert ut folks ud find it eawt,
   Aw wur i' sich a sinkin' state.
Cose when mi childher play'd areawt,
   They'd gether reawnd some choilt wi mayt,

An' every bite it ost to tak
   Their little meawths ud open too;
Their teeth ud wayther, lips ud smack,
   Bo they'd ne'er beg — they'd bear it thro'.

An' when its fyestin's o bin o'er
   They'n turnt tort me sich tearful een,
Aw'd never felt so hurt before,
   Sich longin' looks aw'd never seen.
Mi lot's bin gradely hard to bear,
   An' keep th' grim saycret to misel;
It's happen wrong to nuss mi care,
   Bo weel Theaw knows aw couldno tell.

This tale of o eawr sorrows here —
   Aw blush to tell it neaw to Thee;
Thy help alone eawr souls con cheer,
   We're sunk as low as low con be.
An' soon we'st o dhrop into th' grave, —
   Bo Theaw con stop us wi a breath;
If t'dusno think it reet to save,
   Taytch us to welcome comin' dyeth.

O th' things abeawt depend on Thee,
   O th' hedges, threes, an' th' prattier fleawrs,
An' every buzzart, brid, an' bee,
   An' th' warmin' sun, an' th' coolin' sheawrs.
Theaw knows heaw keen are famine's strings,
   Theaw knows aw've neaw done o aw con;
An' while Theaw cares for o these things
   Theaw'll surely help a sthrivin' mon.

Joseph Burgess
TEN HEAWRS A DAY

From *A Potential Poet? His Autobiography and Verse* (Ilford, n.d.), 26–7. This poem is dated 6 June 1874.

As aw wur hurryin' on i' th' dark
Won mornin' to begin mi wark,
Just turnin' th' corner ov a street,
A facth'ry lass aw chanct to meet,
Carryin' a babby on hur arm,
Lappt in hur shawl to keep it warm,
Which to a nuss hoo had to ta'e
So's hoo met w'ave ten heawrs a day.

To addle her dear babby's bread,
Hoo'd ta'en it gently eawt o' bed,
An' dun hir best to get it dresst
Beawt br'akin' its unconscious rest;
Bu' aw cud yer its wailin' cry,
An' her deep groan as hoo passt by,
To think hoo cudno' wi' it stay,
Bu' had to wa've ten heawrs that day.

Brave heart, aw thowt, theaw bears thi fate
Better nor mony a mon co'ed great;
Theaw doesno' grumble hawve as mich
As lots o' ladies 'at are rich.
Through wind an' rain, through sleet an' snow,
Theaw bears that babby to an' fro,
An' from thy wages has to pay
To have it nusst ten heawrs a day.

Content, when stoppin' toime did coam,
If hoo cud tak' hur babby whoam,
I' wind an' rain, i' snow an' sleet,
Aw met that mother every neet,
An' notist, as hur shawl grew shabby,
Hoo lappt it closer reawnd her babby,
Whoile hur pale lips appeared to pray
For strength to work ten heawrs a day.

Bu' soon the subject o' my tawk
Wur absunt fro' mi mornin' walk,
Nor cud aw yer hur heavy feet,
Returnin' fro' mi wark at neet,
An' soa a sattlt in mi moind
As hoo'd laft facthry wark behind,
No mooar to swallow china clay
Or shoddy dust ten heawrs a day.

Yet hardly had a month gone when
Aw met hur upo' th' road agen;
Aw met hur as a did afore,
Bu' hoo no babby wi' hur bore;
It slept besoide the churchyard tree
Wheer her consumptive husbant lee;
Oh! what a proice hoo had to pay
Throo workin' hard ten heawrs a day.

Shall tragedies loike these disgrace
The vanguart o' the human race?
An' England sacrifoice to greed
Loives 'at hoo will hereafter need?
Up, workin' men, yo'r needs assert,
No moor be tramplt into dirt,
Bu', banded in a bowd array,
Refuse to work ten heawrs a day.

Aw dunno' meeon by a stroike,
Which ruinates booath soides alike;
Nor even mutual arbitration,
Bu' by imperial legislation.
Choose members to draw up yo'r laws
'At feel an interest in yo'r cause,
An' then they'll have a chance to ma'e
An Act agen ten heawrs a day.

Yo' moind 'at M.P.'s arno' sent
To sit for yo' i' Parliament
'At winno' raise their honds to tell a
Vote for the measure ov Mundella.

92

Humanity demands the grant,
Then let no odds yo'r courage da'nt,
Bu' feight until yo'n dun away
Wi' workin' hard ten heawrs a day.

Joseph Skipsey
MOTHER WEPT

From *Songs and Lyrics* (London, Walter Scott, 1892), 19.

Mother wept, and father sighed;
   With delight a-glow
Cried the lad, 'To-morrow,' cried,
   'To the pit I go.'

Up and down the place he sped, —
   Greeted old and young;
Far and wide the tidings spread;
   Clapt his hands and sung.

Came his cronies; some to gaze
   Wrapt in wonder; some
Free with counsel; some with praise;
   Some with envy dumb.

'May he,' many a gossip cried,
   'Be from peril kept;'
Father hid his face and sighed,
   Mother turned and wept.

THE STARS ARE TWINKLING

From *Songs and Lyrics*, 9.

The stars are twinkling in the sky,
   As to the pit I go;
I think not of the sheen on high,
   But of the gloom below.

Not rest or peace, but toil and strife,
    Do there the soul enthral;
And turn the precious cup of life
    Into a cup of gall.

'GET UP'

From *Songs and Lyrics*, 9.

'Get up!' the caller calls, 'Get up!'
    And in the dead of night,
To win the bairns their bite and sup,
    I rise a weary wight.

My flannel dudden donn'd, thrice o'er
    My brids are kiss'd, and then
I with a whistle shut the door,
    I may not ope again.

Chapter Two

THE PARNASSIANS

Standard English poetry by ambitious self-taught writers

W. J. Linton in old age

In this chapter I have set myself the impossible task of illustrating that huge body of poetry produced by working men and self-taught writers, written without specific political intention or affiliation, but with some ambition to distinguish the author as a highly cultured, distinctive, and intellectual member of his (or, very occasionally, her) class. These poems all suggest an endeavour on their authors' part to step beyond the cultural constraints of working-class life into a more ambitious, even universal and trans-historical, poetic discourse. They also suggest a partially contradictory pride in their origins in working-class life, an assertion of the humble and educationally deprived circumstances out of which they were fashioned. These poets both wish to be compared with the highly educated established literary figures and to insist on their distinctiveness as writers who endured low social status and whose educational and cultural deprivations had only been overcome by hard work, coupled with innate talent or 'genius'. I think that it is important for contemporary readers to acknowledge this double focus. At one level, these poems do stand comparison with other Victorian poetry, and any such comparison shows what might be called 'intelligent conservatism' among self-taught writers. The constituents of this conservatism are partly those of verse form and mode — a persisting use of the couplet, the discursive poetic essay, and the eighteenth century pastoral idiom. But more important elements are the continuing use of eighteenth-century kinds of social apprehension and moral indignation. These backward-looking, even anachronistic, poetic modes, served self-taught writers better than their attempts to use Romantic definitions of poetry as a rhapsodic form of self-expression or as a tutelary social force.

Yet at the same time as poetry by self-taught writers stands within this interesting, and almost totally unexplored, relationship with dominant poetic traditions, its links with wider notions of class development clearly require acknowledgement by a modern reader, just as they did for contemporaries. Such a recognition of class implications again results in a double response: admiration for the genuine cultural and often aesthetic achievement of some of this writing, offset against a constant sense of the derivative, apparently inexpressive, impersonal, even mechanical nature of much of the poetry. Often poetry by self-taught writers seems to be nothing more than a piece of cultural display, a class boast, written in an inflated style with cultural pretensions far beyond its artistic achievements. Certainly, as the responses illustrated in Chapter 4 suggest, this was one of the ways in which middle-class contemporaries attacked the writings of working-class poets. I do not think it is any easier now to resolve these conflicting aesthetic, cultural, and political claims on our attention. Many of the poems reprinted here seem to me interesting and worthwhile in their own right. Others come into focus primarily in relation to poetic tradition, and suggest the distinctive use that self-taught writers, with their profound knowledge of British poetry, made of the language and forms available to them. Still other poems seem primarily valuable as statements of a developing cultural and social awareness among working people, a consciousness which, it has to be said, was often expressed in conservative ideologies of temperance, stoicism, domesticity, religious devotion, and quietism.

Yet most obvious of all in this chapter, certainly when compared to the powerful sense of belonging and community expressed in various ways in chapters 1 and 3, is a sense of the poet as an anguished, lonely, and solitary figure, oppressed by the moral and social failings of a wicked world, and haunted by the fear that poetry was not enough of a counterdemanding influence, whatever claims might be made on its behalf. Behind all the rhetoric or poetic confidence, behind the cultural assertiveness of all these poems, lies a deep-rooted sense that they are *just* poems. Poetry may offer release, or consolation, or even a kind of social mobility or localized fame, but it could not offer social resolution or political reform. Poetry itself could not enact a classless world, and often served only to show how deep the divisions between classes were, even for the literate, conciliatory working-class writer. The movement of many of these poems is profoundly pessimistic. At the end of 'The Death of the Factory Child', Prince, for all the intensity of his social concern, recognizes that he has written only an epitaph, remained only a social observer. 'The Poet's Sabbath' is built on a series of contrasts — urban/rural, work/leisure, thought/work — which can only return the poet to his daily, unremitting toil at the expense of his inner life. In 'A Winter Night In Manchester' Connell charts the movement of an artisan's consciousness through several stages which lead from social disgust to terminal introversion. Most powerfully of all, the pastoral poems in this chapter, for all their apparently vigorous celebratory energy, their spiritual vision of the countryside, and their confidence in the established Romantic pastoral idioms, finally celebrate only contemplation, isolation, and retreat not as a restorative but as a debilitating intellectual destination.

The Parnassian self-taught poet, then, might be seen as merely an exaggerating of the Romantic poet, questing in solitude for spirituality, for meaning, and for identity through hopelessly large claims for poetry as a social and moral force. Poetry by self-taught, ambitious writers might be read not entirely as a cultural gesture on behalf of the aspiring artisans, but rather as a desperate quest for an individual sense of coherence and purpose among the earliest and most spectacular casualties of urban industrialism, differing from the Romantics not so much in aim or kind but rather in the more precise location of their alienation in the industrial experience of Manchester, Sheffield, or Leeds. Yet this possible, and important, reading of the poetry that follows must be sophisticated in the ways already suggested: first, by a sense of the extremely conservative ideological position offered by much of this poetry (a conservative position which had been learnt not from the Romantics but from social experience), and second, by the vast range of poetic forms and languages utilized by the self-taught writers, and the ways in which this formal variety could be either an energizing or a destructive force in their work. If the defence of poetry offered here seems to be largely derived from, or rather an exaggeration of, Shelley, Byron, and Wordsworth, the poetry itself shows considerable variety and intelligent self-consciousness, in spite of the uniformly high cultural aspirations which characterize this Parnassian strand in self-taught writing.

It is an understandable simplification to take a poem like Prince's 'To Poesy' as a typical poem in its derivative Romantic subject matter, in the fervency of its rhetoric, in the conventionality of its thought and diction, and in the apparently confident defence of the solace of creativity as an antidote to the realities of industrial life. Yet such a reading acknowledges the poem as fundamentally and inappropriately derivative, a borrowing of conventional Romantic attitudes which do not make sense of the contradictions and complexities of Prince's position as a self-taught, ambitious, competent, working-class writer. The easy solution is to resolve the contradiction between an apparently deeply felt personal vision of poetry and a derivative form and manner by reference to the power of bourgeois notions and values over the working class poetic mentality — in short, by invoking a simple notion of middle-class hegemony. But imitation and allusion to prevalent, or prior, poetic modes is not an entirely adequate way of explaining the poetry in this chapter. If it is impossible to avoid reading literary gestures like these as to some extent statements of the ideological subservience of the working-class point of view, it is also important to recognize that the model of the Romantic artist did not prevent many self-taught writers from using earlier formal and rhythmic models. I feel it important in this chapter not to exaggerate the Romantic element in self-taught writing, but to stress the variety of its sources even at the expense of complicating the ideological relationships between self-taught writers and the dominant literary traditions. Poetry is never a transparent or unmediated statement of political belief, and if, in the end, this chapter only furthers an understanding of how middle class cultural values were disseminated through literary endeavour in early Victorian England, it will have served a useful purpose. But I do not think the poetry represented here works quite as obviously as this in the display of a hegemonic historical model, but rather forces the reader to look more closely at the way in which traditional and conservative elements within artisan cultural history were made relevant to early Victorian industrial culture. Such a process is not always successful in resolving the many contradictions of working-class experience, but it did give rise to a vigorous and varied tradition of writing, less dominated by Romantic pre-conceptions than is usually assumed.

Poems of Social Indignation

Long discursive and meditative poems usually in couplets were some of the most characteristic products of ambitious self-taught writers, for whom the neo-classical idiom was something of a proving ground for their poetic skill. In detaching the following four poems (or extracts) from those in the next section, I wish to focus attention on the results of bringing together an eighteenth-century mode with characteristically early Victorian subject matter. There had been many poems about the rural and even the urban poor written in the late eighteenth century, but the implicit tension between the social problems which formed the subject of the poems and their morally self-conscious, impersonal formal mode had been generally resolved in the fluency and dramatized moral and social concern of the verse. The distinctive element in the poems by self-taught writers is that the poet's anxiety and social concern *does* begin to undermine the confidence of the verse, not just through lack of technical skill but also through the weight of their indignation. J. C. Prince struggles to find a place for himself within his own narrative, but is forced to admit that his main task is that of elegist, chastened by, but not in command of, his own social experience. George Richardson, who was anxious that his subject might be considered 'anti-poetical', can only follow the poetic path of demonstration leading to condemnation of luxury laid out in *The Deserted Village*. Yet the conventionality of Richardson's appeal for more generous and humane employers and for more Christian charity cannot conceal his determination to pursue his 'anti-poetic' subject even at the risk of banality. The modes of neo-classical denunciation are given a very personal energy and ferocity here. Ebenezer Elliott's 'Steam at Sheffield' is probably the best known single poem by a self-taught Victorian writer, and its complex narrative structure and deeply ambiguous analysis justify at least its modest celebrity. An avowed tribute to Crabbe, Elliott's *The Village Patriarch* extended

101

Crabbe's dignified Anglican moralism into a more highly focused kind of social analysis.

To my mind, the continuing use of the neo-classical poetic idioms on into the 1840s and 1850s did bring energy and discipline to self-taught writers at a time when Romantic prescriptions for poetry were being widely accepted or sophisticated by well-educated poets. The argument that the continued use of an outdated eighteenth century idiom precluded self-taught writers from anything other than a deeply moralized social analysis has, of course, to be acknowledged. Yet in admitting the ideological constraints of the modes used here, it is important to see that the attack on fluency and self-confidence, derived from moral concern, was extended into the nineteenth century not by establishment figures like Crabbe but by the self-taught poets. If the appeals to moral justice, to Christian charity, and to common humanity prevent the development of a more rigorous economic or class-based analysis, they do at least sustain poetry as an authoritative moral presence, with a gravity, concern, and moral courage which is, however ineffectual, none the less impressive.

Ebenezer Elliott
STEAM AT SHEFFIELD

From *The Poetical Works of Ebenezer Elliott* (Edinburgh, William Tait, 1840) 91–93. For a detailed account of Elliott and the publication of his works see the entries under Chandler and Klingender in the book-list.

To CHARLES HINDLEY, Esq., M.P., one of our creators of national wealth — who, while they enrich themselves, silently reproach the splendid drones of society, by increasing the productive capital of the State — I inscribe this humble Poem, wishing it were worthier.

I

Well, gaze thou on the hills, and hedge-side flowers!
But blind old Andrew will with me repair
To yonder massive pile, where useful powers,
Toiling unconsciously, aloud declare

That man, too, and his works, are grand and fair.
Son of the far-famed self-taught engineer,
Whose deeds were marvels in the bygone days!
Ill it becomes thee, with ungrateful sneer,
The trade-fed town and townsmen to dispraise.
Why rail at Traffic's wheels, and crowded ways?
Trade makes thee rich; then, William, murmur not
Though Trade's black vapours ever round thee rise.
Trade makes thee sage; lo! thou read'st Locke and Scott!
While the poor rustic, beast-like, lives and dies,
Blind to the page of priceless mysteries!
'Fair is the bow that spans the shower,' thou say'st,
'But all unlovely, as an eyeless skull,
Is man's black workshop in the streeted waste.'
And can the city's smoke be worse than dull,
If Martin found it more than beautiful?
Did he, did Martin steal immortal hues
From London's cloud, or Carron's gloomy glare —
Light-darken'd shadows, such as Milton's muse
Cast o'er th'Eternal — and shalt thou despair
To find, where man is found, the grand and fair?
Canst thou love Nature, and not love the sound
Of cheerful labour? He who loathes the crew
To whose hard hands the toiling oar is bound,
Is dark of spirit, bilious as his hue,
And bread-tax-dy'd in Tory lust's true blue.
'Thou lov'st the woods, the rocks, the quiet fields!'
But tell me, if thou canst, enthusiast wan!
Why the broad town to thee no gladness yields?
If thou lov'st Nature sympathize with man;
For he and his are parts of Nature's plan.
But canst thou love her if she love not thee?
She will be wholly lov'd, or not at all.
Thou lov'st her streams, her flowers; thou lov'st to see
The gorgeous halcyon strike the bulrush tall;
Thou lov'st to feel the veil of evening fall,
Like gentlest slumber, on a happy bride;
For these are Nature's! Art thou not her's too?
A portion of her pageantry and pride;
In all thy passions, all thou seek'st to do,

103

And all thou dost? The earth-worm is allied
To God, and will not have her claims denied,
Though thou disown her fellow-worm, and scorn
The lowly beauty of his toil and care.
'Sweet is the whisper of the breezy morn
To waking streams.' And hath the useful share
No splendour? Doth the tiller's cottage wear
No smiles for thee? 'How beauteous are the dyes
That grove and hedgerow from their plumage shake!'
And cannot the loud hammer, which supplies
Food for the blacksmith's rosy children make
Sweet music to thy heart? 'Behold the snake
Couch'd on its bed of beams.' The scaly worm
Is lovely, coil'd above the river's flow;
But there is nobler beauty in the form
That welds the hissing steel, with ponderous blow;
Yea, there is majesty on that calm brow,
And in those eyes the light of thoughts divine!

II

Come, blind old Andrew Turner! link in mine
Thy time-tried arm, and cross the town with me;
For there are wonders mightier far than thine;
Watt! and his million-feeding enginry!
Steam miracles of demi-deity!
Thou canst not see, unnumber'd chimneys o'er,
From chimneys tall the smoky cloud aspire;
But thou canst hear the unwearied crash and roar
Of iron powers, that, urg'd by restless fire,
Toil ceaseless, day and night, yet never tire,
Or say to greedy man, 'Thou dost amiss.'

III

Oh, there is glorious harmony in this
Tempestuous music of the giant, Steam,
Commingling growl, and roar, and stamp, and hiss,
With flame and darkness! Like a Cyclop's dream,
It stuns our wondering souls, that start and scream
With joy and terror; while, like gold on snow
Is morning's beam on Andrew's hoary hair!

Like gold on pearl is morning on his brow!
His hat is in his hand, his head is bare;
And, rolling wide his sightless eyes, he stands
Before this metal god, that yet shall chase
The tyrant idols of remotest lands,
Preach science to the desert, and efface
The barren curse from every pathless place
Where virtues have not yet atoned for crimes.
He loves the thunder of machinery!
It is beneficent thunder, though, at times,
Like heaven's red bolt, it lightens fatally.
Poor blind old man! What would he give to see
This bloodless Waterloo! this hell of wheels;
This dreadful speed, that seems to sleep and snore,
And dream of earthquake! In his brain he feels
The mighty arm of mist, that shakes the shore
Along the throng'd canal, in ceaseless roar
Urging the heavy forge, the clanking mill,
The rapid tilt, the screaming, sparkling stone.
Is this the spot where stoop'd the ash-crown'd hill
To meet the vale, when bee-lov'd banks, o'ergrown
With broom and woodbine, heard the cushat lone
Coo for her absent love? — Oh, ne'er again
Will Andrew pluck the freckled foxglove here!
How like a monster, with a league-long mane
Or Titan's rocket, in its high career,
Towers the dense smoke! The falcon, wheeling near,
Turns, and angry crow seeks purer skies.

IV

At first, with lifted hands in mute surprise,
Old Andrew listens to the mingled sound
Of hammer, roll, and wheel. His sightless eyes
Brighten with generous pride, that man hath found
Redemption from the manacles which bound
His power for many an age. A poor man's boy
Constructed these grand works! Lo! like the sun
Shines knowledge now on all! He thinks with joy
Of that futurity which is begun —
Of that great victory which shall be won

105

By Truth o'er Falsehood; and already feels
Earth shaken by the conflict. But a low
Deep sigh escapes him; sadness o'er him steals,
Shading his noble heart with selfish woe;
Yes, Envy clouds his melancholy brow.
What! shall the good old times, in aught of good,
Yield to the days of cant and parish pay,
The sister-growth of twenty years of blood?
His ancient fame, he feels, is passed away;
He is no more the wonder of his day —
The far-praised, self-taught, matchless engineer!

V

But he is still the man who planted here
The first steam-engine seen in all the shire —
Laugh'd at by many an Eldon far and near —
While sundry sage Newcastles, in their ire,
Swore that a roasting in his boiler fire
Would best reward the maker. Round his form
The spirit of the Moors wrapped fold on fold
Of thund'rous gloom, and flash'd th'indignant storm
From his dilating eyes, when first uproll'd
The volum'd smoke, that, like a prophet, told
Of horrors yet to come. His angry scowl
Cast night at noon o'er Rivelin and Don,
And scar'd o'er Loxley's springs the screaming fowl;
For rill and river listen'd, every one,
When the old Tory put his darkness on.
Full soon his deep and hollow voice forth brake,
Cursing the tilting, tippling, strange machine;
And then the lightning of his laughter spake,
Calling the thing a 'Whimsy!' to this day
A 'Whimsy' it is called, wherever seen;
And strangers, travelling by the mail, may see
The coal-devouring monster, as he rides,
And wonder what the uncouth beast may be
That canters, like a horse with wooden sides,
And lifts his food from depths where night presides,
With winking taper, o'er the in-back'd slave,
Who, laid face upward, hues the black stone down.

Poor living corpse! he labours in the grave;
Poor two-legged mole! he mines for half-a-crown,
From morn to eve — that wolves, who sleep on down,
And pare our bones, may eat their bread-tax warm!

VI

But could poor Andrew's 'Whimsy' boast an arm,
A back like these? Upstart of Yesterday!
Thou doubler of the rent of every farm,
From John o' Groat's to Cornwall's farthest bay!
Engine of Watt! unrivall'd is thy sway.
Compared with thine, what is the tyrant's power?
His might destroys, while thine creates and saves.
Thy triumphs live and grow, like fruit and flower;
But his are writ in blood, and read on graves!
Let him yoke all his regimented slaves,
And bid them strive to wield thy tireless fly,
As thou canst wield it. Soon his baffled bands
Would yield to thee, despite his wrathful eye.
Lo! unto thee both Indies lift their hands!
Thy vapoury pulse is felt on furthest strands!
Thou tirest not, complainest not, though blind
As human pride (earth's lowest dust) art thou.
Child of pale thought! dread masterpiece of mind!
I read nor thought nor passion on thy brow!
To-morrow thou wilt labour, deaf as now!
And must we say 'that soul is wanting here?'

VII

No; there he moves, the thoughtful engineer,
The soul of all this motion; rule in hand,
And coarsely apron'd — simple, plain, sincere —
An honest man; self-taught to understand
The useful wonders which he built and plann'd.
Self-taught to read and write — a poor man's son,
Though poor no more — how would he sit alone
When the hard labour of the day was done,
Bent o'er his table, silent as a stone,
To make the wisdom of the wise his own!
How oft of Brindley's deeds th'apprenticed boy

Would speak delighted, long ere freedom came!
And talk of Watt! while, shedding tears of joy,
His widow'd mother heard, and hoped the name
Of her poor boy, like theirs, would rise to fame.
Was not her love prophetic? Is he famed?
Yea; for deep foresight, and improving skill,
And patience, which might make the proud ashamed,
Built by himself, lo! yonder, from the hill
His dwelling peeps! — and she is with him still;
Happy to live, and well prepared to die!

VIII

How unlike him is Grip, the upstart sly,
Who on the dunghill, whence he lately rose,
Lost his large organ of identity,
And left his sire to starve! Alas he knows
No poor man now! But every day he goes
To visit his nine acres, pitiless
Of him who tills the road, that shoeless boor
Who feeds his brother exile in distress.
Hark, muttering oaths, he wonders why our poor
Are not all Irish! Eyeing, then, the moor,
He swears, if he were king, what he would do!
Our corn-importing rogues should have a fall;
For he would plough the rocks, and trench them too.
And then of bloody papists doth he bawl;
If he were king, he'd (damn them!) shoot them all.
And then he quotes the Duke! and sagely thinks
That princes should be loyal to the throne.
And then he talks of privilege — and winks:
Game he can't eat, he hints; but kills his own.
And then he calls the land a marrow bone,
Which tradesmen suck; for he no longer trades,
But talks of traffic with defensive sneer.
Full deeply is he learn'd in modes and grades,
And condescends to think my Lord his peer!
Yet, lo! he noddeth at the engineer —
Grins at the 'fellow' — grunts — and lounges on!

From THE VILLAGE PATRIARCH

From *The Poetical Works of Ebenezer Elliott* (Edinburgh, William Tait, 1840), 61. This extract is from Book Three of the poem.

III

Hail, Sabbath! day of mercy, peace, and rest!
Thou o'er loud cities throw'st a noiseless spell.
The hammer there, the wheel, the saw, molest
Pale thought no more. O'er trade's contentious hell
Meek quiet spreads her wings invisible.
But when thou com'st, less silent are the fields
Through whose sweet paths the toil-freed townsman steals.
To him the very air a banquet yields.
Envious, he watches the pois'd hawk, that wheels
His flight on chainless winds. Each cloud reveals
A paradise of beauty to his eye.
His little boys are with him, seeking flowers,
Or chasing the too venturous gilded fly.
So by the daisy's side he spends the hours,
Renewing friendship with the budding bowers;
And — while might, beauty, good, without alloy,
Are mirror'd in his children's happy eyes —
In his great temple, offering thankful joy
To Him, the infinitely Great and Wise,
With soul attuned to Nature's harmonies,
Serene, and cheerful, as a sporting child.
His *heart* refuses to believe, that man
Could turn into a hell the blooming wild,
The blissful country, where his childhood ran
A race with infant rivers, ere began
King-humbling, blind misrule his wolfish sway.

IV

Is it the horn that, on this holy day,
Insults the songs which rise, like incense sweet,
From lowly roofs, where contrite sinners pray,
And pious rustics, poor, yet clean and neat,
To hear th'apostle of the hamlet, meet?
They come, they come! behold, hark! — thundering down

Two headlong coaches urge the dreadful race;
Woe to outsiders, should they be o'erthrown!
Be ready, Doctor, if they break a trace!
Twelve miles an hour — well done; a glorious pace!
Poor horses, how they pant, and smoke, and strain!
What then? Our jails are full, and England thrives.
Now, Bomb! now, Bomb! Defiance lends again;
Hurrah! Bill Breakneck or the Devil drives!
Whip! — populous England need not care for lives.
O blessed Sabbath! to the coach-horse thou
Bringest no pause from daily toil. For him
There is no day of rest. The laws allow
His ever-batter'd hoof, and anguish'd limb,
Till, death-struck, flash his brain with dizzy swim,
Lo, while his nostrils flame, and, torture-scor'd,
Quivers his flank beneath the ruthless goad,
Stretch'd, on his neck each vein swells, like a cord!
Hark! what a groan! The mute pedestrian, aw'd,
Stops — while the steed sinks on the reeling road,
Murder'd by hands that know not how to spare!

V

Now landed Trader, that, with haughty stare,
Thron'd in thy curtain'd pew, o'erlook'st the squire!
Be kind and saintly; give, for thou can'st spare,
A pittance to the destitute; enquire
If yon pale trembler wants not food and fire?
Though thou could'st thrive, say not all others can,
But look and see how toil and skill are fed;
Lo, merit is not food to every man!
Pious thou art, and far thy fame is spread;
But *thy* Saint Peter never preach'd cheap bread.
Though bright the sun, cold blows the winter wind:
Behold the tramper, with his naked toes!
Where for the night shall he a lodging find?
Or bid that homeless boy relate his woes;
O try to feel what misery only knows,
And be like him of Wincobank, who ne'er
Sent a fall'n brother heart-struck from his door!
Or be like Wentworth's lord, a blessing here!

110

O imitate the steward of the poor,
According to thy means, heav'n asks no more!
Think of the hope of ten, the sire of nine,
The proud, skill'd man, wheel-shatter'd yesterday:
His wife will wring her hands ere eve decline;
And ah! the next week's wages, where are they?
O soothe her, help her, name not parish-pay!
Think, too, of her, the maid who dwelt alone,
Whose first, sole, hopeless love was Enoch Wray.
Forgotten ere she died, she liv'd unknown,
And told her love but once, passing away
Like a slow shadow, in her tresses gray.
Proud, though despis'd she sternly paid for rent
Her all, her weekly eighteenpence, and died,
Rather than quit the home where she had spent
Twice forty years. Her last pawn'd rug supplied
A fortnight's food. None heard her if she sigh'd;
None saw her if she wept; or saw too late
That tears were ice upon her lifeless face.
Her Bible on her lap, before the grate
That long had known no fire, gnawing a lace
With toothless gums — the last of all her race —
She died of cold and hunger in her chair.

John Critchley Prince
THE DEATH OF THE FACTORY CHILD

From *The Fleet Papers* (ed. Richard Oastler) vol. 1, no. 29, July 17
1841, 3–4.

'The Death of the Factory Child' is an interesting poem for a number
of reasons. Its origins as a commissioned poem for Oastler's propagandist campaign on factory legislation, conducted through the pages
of his unstamped journal *The Fleet Papers*, give it an unusual resonance
as a direct attempt at specific political intervention associated with
legislation, rather than the more unfocused political consciousness-
raising of most Chartist poetry. The complex nature of such poetic
interventions is reflected in the difficult relationships of the poet to his
poetic task — the poet actually breaks into the narrative as a par-

ticipant as well as trying to distance himself sufficiently from his subject to write with Augustan dignity and objectivity. Furthermore, the poet is uncertain whether he is writing a moving but ineffectual epitaph or a politically interventionist polemic. Nor is Prince sure whom he is addressing — 'the firm and uncorrupted few' of his opening paragraph are regarded as the primary audience, but the pathos and sympathy of the poem suggest an artisan readership as well. For all these uncertainties, the poem manages to sustain an impressive level of both moral indignation and poetic energy. Imitative in many ways, and drawing especially on Goldsmith's *Deserted Village*. Prince none the less shows considerable command of the dramatic and pathetic narrative, modulating between melodrama, pathos, and humane outrage. A further interest in the poem is that it was the only considerable poem of Prince's not collected either by Prince himself in his numerous miscellaneous volumes, or by the industrious Lithgow who edited Prince's memorial *Works* in 1880. There could be many reasons for this neglect, but it is tempting to believe that the explicit political context in which the poem was written, as well as the views expressed in the poem, might have caused Prince some embarrassment with his patrons and subscribers. What we might now read as impressively sustained moral indignation might well have been read by mid-Victorian readers as political impertinence. A study of the poem by A. S. Crehan and B. E. Maidment was published in pamphlet form by Manchester Polytechnic in 1978.

The following affecting story, so well told by a poor operative, is copied from that excellent publication, *The People's Magazine*, for July, 1841, by the Rev. J. R. Stephens. I well remember poor Prince telling me the tale; and when I desired him to versify the same, how readily he complied with his 'King's' request. My readers will judge how well he performed the task — *R.O.*

> Hear me! ye firm and uncorrupted few,
> Followers of freedom! and of virtue too!
> Ye, who are pleading with a noble zeal
> For poor men's rights — rejoicing in their weal;
> Friends of the parent — guardians of the child —
> Whose frames are wasted, and whose souls defiled
> Within these halls of tyranny which stand,
> Gloomy and vast, o'er all the sinking land.
> Too long, my harp hath breath'd of fancy's dreams,
> Too long responded to unworthy themes.

112

Farewell! ye once-lov'd fictions of my youth,
Its future tones shall harmonise with truth.
To rouse the Labourer in peril's hour;
To cheer the victims of a lawless pow'r;
To wake that slumbering energy of soul
Which brooks no wrong, and spurns unjust controul;
To add my feeble voice to that which rings
With awful thunder in the ear of kings;
This is my hourly hope, my daily aim;
If virtuous men approve, I seek no higher fame:

The long drear winter night was gathering fast;
The snow danced wildly on the fitful blast;
Within yon Bastile's suffocating walls,
(Whose very name my sickening soul appals,)
The gas which burns to light these living graves
Gleam'd on the faces of a thousand slaves.
I saw, and knew one gentle victim there,
The youngest of a widow'd mother's care:
Hard had he labour'd since the morning hour, —
But now his little hands relax'd their pow'r —
Yet, urg'd by curses or severer blows,
Without one moment's brief, but sweet, repose,
From frame to frame the exhausted sufferer crept,
Piec'd the frail threads, and, uncomplaining, wept.

While yet the night was boisterous and chill —
While winds were loud, and snows were drifting still,
The bell gave out its long expected sound,
The mighty engine ceased its weary round.
Forth rush'd the captives, — a degraded train! —
Till morn should summon them to toil again.
Some to the maddening ale-cup rashly sped;
Some to the short oblivion of their bed;
But he whose tale is woven in my song —
The first to fall, of that devoted throng —
With mingl'd cold and pain his tears ran o'er,
As the keen ice-wind entered every pore.
I ask'd his ailment, but he did not speak;
His fate was written on his ghastly cheek, —

I strove to help him with a friendly hand:
Alas! poor boy! he could not walk or stand.
I clasp'd my arms around his wasted form,
And bore him through the fury of the storm;
Up the dark street my eager footsteps bent,
Cursing the power that doom'd him, as I went;
His mother met me, with unfeign'd alarms,
And snatch'd the slaughter'd victim from my arms,
Kiss'd his pale lips, and call'd upon his name;
He murmur'd faintly, but no answer came.
I turn'd in grief from her imploring cries;
Unbidden tears were springing in my eyes;
Yet, breathing words of hope, I sought my home,
To ponder upon miseries to come.

The wond'rous wizard, Sleep, had now unfurl'd
His drowsy pennons over half the world;
The widow's children to their beds were gone,
And left her calm, yet mournfully, alone —
Alone with him, the idol of her heart.
Whose sinless soul was yearning to depart;
She, mute at length, with sorrow and dismay,
Wept, o'er his shattered frame, the night away.

Time was, ere commerce seal'd his early doom;
Shut up in Moloch's life destroying womb;
Ere yet the roses of his cheeks were pale,
He ran uncurb'd o'er mountain, moor, and vale:
Lur'd by the hives of bees, the voice of birds,
Sweet and familiar, as his mother's words, —
With buoyant step he sallied forth at morn,
And pluck'd his hasty dinner from the thorn;
He knew each sylvan and sequester'd nook;
He watch'd the secret mazes of the brook
Thread the dark forest; roam'd the laughing fields,
Deck'd with each golden bud that summer yields,
The same, though changeful nature frown'd or smil'd,
A healthful, innocent, and joyous child.

Thus, in the mourner's harass'd mind were glass'd,
These sad, yet sweet, reflections of the past,
Until these thrilling words her vision broke: —
'Mother! dear mother!' — twas her boy who spoke.
With fever'd lips he ask'd the cooling draught,
And, long and deeply, from the cup he quaff'd;
But, scarcely had he turn'd his head to rest:
Fondly secure upon his mother's breast,
A sound, which woke no feeling but of fear,
With well-known import smote his startled ear —
A sound alas! which prov'd his dying knell, —
The horrid clangour of the Bastile bell!
Then, starting up, he gaz'd on vacant space,
Cried, as he listen'd with bewilder'd face,
'Oh! mother, mother, I can work no more,
My head is painful, and my feet are sore;
Forgive me, mother, if I thus complain —
I fear I never shall be well again;
And if I die, O! do not weep for me,
But make my grave beneath some pleasant tree,
Where summer flowers around its roots may spring,
And summer birds within its branches sing;
And tell my loving sisters when they weep,
I saw my gentle father, in my sleep;
And, as he kindly looked and sweetly smil'd;
I thought he call'd me his own happy child.'
The suff'rer spake his last — his eyes grew dim;
The cruel spoiler palsied ev'ry limb;
One sigh — before the victory was won, —
One gentle tremor — and the strife was done; —
Whilst the glad spirit, freed from chains of clay,
Soar'd to her native realms, away, away.

My painful task is drawing to a close;
I would not dwell upon a parent's woes.
She mourned for him, as mothers always mourn,
Yet, did not seem to wish for his return.
She laid him in the earth with decent pride,
For poor men's charity the means supplied;

And one poor bard to whom the child was known,
Inscrib'd these lines upon his humble stone: —

EPITAPH

Here sleep the relics of an orphan flower,
Crush'd by the brutal foot of lawless pow'r;
Another victim to the thousands slain
Within the mighty slaughterhouse of gain.
O! come ye kind philanthropists, who feel
The noblest int'rests in the people's weal,
Pause on this infant-martyr's new turn'd grave,
Swear to emancipate the British slave;
Tell the oppressor, that the widow's God,
In justice, wields an all-avenging rod.
And if the pow'rs of human virtue fail,
The hand of heaven will certainly prevail.

'John Critchley Prince.'

George Richardson
From PATRIOTISM

From *Patriotism and Other Poems* (London, W. J. Adams and
Manchester, G. and A. Falkner, 1844), 39–43.

George Richardson was a Manchester contemporary of Charles Swain,
Sam Bamford, Elijah Ridings, and J. C. Prince, who had risen from a
poor background to become a respectable clerk. His account of his
enormous respect for learning, poetry and painting in particular,
forms a Preface to *Patriotism*, a book published with some style
despite its provincial origins. The title poem is inspired by both
orthodox Christianity and a conservative vision of a settled agrarian
Britain (there are sections of Canto II called 'The dread and curse of
Rebellion' and 'The horrors of Civil War') but Richardson's social
vision, like that of Chartism, defends social criticism and denunciation
of injustice as a patriotic act, as the following section describing the
plight of the handloom weavers suggests.

England! my persecuted isle,
When will thy light of freedom smile?
Alas! the mighty of the land
Disdain the lowly straggling band!
When will thy stricken sons be free,
By rightful, legal, wise decree,
The flag of Justice wave unfurled,
And Peace enfold the jarring world?

Lo! The pale weaver at his loom,
In the damp cellar's sickly gloom,
Toiling for bread from early light,
Through lurid day to darksome night;
Look on his dewy brow, where care
Hath stamped the impress of despair,
And in his eye, too stern to weep,
Behold a canker keen and deep!
His bosom throbs with conscious pain,
As under currents swell the main;
Unheeded grief, with racking tone,
Hath torn his heart — with vigour gone;
His frame, by ceaseless turmoil bent,
Nerve, life, and spirit — all are spent;
To cruel vassalage a prey,
Drooping with premature decay.
Sad baffled hope, without redress,
Concludes each day of bitterness —
The irksome day, the restless night,
And hunger comes with morning light —
A human sacrifice! a slave
Living immured within a grave,
As one within a dungeon's gloom
Is fated to a dismal doom!

Look in his cot, where pining dearth
Is seen beside the wretched hearth,
Where, comfortless, his tender band
Around the dying embers stand;
They ask for bread! O, God of Heaven,
When thou for all has plenty given!

Behold, his agony of mind
To utter penury consigned,
To know his wife and infant brood
Must feel the dreadful want of food;
Whilst ye, base lordlings, 'mid their strife,
Gloat on the luxuries of life!
Behold the broken walls and door,
The shattered panes, the dark, damp floor,
The homely table, rugged chair —
Not even common food is there;
With roof scarce sheltering their head,
Nor covering for their darksome bed!
Oh, thus the skilful weaver lives —
This is the boon that England gives!

Descend to the home, and narrowly scan
The cell of the labouring artisan;
The humble hovel, cold, clammy, and bare,
Calls loud for your mercy and friendly care;
How dingy and drear, with scarcely a ray
Of the cheering and blessed light of day!
What joy hath he through the season of life,
'Mid months and years of harassing strife,
Whilst the utmost effort of human power
Scarce yields relief for the wants of each hour,
And hunger, with heart-stirring moan, is there,
With fleshless fangs on the wrinkles of care;
There, on the pallet bed huddled and low,
Sweet rest is encumbered with visions of woe,
Till morning appears, when, faint and aghast,
The lab'rer creeps forth with a hopeless repast.
   Thus journies the poor, suffering man,
   A victim to a selfish ban;
   Thus, patient, curbs with calm control
   The burning fervour of his soul!
Ye proud voluptuaries of earth
Who boast, how vainly boast of birth!
Yet ask Protection! shame, oh, shame!
Degraded and perverted name;
Protect ye, minions of the land,

Against a trammelled, hungry band!
Protect ye, in your chariot pride,
Against the houseless at your side!
Protect ye, at your orgeian rites,
Against the squalid foodless wights!
Protect ye, 'gainst the low, obscure,
The weakly, harassed, prostrate poor!
Protect ye, while ye dare to hold
Heaven's bounty for the lust of gold;
What know ye in your princely domes
Of thousands and their narrow homes?
What know ye of the common want —
Of wages, or of warmth the scant?
What know ye of the lack of bread,
The throb of woe, the fevered head!
No anxious days, no nightly throes,
Perplex your minds, or wound repose,
Tho' near, yet far, ye swell apart,
And 'reck not of the anguished heart!
Vouchsafe to ope 'one cottage door,'
And yield some solace to the poor;
Approach with sympathetic care,
And see the sickly misery there!

Philosophical, Discursive and Historical Poems

This section offers a glimpse of the more ambitious and extended poems written by self-taught writers. All four of the poems here are eighteenth-century in feel, and the verse forms and diction confirm this sense of a conservative tradition of meditative and philosophical poetry emerging among artisan poets. Cooper's *The Purgatory of Suicides* clearly makes larger poetic claims than the others. All the poems are allusive in method, echoing *The Deserted Village* and Gray's 'Elegy' in particular, and seek to make available a harmonizing vision which will make sense of, if not resolve, social conflicts and hardships. In this, they borrow the ideological purpose of their eighteenth-century models. As with the poems of moral indignation in the previous section, the predominant values are moral and humanitarian, which inevitably leads to a conservative analysis of social relationships. Both Cooper and Ridings invoke the Chartist tradition of Edenic vision and use the Chartist rhetoric of exhortation, but neither poet, in these longer ruminative poems, is bound to specific local political purpose. All four poems reinforce their conception with competent versification, which authenticates their claim to be taken seriously as part of an established poetic discourse, but the outmoded formality of this kind of verse in the 1840s and 1850s is immediately obvious. Without the driving force of specific political occasion or a dominating vision of social injustice, the conservative poetic forms used here seem to predetermine what can and cannot be said. There is little tension here between form and content of the kind which energizes the poems in the previous section.

Charles Swain
From THE MIND

From *The Mind and Other Poems* (Fifth edition, London, Simpkin Marshall; Manchester, A. Ireland, 1870). First published as 'Beauties of the Mind' in 1831, the poem was revised and extended into 'The Mind' in 1832, and was frequently reprinted in its later form.

Born in Manchester, Swain was one of the small number of artisans who escaped into a substantial career in London, working as an engraver on many of the major book-illustrating ventures of the mid-Victorian period. Swain's London contacts ensured that his work was kept in print, and he was a widely published magazine and album poet. His verse tends to be vapid and conventional in expression and attitude, and, for all its portentous claims, *The Mind* is really little more than a series of well-worn if competently versified platitudes, its subject and manner largely drawn from Campbell and Rogers. Swain's books are produced in imitation of such illustrated best-sellers as Rogers's *Poems* and *Italy*, and Swain is unusual in retaining his urbanity and poise despite his social origins and his move to London. His poetry continued to be admired in Manchester and its environs long after Swain had moved to London. *The Mind: its Powers, Beauties, and Pleasures* is written in the Spenserian stanzas used by Cooper for 'The Purgatory of Suicides', but the tone is genial and bland, reducing the intensity of the discussions about art, patriotism, and cultural purpose so central to self-taught writers to a series of vapid celebratory remarks. The following section is from the First Part of the poem, which comes complete with a preliminary 'Analysis' of the argument to emphasize its origins in eighteenth century reflective verse.

> Thine are, oh Mind! — the colours which delight
> The artist in his visionary mood! —
> Thou art the inspiration and the might —
> The deep enchantment of his solitude!
> What time nor breath, nor sounds of life intrude —
> Where Alps on Alps eternally seemed piled —
> Then is thy best — thy holiest impulse wooed!
> Amid the grand, the wonderful, the wild,
> For ever have thy loftiest revelations smiled.

Thy mighty and immortal energies
That crowned the genius of young Angelo,
And steep'd his spirit in the richest dyes
That nature's wealthiest fountains could bestow;
The tastes, the passions, sentiments which show
The eloquence of colours — and those fine
Mysterious sympathies that thrill and glow,
Like stars which burn and tremble as they shine, —
Gifting the painter's sight with glories all divine.

Who may behold the works of Raphael's hand
And feel no mountings of the soul within;
Find not his sphere of intellect expand,
And the creations of the pencil win
His thoughts towards heaven — to which they are akin!
Ennobling his whole being, — touching chords
Of holiest sweetness, — purifying sin —
Raising a deathless moral that records
The majesty of truth, in *tints* surpassing words! —

Hues which are immortalities! — for age,
That moulders the high hand which gave them birth,
Consigns to dust the painter, poet, sage,
Increases but their glory and their worth: —
They are the gifts which dignify the earth! —
Exalt humanity, refine, inspire;
And lend a charm to grief — a grace to mirth!
That wake the finest echoes of the lyre —
And stir the kindling heart with Hope's Promethean fire.

What though pale penury may haunt the spot
That genius hallows with its earliest flame,
Correggio lives while princes are forgot —
The canvas speaks when kingdoms lose their name.
Where lie the great whose gold was all their fame? —
May costly cenotaph — can sculptur'd tomb —
Save titled ashes from oblivion's claim? —
Yet there be names that years may not consume,
Nor misery corrode — nor death despoil their bloom.

West, Reynolds, Wilson, Lawrence — these are names,
My country! — dear — ay, doubly dear, to thee;
Gems of thine own heart's mine, whose lustre shames
The earlier record of thine history;
High denizens of immortality, —
Enduring pillars of their native shore —
Whose memories are a people's legacy! —
A rich bequeathment, and beloved the more,
For they were good as great, brave spirits born to soar.

'T is not alone the poesy of form —
The melody of aspect — the fine hue
Of lips half blushing, odorous and warm,
Of eyes like heaven's own paradise of blue;
Nor all the graces that encharm the view
And render beauty still more beautiful;
But the *resemblances* that can renew
Past youth, past hopes, past loves, no shade may dull;
Affections years may dim — but never quite annul! —

Wresting from death and darkness, undecayed,
The kindred lineaments we honoured here;
The breast on which our infant brow had laid,
The lips that kiss'd away our first brief tear —
The all we lost, ere yet the funeral bier
Convey'd to our young souls how great a blow
Laid desolate the homes we loved so dear; —
Oh, heart! — too early wert thou doom'd to know
The grave that held thy sire, held all thy hopes below!

Then, ah! — for ever sacred be the Art
Which gave me all the grave had left of mine!
I gaze upon this portrait till my heart
Remembers every touch and every line;
And almost do I deem the gift divine,
Direct from heaven, and not from human skill: —
Instinct with love, those noble features shine —
The eyes some new expression seems to fill —
And half I know thee dead — half hope thee living still!

Through all the orphan loneliness of years
The lyre breath'd first to glad my silent way;
Dispell'd the gathering night of doubts and fears,
And, like Aurora, wreath'd the wings of day! —
No longer drooped my heart to gloom a prey:
That charm smiled o'er me, even in my dreams —
The source and spirit of all harmony —
Touching the future with romantic beams,
And pouring freshness forth as from exhaustless streams.

Thomas Cleaver
From NIGHT

From *Night and Other Poems* (London, Simpkin Marshall; Stokesley, W. Braithwaite, 1848), 17–21.

Thomas Cleaver's 'Night' clings without diffidence to a very eighteenth-century mode. A meditative poem in pentameter couplets, its narrative voice and objectified, impersonal moral tone, and its subject matter, all declare its neo-classical models. Ideologically, too, the stress on domesticity, on humanitarian and Christian social values, and the perception of social relationships in almost exclusively moral terms emphasize the poem's conservatism. Yet for all its reflex Augustan responses, this is a poem which does admit the urban and the industrial, and there are clear moments when the old social perceptions have to confront new realities like 'the pale mechanic' who might 'reform the laws'. But it is the untroubled way in which Cleaver can persist in his eighteenth century poetic mode and moral certainties which is, I think, the most interesting aspect of this poem. In borrowing the diction, form, and voice of eighteenth century reflective poetry, it was almost impossible for self-taught writers to formulate any other social vision than that offered to them by their poetic models. Cleaver's adherence to the neo-classical mode, in Stockton, in 1848, shows how a self-taught poet perceived literary form as being free from historical specificity. All literary modes were equally available to the writer whose reading was omnivorous and not constrained by the flow of fashion or theoretical polemic. Cleaver's poem is dedicated to Charles Swain.

The Day is o'er! yet pleasure, commerce, gain,
Still cheat the heart and press the weary brain;
The arm of toil pursues its constant trade,
Heedless of rest, or Night's intrusive shade;
Life's stir and tumult ceaseless yet prevail,
Swell through the street, and float upon the gale;
Still Fashion shines in all its vain display
Where Pomp and Title boast their rich array;
Still murmuring pours the human tide along,
As different aims impel the varied throng.
The trifling lounger and the painted fair,
The pale mechanic, and the man of care;
The vain — the great — the wealthy and the proud —
The thief — the outcast, mingle in the crowd!
The loitering vagrant skulks with jealous eye,
Or boldly importunes the passer-by;
Some blind old suppliant whines his rueful case,
And, as he pleads, upturns his sightless face.
And now, when placid Nature woos to sleep,
What thousands wake to tremble, watch, and weep;
Tend the loved form in illness prostrate bowed,
Or mourn the pallid inmate of the shroud
Wrapt in that solemn sleep of voiceless Night,
Which half appals affection's aching sight;
While some to scenes of mirth and vice repair,
To add another night to life's despair,
Lend to the cheek a sickly pallor wan,
Bedim the God-ray, and degrade the man!
  Now where the tavern swells its motley din,
Dispute and song discordant reign within;
The brain is tortured for the ribald jest;
If wit be dull, the laugh supplies the rest;
There seeks the troubled mind a false repose,
Woos in the cup Oblivion of its woes.
The politician prompts the keen debate,
Reforms the laws and renovates the State.
See there the man debased — the spendthrift sot,
While by his hearth, forsaken and forgot,
Pines the lone form of her, the grief-distressed,
Her cherub infant sleeping at her breast;

Turns her sad eye to days when all was bright,
And weeps and watches through the weary night.
  In smiling contrast view the worthy sire,
True to each noble aim, each wise desire,
Seek at the evening hour the peaceful charms
That sanctify his home! Affection's arms
Receive him with delight, no ills annoy,
To banish from his hearth the light of joy;
Here social converse cheers, devotion sways,
And sweet ascends the voice of evening praise;
Here magic tale and poet's verse engage,
Or deep reflections from the sterner page;
Kind words, and deeds of fondness, all endear
The quiet current of each passing year;
And oh! let troubles darken as they may,
There's one whose smile can chase them all away;
She that to home lends loveliness and grace;
The guardian spirit of that hallowed place!
His the delight to gather round his knee
His blooming children, innocent and free,
And, led by Admonition's gentle hand,
See how the mind's young energies expand,
While hope points onward into future years,
That when the almond flower of age appears,
They all shall stand, in honor and in praise,
The pillar of his fast-declining days!
  Beloved Home! where'er our steps may be,
We find no joy in life can equal thee; ·
When virtue, peace, and mild contentment dwell,
To weave o'er every hour their sacred spell;
Refine the manners, captivate the soul,
And guide the passions by a wise control!

Thomas Cooper
From THE PURGATORY OF SUICIDES

From *The Poetical Works of Thomas Cooper* (Second edition, London, Hodder & Stoughton, 1886), 57–61. First published 1845.

The Purgatory of Suicides is one of the most famous monuments to the development of working class cultural aspirations, as Cooper himself predicted it would be. The reasons for its celebrity are easy to understand. It is, first of all, a very ambitious undertaking, in ten books, sustained in the difficult Spenserian stanza; it stands out among the occasional lyrics, pastoral melodies, Chartist hymns, and exhortations of his contemporaries for both its epic scale and its poetic achievement. Secondly, the poem had what might in retrospect be called a very romantic origin, being written while Cooper was imprisoned in Stafford gaol for his political activities as a Chartist in the early 1840s. The poem was part an act of localized defiance, partly amuch wider cultural challenge on behalf of all self-taught and working-class writers, and the Preface of successive editions insisted on its origins as a 'greater prison rhyme', as Cooper himself styled it. Thirdly, Cooper was very well known not only in the 1840s, but throughout the century as he developed a post-Chartist career as a lecturer, preacher, and writer. Thus the poem achieved an iconic stature as an emblem of social progress, living proof that humbly born and poorly educated writers could discourse with all the allusiveness, high seriousness, learning, and sustained poetic energy which had seemed to belong only to an educated élite. Despite the revisionism of Cooper's later accounts of his early career, especially expressed in his superb *Life of Thomas Cooper Written by Himself* (1872), *The Purgatory of Suicides* retained its symbolic cultural prominence in accounts of the achievements of working-class culture, its specific political context having been dispersed into more acceptable admiration of its epic scale and ambitions. *The Purgatory* is not an easy poem to represent by extracts. It is tempting to use the inspirational, if not very specific, exhortations to working people with which each book opens, but the range of the poem is better represented by one of the many dialogues which the poet witnesses and records on his prolonged intellectual wanderings round a Dantesque purgatory, peopled by the carefully invoked shades of the world's suicides. Cooper manages to create an epic vision of history which is self-consciously revealed as an act of poetic endeavour, 'the birth of intellection' as he puts it in this passage. *The Purgatory of Suicides* is to be read as much as a defence of poetry at its most elevated as for its commentary on history and on human aspirations.

127

Methought, on this aspiring form I gazed
Until a youth, who downcast looked, and coy,
Came near; when wondering that he never raised
His eyes, I asked what thoughts might him employ:
The minstrel said, 'twas 'he who to enjoy
'Plato's Elysium leapt into the sea —
'Cleombrotus' — and, the fanatic boy
Thus briefly named, my minstrel guide from me
Departed. I, to follow felt I was not free.

Perplexed, I seemed a while to look around,
And wistfully to think of mother Earth;
But soon all thought and consciousness were bound
Unto that mountain region: I felt dearth
Of earthly sense, as heretofore, but birth
Of intellection; for the spirits twain,
Of Hellas sprung, seemed now, in words of worth,
Though without mortal sound, of their soul's stain
And essences of things, to speak in fervid strain. —

'Sage Agrigentine, shall we never leave
Our earth-born weaknesses?' — the youth began:
'Ages of thought, since Hades did receive
Our spirits, have elapsed, by mortal span, —
Still, from the great disciplinarian
Stern Truth, we slowly learn! A juggler's dupe
Thou art, ev'n now — thyself the charlatan!
Nay! — like an intellectual eagle, stoop
Upon thy quarry, Self-Deceit, with conquering swoop!

'Vainly, thou knowst, thou wilt seek worshippers
Of thy proud foolery, here. Before thee fall
No votaries; and thy erring spirit stirs,
In vain, her sovereignty to re-enthral
By harbouring old thoughts terrestrial:
None will thy godship own! Thy rock descend,
Laying stale follies by, and let us call
Forth from the mind the vigorous powers that rend
Fate's curtain; and our ken beyond these shades extend!' —

The younger Hellene ceased; and, while he spake,
The elder changed, like one who having quaffed
The maddening cup, up, from his couch doth wake,
And — told by crowds that old Lyaean craft
Beguiled him, till he skipt, and mouthed, and laught,
As one moon-struck, — now, ebriate with rage,
Dashes to earth the foul venemose draught;
So changed, from pride to ire, the thought-smit sage:
As if the soul now spurned her self-wrought vassalage.

Descending his imaginary throne
With haste, upon the rugged granite peak
He seemed to have laid his fancied godhead down;
For, like to glow that crimsons mortal cheek,
A glow of shame came o'er the lofty Greek,
When, 'midst the grove, upon the mountain's sward
He stood, and, couched in phrase antique,
Poured forth his inmost thoughts. A rapt regard
Rendered the youth while thus discoursed the ancient bard:

'Cleombrotus, thou humblest me; yet I
Thy debtor am; fraternal chastisement
Our spirits need, even here — O mystery
Inexplicable! Vainly, on earth outwent
The mind on high discovery, prescient
Herself esteeming of her after-state;
For Ease, Pain's issue, here, is incident,
As to Earth's clime; and all unlike our fate
To what we did in mortal life prognosticate.

'Thou findst not here deep ecstacy absorb
With ravishment perpetual the soul;
Although Elysian dreams yon dreaming orb
Enticed thee to forsake, and flee to goal
Eternal. Neither do fierce fires control
Our thought with mystic torture, as they feign
On earth, who now affright, and then cajole
Poor trampled earthworms — picturing joy or pain
Ghostly, until the mind subserves the body's chain.

'Here, as on earth, we feel our woe or joy
Is of and from ourselves: the yearning mind
Her own beatitude, and its alloy,
Creates, and suffering ever intertwined,
She proves with error. Fool — I am, and blind —
Amidst my fancied wisdom! What impels
The soul to err? If in the right she find
Her happiness concentred, why rebels
The will against the judgment till it foams and swells?

'A tempest, — aided by the raging blast
Of passion, — and the yielding soul is whirled
Helplessly into guilt's black gulf, or cast
On death's sharp breakers? What hath hither hurled
Thy bark and mine? Our senses' sails upfurled
We did esteem, by sage Philosophy,
Yet was our vessel caught where fiercest curled
The furious billows, and poor shipwrecks we
Were left — even while we boasted our dexterity!

'Thou, whilst aspiring after fuller bliss
Than earth affords, wert maddened with desire
To realise some pure hypostasis
Platonic dreamers fable from their sire,
The Academian: I consuming fire
Felt daily in my veins to see my race
Emerge from out the foul defiling mire
Of animal enjoyments that debase
Their nature, and well-nigh its lineaments efface.

'I burned to see my species proudly count
Themselves for more than brutes; and toiled to draw
Them on to drink at Virtue's living fount,
Whence purest pleasures flow. Alas! I saw
Old vice had them besotted till some awe,
Some tinge of mystery, must be allied
With moral lessons; or, a futile law
My scholars would esteem them. Not in pride
To Etna's yawning gulph the Agrigentine hied:

130

'I loved my kind; and, eager to exalt
Them into gods, to be esteemed a god
I coveted: thinking none would revolt
From godlike virtue when the awful nod
Divine affirmed its precepts. Thus, to fraud
Strong zeal for virtue led me! Canst thou blame
My course? I tell thee, thirst for human laud
Impelled me not: 'twas my sole-thoughted aim
To render Man, my brother, worthy his high name!' —

So spake Empedocles; and him the youth
Thus answered: — 'Mystery, that for ever grows
More complex as we, ardent, seek for truth,
Doth still encompass us! Thy words disclose
A tide of thoughts: and o'er my spirit flows
Wave after wave, bearing me, nerveless, from
My fancied height: as when, by acheful throes,
Self-castaway, the shelving rock I clomb,
The sea asserted o'er my limbs its masterdom.

'My chiefest marvel is that Wisdom's son,
Thyself, should, after ages have gone o'er
Him, and his race unto the tomb is run,
Still feels anxieties which earth's old shore
Convert to hell. Empedocles, no more
Mix palliation with confession, guise
Of fraud with truth! If, in thy heart's deep core,
Thou hadst not erred, why, by the grand assize
Of the soul's Judge, dost thou in Hades agonise?

'No longer from thy judgment seek to hide
The truth indisputable — that thy heart
Was moved, like every human heart, by pride —
That subtle poison which with fatal smart,
Man's spirit penetrates, and doth impart
Its hateful tinct even to his pearliest deeds.
Whence rise the spectrous forms that flit athwart
Thy mental vision here? Thy thought — why breeds
It still Pride's haughty plant, unless from earth-sown seeds?

'I question not the truth of thy deep love
For virtue, for man's happiness thy zeal.
Empedocles, thou knowst my soul hath clove
To thine for ages, in these shades: we feel
Our heart congenial while we thus reveal
Its throbbings to the core. Oh! not in hate
Or mockery do I once again appeal
Unto thy nobler thought. Though sad our state,
Let us from self-deceit the soul emancipate!'

He ceased . . .

Elijah Ridings
From THE ISLES OF BRITAIN

From *The Village Muse — the Complete Poetical Works of Elijah Ridings* (Third edition, Macclesfield, Thomas Stubbs, 1854), 68–72.

Elijah Ridings, along with Samuel Bamford, was one of the two local writers of the Manchester region most widely respected by their own class in the early Victorian period. In contrast to writers like Charles Swain or J. C. Prince, Ridings and Bamford sought a primarily local and artisan readership, as the title of Ridings's collected works suggest. Such a rejection of metropolitan or even universal aspirations does not prevent Ridings from being an allusive or ambitious poet. His sense of his audience brings a sanity and sturdiness to his poetry which saves it from the inflated claims or pretentious diction of the most ambitious self-taught writers. 'The Isles of Britain' brings together a conventional patriotism with a more radical reading of British history and a vision of peace and brotherhood. Thus conservative, chauvinistic, anti-Catholic John Bullishness is brought into alliance with a sub-Chartist vision of an Edenic, reformed society in which community, co-operation, and peace are paramount. Ridings's poem makes an interesting contrast with the more explicitly radical poems in the 'Historical Narratives' section in Chapter 2. 'Sardanapalus' in stanza three is George IV.

Hail! muse of my Lancastria fair;
    No more may lie the bleeding flowers;
Born but to breathe one native air,
    They intertwine in their own bowers.

132

Red rose and white, commingling well,
     Another beauty shall be born,
And all shall praise and love to tell
     They have escaped the wounding thorn.
No more in England's genial vales
Vex'd feud or civil broil prevails;
Then all unite, as if in one —
Let all be free beneath the sun!

In by-gone years the tyrants reigned,
     And with a cruel hand held sway;
With blood of innocence were stained
     The savage lictors of the day.
On the three isles — the world-renowned —
     The triune home of famous men,
The visage of the statesman frowned,
     And none durst use the tongue or pen.
Unnumber'd pris'ners of the state —
Unnumber'd martyrs met their fate;
The victims of suspended laws,
Their lives devote to virtue's cause.

Then our Sardanapalus loved,
     And drank his wine and ate his fill,
While Sidmouth, placid and unmoved,
     Sent forth his myrmidons of ill.
Now bloom the vallies of the free,
     And clouds of darkness flee the land;
Britannia smiles o'er land and sea,
     To exercise a mild command.
There beams around another sun,
Dread times are numbered with the gone;
The moaning voice of Castlereagh,
In his blood welt'ring at North Cray,
Sounds in mine ears his myriad crimes —
A tragic tale of other times.

In city Metropolitan
     Behold a Crystal Palace rise,
That beggars every ancient fane,
     In high commercial mysteries:

Now realised is Chaucer's dream
    Upon this moral battlefield:
From Baltic and from Ganges' stream,
    The universal nations yield:
Freedom and Commerce here shake hands,
And nation, nation understands;
No more confounded are the tongues;
For love and friendship righteth wrongs;
Disorder, order soon appears;
The human face an aspect wears,
As if *were not* the lictor's rod,
And men deserved the smiles of God.

The fairy palace of old times
    Had taught my heart the better way;
Yet other themes provoke my rhymes,
    And rouse me from the lethargy,
That peaceful meditations brought,
    To lull me in the outward sense; —
Hence, diabolic evils, wrought
    Within the halls of indolence!
Ah! may I speak from wounded pride,
With feelings unto rage allied —
When nature cries to all around,
In the expressive bleeding wound?

Peace would extend her realms afar,
    Mid mild ameliorated laws,
The stains incarnadine of war,
    To cleanse in Christian mercy's cause;
A princely word of love to man
    Had called each nation and each clime —
Each creed and colour, dark and wan,
    To grace his own Victoria's time.
They met — not on Marengo's plain,
Where, erst lay thousands madly slain —
But near his own adopted home:
Oh! noble words — 'Come, hither, come —
Come, to the kingdom of my bride;
See, Queen and Subject, side by side,

'Lo! view the arts of peace awhile!
        The product of the loom and mine;
Lo! view the arts triumphant smile
        In this emporium crystalline.
Mechanic, or artificer,
        Ploughman, or poet, may behold —
Clerk, merchant, auditor, or peer,
        May view much more than mines of gold, —
What dextrous hand, or cultured mind,
Our natural gifts by heaven designed,
Can work, or mould, or form at will,
By efforts of superior skill:
Here are the treasures of the earth,
What mother Nature brings to birth.

'Come, to this land of chaste delight,
        And in her consecrated halls
Behold what charms the human sight,
        Yet ne'er the human heart appals;
The civil bond in each degree
        Reciprocating *mine* and *thine*,
In welfare liberal and free —
        Oh what a glorious work divine!
Oh may the arts of love and peace
Make every savage warfare cease!
Come, to the kingdom of my bride —
See, Queen and Subject, side by side.'

'Such Gems as Morland Drew':
nature poetry, pastoral, and self-taught writers

The pastoral mode is endemic in the work of self-taught writers. Even where not explicitly present as a subject, many other subjects are seen through the corrective or restorative implicit presence of the countryside. At first glance, the pastoral vision of the self-taught writers seems like an attempt to conceal or destroy ideology, for the kind of pastoral most usually evident is an untroubled Romantic celebration of the countryside very different from the ideologically weighted countryside of Pope's 'Windsor Forest' or Goldsmith's *Deserted Village*. It is indeed one of the central paradoxes of poetry by self-taught writers that in their poetic models they should follow Pope and eighteenth century neo-classic modes in their reflective and social poetry, but the Romantics, whose politics were much admired, largely for their pastoral and devotional poetry. In this attempt to empty the countryside of social weight, and invest it with a spiritual one, several strands can be identified. First of all, pastoral poetry by self-taught writers is the main site for religious and devotional poetry — a strand in working-class writing which is perhaps under-represented in this anthology. Although much working-class writing is underpinned by an unquestioned religious faith, pastoral's celebration of the beauty of the created world leads to an explicit devotional mode within poetry about the countryside which can only be sustained by the absence of people either as individuals or, more explicitly, as social organizations. The pastoral produced by self-taught writers is peopled only by solitary poets. Pastoral is the prime site in working-class writing for the exploration of Romantic ideas of poetic and social alienation. Secondly, the countryside is almost invariably viewed in explicit or implicit contrast to the city, as an antidote to the devastation and confusion of the city. Such contrasts are made explicit in many poems apparently about the city — in Prince's 'Death of the Factory Child' for instance, the child dies after recounting a vision of Edenic innocence. Many other poems in this chapter use pastoral/urban contrasts as a basic structure. Thirdly, the countryside becomes a metaphor for Edenic states of mind — especially focused in the images of childhood and freedom so common in Romantic pastoral, so that a constant elision takes place between not just city and country but also between present and past, knowing old age and innocent childhood. All these elements suggest a drive towards pure lyricism, and an attempt to subdue the human and social presence in the countryside to a spiritualized, if alienated, vision of purity and beauty. The content of pastoral poems by self-taught writers, then, for all its apparent innocence and simplicity, might well be read as an attempt to find a location outside the social and ideological where the celebratory role of poetry can be sustained without challenge.

In accepting the Romantic formulation of pastoral, it is nevertheless hard to find rural poetry by self-taught writers which proceeds from an obviously deep sense of conviction. The conventions of Romantic pastoral are everywhere apparent, but the ability to use pastoral as a form of self-exploration is seldom found. Most of the following poems read like the fulfilment of a poetic expectation rather than suggesting any compelling vision of the countryside. The poems which seem to contain a more complex analysis of the rural impulse are to be found in other sections of this anthology: poems which deliberately pose the countryside against the city, poems which explore poetry itself and the role of the poet, and even a few poems which deal with rural poverty. Generally, the landscape of the many hundreds of rural lyrics produced by self-taught writers is a de-politicized one of an Edenic, pre-social world, in which human perfection can only be achieved without the presence of Man. Thus, for all the celebratory energy, the constant stress on the restorative powers of nature, on the spiritualizing capacity of the countryside, most of the following poems seem to me extremely pessimistic in their account of the alienated, if rapturous, bard, alone with his thoughts which do not, unfortunately, lie too deep for words. It is a relief to find a poem like Edward Capern's jaunty 'My Latest Publication', in which cultivation and husbandry are an essential part of the natural scene. Given the endless Romantic lyrics of isolation, introspection, and consolation to be found among the works of self-taught poets, it is to be regretted that neo-classical pastoral, for all its conservative ideological vision, seldom energized self-taught writers in the way that neo-classical discursive poetry had done. Much of this anthology stresses the debt owed to eighteenth-century poetry by Victorian self-taught writers, a debt that not only gave focus to social indignation but also allowed self-taught poets to display their poetic competence and to subvert their neo-classical models on many occasions. The worship of Byron, Shelley, and other Romantic poets so often revealed in prose commentaries is not greatly evident in self-taught writing, except in the symbolist discourse of some Chartist writing. The Romantic debt does, however, dominate writing in the pastoral mode, though much of what was produced by self-taught writers merely confirms that they were better able to develop and adapt more conservative poetic forms than to develop the expressive, confessional modes of Romanticism.

John Bethune
A SPRING SONG — 1834

From *Poems by the Late John Bethune* (Edinburgh, Adam and Charles Black, 1840), 205–207.

John Bethune's tragically short and miserable life (1812–39) aroused rather more interest than his poetry, and his brother's lengthy account of his Christian virtues, patience, respectability, and longing for cultural advancement in the face of disease and poverty forms the source of Alton Locke's poetic ambitions in Kingsley's novel. Bethune's hard-won poetic skills seldom reached beyond competent pastoral and devotional poems, but in its exemplary pursuit of culture under the most appalling hardships, his life became a rallying point for middle-class defenders of the writing of poetry as a helpful and morally rewarding activity even for the very poor.

> There is a concert in the trees —
>   There is a concert on the hill —
> There's melody in every breeze,
>   And music in the murmuring rill.
>   The shower is past, the winds are still,
> The fields are green, the flowerets spring,
>   The birds, and bees, and beetles fill,

The air with harmony, and fling
  The rosied moisture of the leaves
In frolic flight from wing to wing,
  Fretting the spider as he weaves
His airy web from bough to bough;
  In vain the little artist grieves
Their joy in his destruction now.

Alas! that in a scene so fair
  The meanest being e'er should feel
The gloomy shadow of despair,
  Or sorrow o'er his bosom steal.
  But in a world where woe is real,
Each rank in life, and every day,
  Must pain and suffering reveal,
And wretched mourners in decay;
  When nations smile o'er battles won —
When banners wave, and streamers play,
  The lonely mother mourns her son
Left lifeless on the bloody clay;
  And the poor widow all undone,
Sees the wild revel with dismay.

Even in the happiest scenes of earth,
  When swell'd the bridal song on high —
When every voice was tuned to mirth
  And joy was shot from eye to eye,
  I've heard a sadly stifled sigh;
And 'mid the garlands rich and fair
  I've seen a cheek, which once could vie
In beauty with the fairest there,
  Grown deadly pale, although a smile
Was worn above to cloak despair;
  Poor maid! it was a hapless wile
Of long conceal'd and hopeless love,
  To hide a heart which broke the while
With pangs no lighter heart could prove.

The joyous spring, the summer gay
  With perfumed gifts together meet,

And from the rosy lips of May
    Breathe music soft, and odours sweet:
    And still my eyes delay my feet
To gaze upon the earth and heaven,
    And hear the happy birds repeat
Their anthems to the coming even:
    Yet is my pleasure incomplete —
I grieve to think how few are given
    To feel the pleasures I possess,
While thousand hearts, by sorrow riven,
    Must pine in utter loneliness,
Or be to desperation driven.

Oh! could we find some happy land,
    Some Eden of the deep blue sea,
By gentle breezes only fann'd,
    Upon whose soil, from sorrow free,
    Grew only pure felicity;
Who would not brave the stormiest main
    Within that blessful isle, to be
Exempt from sight or sense of pain?
    There is a land we cannot see,
Whose joys no pen can e'er pourtray,
    And yet, so narrow is the road,
From it our spirits ever stray.
    Shed light upon that path, O God!
And lead us in the appointed way.

There only, joy shall be complete,
    More high than mortal thoughts can reach,
For there the good and just shall meet
    Pure in affection, thought, and speech;
    No jealousy shall make a breach,
Nor pain their pleasure e'er alloy —
    There sunny streams of gladness stretch,
And there the very air is joy.
    There shall the faithful, who relied
On faithless love, till life would cloy,
    And those who sorrow'd till they died,

O'er earthly pain, and earthly woe,
   See pleasure, like a whelming tide,
From an unbounded ocean flow.

Thomas Miller
From SUMMER MORNING

From *Poems* (London, Thomas Miller, 1841), 67–71.

Thomas Miller (1807–74) formed part of the group of writers known
as the Sherwood Foresters, who were based in Nottinghamshire and
included such literary celebrities as William and Mary Howitt and
Spencer Hall. The group is described in Christopher Thomson's *The
Autobiography of an Artisan* (1847). Miller was one of those few artisan
authors like Gerald Massey and Thomas Cooper who rose into
literary celebrity of a limited kind, and he produced a wide variety of
books, many of which he published himself. Miller's early poems are
largely collected magazine contributions, and 'Summer Morning' is
almost a compendium of popular conceptions of pastoral, containing
devotional, patriotic, Edenic, and celebratory elements. Miller does,
however, bring a momentary sense of history into his rural celebration,
even at the expense of his rhapsodic impulse.

See yonder smoke, before it curls to heaven
Mingles its blue amid the elm-trees tall,
Shrinking like one who fears to be forgiven;
So on the earth again doth prostrate fall,
And mid the bending green each sin recall.
Now from their beds the cottage-children rise,
Roused by some early playmate's noisy bawl;
And, on the door-step standing, rub their eyes,
Stretching their little arms, and gaping at the skies.

The leaves 'drop, drop,' and dot the crisped stream
So quick, each circle wears the first away;
Far out the tufted bulrush seems to dream,
And to the ripple nods its head alway;
The water-flags with one another play,
Bowing to every breeze that blows between,

141

While purple dragon-flies their wings display:
The restless swallow's arrowy flight is seen,
Dimpling the sunny wave, then lost amid the green.

The boy who last night passed that darksome lane,
Trembling at every sound, and pale with fear;
Who shook when the long leaves talked to the rain,
And tried to sing, his sinking heart to cheer;
Hears now no brook wail ghost-like on his ear,
No fearful groan in the black-beetle's wing:
But where the deep-dyed butterflies appear,
And on the flowers like folded pea-blooms swing.
With napless hat in hand he after them doth spring.

In the far sky the distant landscape melts,
Like piled clouds tinged with a darker hue;
Even the wood which yon high upland belts
Looks like a range of clouds, of deeper blue.
One timbered tree bursts only on the view, —
A bald bare oak, which on the summit grows,
(And looks as if from out the sky it grew:)
That tree has borne a thousand wintry snows,
And seen unnumbered mornings gild its gnarled boughs.

Yon weather-beaten grey old finger-post
Stands like Time's land-mark pointing to decay;
The very roads it once marked out are lost:
The common was encroached on every day
By grasping men who bore an unjust sway,
And rent the gift from Charity's dead hands.
That post doth still one broken arm display,
Which now points out where the new workhouse stands,
As if it said 'Poor man! those walls are all thy lands.'

Where o'er yon woodland-stream dark branches bow,
Patches of blue are let in from the sky,
Throwing a chequered underlight below,
Where the deep waters steeped in gloom roll by;
Looking like Hope, who ever watcheth nigh,
And throws her cheering ray o'er life's long night,

142

When wearied man would fain lie down and die.
Past the broad meadow now it rolleth bright,
Which like a mantle green seems edged with silver light.

All things, save Man, this Summer morn rejoice:
Sweet smiles the sky, so fair a world to view;
Unto the earth below the flowers give voice;
Even the wayside-weed of homeliest hue
Looks up erect amid the golden blue,
And thus it speaketh to the thinking mind: —
'O'erlook me not! I for a purpose grew,
Though long mayest thou that purpose try to find:
On us one sunshine falls! God only is not blind!'

England, my country! land that gave me birth!
Where those I love, living or dead, still dwell,
Most sacred spot — to me — of all the earth;
England! 'with all thy faults I love thee well.'
With what delight I hear thy Sabbath bell
Fling to the sky its ancient English sound,
As if to the wide world it dared to tell
We own a God, who guards this envied ground,
Bulwarked with martyr's bones — where Fear was never found.

Here might a sinner humbly kneel and pray,
With this bright sky, this lovely scene in view,
And worship Him who guardeth us alway! —
Who hung these lands with green, this sky with blue,
Who spake, and from these plains huge cities grew;
Who made thee, mighty England! what thou art,
And asked but gratitude for all His due.
The giver, God! claims but the beggar's part,
And only doth require 'a humble, contrite heart.'

Robert Story
MY OWN HILLS

From *Love and Literature* (London, Longman, Brown, Green and Longmans, 1842), 71–72.

Robert Story (1795–1860) was another of the self-taught poets whose career was quite well known among middle-class critics and writers. *Love and Literature* is a curious mixture of poetry, prose comment, and opinion narrated by a third person 'bard' instead of by Story himself. 'My Own Hills' links landscape with childhood, patriotism, and local pride in a half-apologetic statement of a modest local identity. In using pastoral to shape a sense of self, Story follows the dominant pattern of pastoral lyrics by self-taught writers.

These are not my own hills,
    Fair though their verdure be;
Distant far my own hills,
    That used to look so kind on me!
These may have their rock and cairn,
Their blooming heath and waving fern;
But O! they stand so strange and stern,
    And never seem like *friends* to me!

'Where, pr'ythee, rise thine own hills?
    In France, or brighter Italy?
What fruit is on thine own hills
    That we must deem so fair to see?
Grows, in summer's constant shine,
The orange there, or purpling vine?
Does myrtle with the rose entwine
    On mountains so beloved by thee?'

All bleak along my own hills
    The heather waves, the bracken free;
The fruit upon my own hills
    Is scarlet hip and blaeberry!
And yet I would not those exchange,
Mid gay Italian scenes to range —
No, vine-clad hills would look as strange,
    As stern and lone as *these* to me!

In boyhood on my own hills
    I plucked the flower, and chased the bee;
In youth upon my own hills
    I wooed my loves by rock and tree;
'Tis thence my love — to tears — they claim;
And let who will the weakness blame,
But when in sleep I dream of *them*,
    I would not wake *aught else* to see!

Robert Nicoll
THE MOSSY STANE

From *The Poems of Robert Nicoll* (Second edition, Edinburgh,
William Tait, 1842), 225–7.

Nicoll's precocious career as a newspaper editor and journalist of
distinction was brought to an end by his death of consumption at the
age of twenty-three in 1837. As his early death echoes that of
Bethune, so the celebrity of his career underlines the kind of fame that
Story enjoyed as a result of middle class interest. Nicoll's swift rise
from a Scottish peasant background to a newspaper editorship in
Leeds, then his early death, attracted both by its exemplary success and
its tragic conclusion the interest of Kingsley and Smiles among many
other essayists, and the goodwill of the publisher William Tait, who
published Elliott, Overs, and other self-taught poets. Nicoll's poems
show little of his passionate journalistic and political interests, but the
energy of the dialect gives 'The Mossy Stane' more than usual
pastoral energy. Interest in Nicoll's career long outlasted his death,
and his work was reprinted often in the latter half of the century.

That ill-faur'd lump of mossy stane
Has lain amang the breckans lane,
And neither groan'd nor made a mane,
    For years six thousand!
That's fortitude — the stoics, gane,
    Wad wagg'd their pows on't!

The heather-blossom fades awa' —
The breathing winds of Summer blaw —

The plover's wail — the muircock's craw —
    I'll lay a bodle,
It snoozes on through rain and snaw,
    Nor fykes its noddle!

It's pleasant wi' a stane to crack,
It ne'er objects to word or fact;
And then they ha'e an unco knack
    Of listening well —
They a' the story dinna tak'
    Upo' themsel'.

Aweel, whinstane! since there ye lay,
The world's gane monie an unco way:
We've a' been heathens — now we pray,
    And sing and wheeple,
And mak' a lang to do and say
    Beside the steeple!

And there cam' men o' meikle power,
Wha gart the frighted nations glowr,
And did wi' swords mankind devour:
    Snoozed thee through all?
Faith! ye think little of a stour,
    Upon my saul!

Stane! if your lugs could better hear,
I doubt me if't wad mend your cheer,
If ye but kent — I fear, I fear —
    That sorrow's round ye;
Though hard as tyrants' hearts, fu' sair
    The tale wad wound ye!

How priests, and kings, and superstition,
Have marr'd and ruin'd man's condition,
If I could tell, ye'd need a sneeshin'
    To clear your een:
Lord, stane! but they deserve the creeshin'
    They'll get, I ween.

146

Look, there's the sun! the lambkins loupin'
Are o'er amang the heather coupin';
The corbies 'mang the rocks are roupin'
    Sae dull and drowsy;
This Summer day, my cracks, I'm houpin',
    To life will rouse ye!

Na, there ye lie — naught troubles thee:
Ye hae some use as well as me,
Nae doubt; but what that use can be
    The thought doth rack me;
Wi' a' my een I canna see,
    The devil tak' me!

I'm sure there's naething made in vain —
Not even a mossy auld whinstane:
Ye Powers aboon! I ken, I ken —
    Auld stane sae bonnie,
Ye just was made that I fu' fain
    Might rhyme upon ye.

Edward Capern
MY LATEST PUBLICATION

From *Wayside Warbles* (Second edition, London, Simpkin Marshall;
Birmingham, E. C. Osborne, 1870), 238–40.

Edward Capern seems to have been something of a rarity — a
self-taught working-man poet whose work did not cause him any
great anguish, and seems instead to have brought him modest
pleasure and slight celebrity. After many years as a rural postman in
Bideford, Capern moved to Birmingham, where he maintained his
steady output of largely inconsequential and occasional poems, with a
few more ambitious personal lyrics thrown in. The following poem
is unusual in using husbandry as an image of poetic production —
self-taught writers far more commonly use wild unpeopled Nature as
a metaphor for their own creativity. 'My Latest Publication', with its
jocular dedication and refusal to take itself seriously, offers an antidote
to the troubled celebration of most pastoral writing by self-taught
writers.

147

My dear brother BURRITT, you asked me to-day,
If the muse was propitious and jingling away.
Well, yes; she is lively; how can she be less?
To tell you the truth, friend, I'm just out of press.
My work has been published by Mattock and Hoe,
And brought out in hawthorn, embossed with the sloe;
And, if I am spared in a healthy condition,
Next summer shall see out another edition.
'Well, what is the title?' I hear you inquire;
'An Essay on Nature,' which you will admire.
When first I commenced, it was tug, tug, and toil;
A spade was my steel pen, my paper the soil.
But after a scratch or two made with good will,
I found that my metal would write like a quill.
As thoughts from a thought, friend, will oftentimes breed,
So charlock in acres is raised from one seed.
'Ill weeds grow apace;' and, to kill out the crop,
I burnt it together with 'scutch' on the top.
Next into the ground with a purpose I went,
Till over my task all aweary I bent;
And found that my thoughts sought expression in lines
All dotted with quaint hieroglyphical signs.
'Tis true, I first purposed commencing in prose,
When, finding a cabbage was but a green rose,
I started in verse, and discovered that greens
Was a very fair rhyme after carrots for beans;
And talk about fancy, why look at my peas;
I've old 'Dan, the Irishman,' blowing at ease:
While 'Progress' is seen in 'McClean's' great 'Advancer,'
As well as his 'Wonderful,' such a sweet dancer!
For 'Champions' of all sorts I have an affection,
And therefore I glory in 'Veitch's Perfection.'
I have stanzas of lettuce, and parsnips, and leeks,
And a canto of onions, a study for weeks.
I have sonnets of celery, turnips and sage;
And sweet mint and savory — what a sweet page!
I have raspberries blushing like love on their stalks,
And strawberries creeping all over the walks;
And, if you are loyal, 'twill gladden your sight
To see my potatoes — red, purple, and white:

148

There are 'Regents,' 'Victorias,' 'Prince Rocks,' and 'King Flooks,'
And a host of 'self-setters' abloom in the nooks,
The bright 'scarlet runner' — a fancy run wild —
Is having her fling like a frolicsome child;
While the artichoke lifts up her head to the sky,
As if in proud scorn of the marrows hard by;
And as for my parsley, 'twill just suit your mood,
'Tis such a sweet miniature, friend, of a wood.
So much for the matter my new book contains,
A work of the muscles far more than the brains;
And maybe 'twill please you to learn by the way,
That the critics have not had an ill word to say.
Thanks, thanks to a rake that revised all for me,
Not the sign of an unfinished thought can you see;
'A work' the reviewers say, 'suiting the taste.'

Yours aye in good fellowship, — E.C.

The City Observed, the City Repressed: poems about Manchester

On first thoughts, the city itself might seem to be the obvious theme for the aspiring self-taught writer. Yet in the event there are relatively few poems which describe the industrial city, and even fewer which analyse it as an economic or social system. The subject matter of the self-taught writers remained resolutely abstract, rural, or domestic. None the less, it is worth looking more closely at a group of poems which try to make sense of the city, as they quickly reveal tensions and confusions which are identifiable more widely in the writings of self-taught poets. Philip Connell's 'A Winter Night in Manchester' presents a paradigm for these problems. Connell was an immigrant Irish plasterer who published his book, revealingly called *Poaching on Parnassus*, in a tiny subscription edition in 1865. Connell begins his poem by attempting to comprehend Manchester as an unusual but rewarding aesthetic spectacle, a task rendered impossible not only by intrusive social realities, but more particularly by a conflict between a neo-classical verse form, a mock heroic tone, and a vocabulary drawn largely from Romantic pastoral verse. The problems of assimilating his reading also haunt Connell: the specific echo of Gray's 'Elegy' ('Then leaves the world to cold and darkness soon') is only slightly more obvious than allusions to Wordsworth and Bloomfield, to say nothing of a more general sense of feeble imitative recollections of many other poets indiscriminately parcelled together to describe the urban scene. (Another of Connell's poems is called 'The Cotter's Sunday Morning'.) Connell then proceeds to a ringing denunciation of the city, concentrating particularly on the lack of respectable recreation for the poor. For a moment, the poem rises into a fierce tone of moral indignation strengthened by some almost Blakean puns and paradoxes ('meet recreation' and 'tawdry' against 'alluring'). But even here Connell cannot sustain his vision, and shifts the focus of his indignation from the industrial system on to his own class, its coarsenesses, and immoralities. This is a focus which can only force Connell into retreat, and the poem shifts again to a description of an obsessively neat and orderly cottage interior, where the glib couplets tidy the city away out of sight if not out of mind. But even the comforting, and quite powerfully realized, platitudes of domestic order and harmony cannot eradicate the threat of Manchester, and Connell retreats still further, first into a course of extremely ambitious reading ('all the classic minds of Greece and Rome'), and finally into that last refuge of urban alienation, the mind itself. Introversion was, of course, the very state that Mrs Gaskell pointed to as the source of John Barton's decline in *Mary Barton*, and, as F. W. Robertson and Kingsley among other critics had suggested, morbidity was understood to be the first step towards ill-health, bitterness, and despair.

Connell is clearly a poet of limited ability, and he does not seem conscious of the emblematic progress of his poem's narrative. Yet he unconsciously reveals how hard it was for self-taught poets, who saw their main function as celebratory, to sustain any confident or optimistic way of reading the industrial city, even from a politically conservative point of view. Others in this group of city poems show similar, if less obvious, failures of confidence. J. B. Rogerson's attempt to encompass the history and recent achievement of Manchester in lyric celebration concludes bathetically with an appeal to the 'tuneful murmurings' of the poet as a force of cultural opposition to the 'busy throng' of 'Commerce'. His claims for the weight and force of poetry are overwhelmed by his earlier invocation of 'clamorous confusion' peopled by 'pallid slaves'. Rogerson can only elaborate and re-state his antithetical vision, for he lacks the poetic authority to resolve it into a version of either despair or of hope — the two cannot be separated. 'Fanny Forrester' (a female operative in a Pendleton dye-works, who contributed regularly and pseudonymously *to Ben Brierley's Journal*) and John Owen both elaborate the implicit conflict between poetry and the city, finding resolutions largely by appeal to religious or pastoral metaphors of consolation. William Billington, an ambitious and relatively accomplished Blackburn poet, locates himself like Connell on Victoria Bridge, between Manchester and Salford, but fails to see the city at all because of his revulsion from the people who inhabit it. As Connell's poem suggests, a sense of class solidarity was seldom present in Parnassian writing, as the act of writing itself de-classed the author to some extent. Billington's Parnassian concentration on the good, the elevated, and the beautiful made Victoria Bridge a poor vantage point. He sees only a vision of urban alienation from there.

Billington's disgust stands in interesting contrast to a vivid broadside ballad called 'Victoria Bridge on Saturday Night', in which the famous resort for the idle and criminal poor is celebrated for its urban energy. (There is a version of this ballad on Harry Boardman's record *A Lancashire Mon*, Topic 12TS236.) Reading the anguished and self-conscious poetic attempts to resolve the contradictions of the urban industrial complex, one often longs for the unclouded energy, good humour, and wry scepticism found in many of the urban ballads describing Manchester. The ambitious poetry is, however, an important reminder of the differences within what would be too glibly characterized as the urban working class. Neither the ballads nor the poetry offer anything more than a partial and confused reading of a complex phenomenon which was, as many writers admitted, in some ways beyond the power of language to describe. Thus, in these poems, we have Blake's 'London' or Wordsworth's 'Westminster Bridge' writ small, but writ revealingly.

A recent critical account of Manchester Poetry can be found in B. E. Maidment's chapter 'Poetry in Victorian Manchester' in A. Kidd and K. Roberts eds, *City, Class, and Culture* (Manchester, 1985).

Philip Connell
A WINTER NIGHT IN MANCHESTER

From *Poaching on Parnassus* (Manchester, John Heywood, 1865), 29–32.
The book contains a list of about 150 subscribers.

> When surly Winter o'er the naked earth
> Sends forth the stormy terrors of the North;
> When Irwell thundering from the Yorkshire hills
> Victoria Bridge up to the keystone fills.
> When fogs in Deansgate veil the dusky air,
> And winking gaslights yield a sickly glare;
> When names of streets no more on corners guide,

Bewilder'd housewifes wandering far and wide;
When colour'd lamps, with faintly lurid ray,
But dimly shew the blinking drunkard's way.
When mufflers, furs, and asthmas are the mode,
And dark umbrellas hide the miry road;
When mid a wilderness of chimneys high
The palid sun beneath a troubl'd sky —
Just peeps above the snow-cap'd roof at noon;
Then leaves the world to cold and darkness soon.
While sleet and snowdrifts usher in the night,
Then shivering Winter is established quite: —

At Evening bell when Warehouse, Office, Forge,
Workshop and Mill their thousand hands disgorge;
Where may these countless sons of toil repair
Meet recreation for the night to share?
If to the streets there rang'd on either hand
In tawdry shreds alluring harlots stand
With aching hearts and palid faces veil'd
In paint and smiles, alas, how ill conceal'd!
If to the Beerhouse there a maudlin crew
Their ribald, rank, disgusting jests renew;
If to the Theatre — with Shakespeare's art,
Tho' Brook and Dillon try to touch the heart,
Their grandest strokes what feeling heart enjoys
While ruffian, ragged gods renew their noise?

Far other scenes now bless the workman's night,
In slippers easy, chair, and shirtsleeves white,
With hair to one side comb'd, and well-wash'd face
Radiant with happiness — whilst in her place
The very cat enjoys her evening nap,
Purring her grateful anthems in his lap.
And ever as he casts around his eyes
A look meets his, beaming with hopes and joys,
And quiet happiness — his own dear Bess
Nursing their baby boy in fond caress,
His vermil' lips around the nipple press'd,
And half his cheek hid in her milkwhite breast:
There sits the workman in his happy home,

153

The fire fair blazing round the cheerful room,
The carpet brush'd, the grate and fender bright,
The polish'd table glancing to the light,
The hearth pure white, the chimneypiece array'd
With dogs and shepherds nestling in the shade;
The simple shelves with glass and china bright,
The busy bare-faced clock not always right;
The baywood bookcase, full, select, but small,
Curtain'd with crimson, pendant on the wall,
And hung around — the lovely, good, and wise
Look from their maple frames, with living eyes.
Midst maps unroll'd that to his eyes display
Leagues upon leagues of countries far away.
Nor these alone endear the workman's home.
Behold what friends to cheer his evenings come
From 'The Free Library' lo! Johnson, Blair,
Rollins, Macaulay, Robertson appear,
Boyle, Newton, Bacon, Tillotson and Hume,
With all the classic minds of Greece and Rome;
While Bulwer, Ainsworth, Lever, Boz and Scott
Recite their Thousand tales in social chat.

Behold him next wrapt up in scenes sublime!
Scenes that from Poet's brain in olden time
Flash'd forth electric, and in verse enshrin'd
Still holds a magic influence over mind,
With Homer now he mounts the Trojan wall,
Now sails with Virgil where strange oceans roll;
Now Shakespeare's magic bids his bosom swell,
Now follows Milton thro' the gloom of hell;
With Job sublimely rapt, in wonder gaze,
Or join the son of Jesse in prayer and praise.

John Bolton Rogerson
MANCHESTER

From *The Wandering Angel and Other Poems* (London, Thomas Miller, 1844), 35–36.

And this, then, is the place where Romans trod,
    Where the stern soldier revell'd in his camp,
Where naked Britons fix'd their wild abode,
    And lawless Saxons paced with warlike tramp.
Gone is the castle, which old legends tell
    The cruel knight once kept in barbarous state,
Till bold Sir Launcelot struck upon the bell,
    Fierce Tarquin slew, and oped the captives' gate.
No trace is left of the invading Dane,
    Or the arm'd followers of the Norman knight;
Gone is the dwelling of the Saxon thane,
    And lord and baron with their feudal might:
The ancient Irwell holds its course alone,
And washes still Mancunium's base of stone.

Where once the forest-tree uprear'd its head,
    The chimney casts its smoke-wreath to the skies,
And o'er the land are massive structures spread,
    Where loud and fast the mighty engine plies;
Swift whirls the polish'd steel in mazy bound,
    Clamorous confusion stuns the deafen'd ear,
The man-made monsters urge their ceaseless round,
    Startling strange eyes with wild amaze and fear;
And here, amid the tumult and the din,
    His daily toil pursues the pallid slave,
Taxing his youthful strength and skill to win
    The food for labour, and an early grave:
To many a haggard wretch the clanging bell,
That call'd him forth at morn, hath been a knell.

But lovely ladies smile, in rich array,
    Fearing the free breath of the fragrant air,
Nor think of those whose lives are worn away,
    In sickening toil to deck their beauty rare;

And all around are scattered lofty piles,
   Where Commerce heapeth high its costly stores —
The various produce of a hundred isles,
   In alter'd guise, abroad the merchant pours.
Learning and science have their pillar'd domes;
   Religion to its sacred temples calls;
Music and Art have here their fostering homes,
   And Charity hath bless'd and sheltering halls;
Nor is there wanting, 'mid the busy throng,
The tuneful murmurings of the poet's song.

'Fanny Forrester'

THE LOWLY BARD

From *Ben Brierley's Journal* (Manchester, November 1873), 265.

He tunes his lyre within his lowly dwelling,
   He sings of hopes all rosy–hued but vain,
And, while the thrilling melody is swelling,
   His soul is burning for a loftier strain.
Ye mighty dead, that haunt the poet's slumber,
   His efforts cheer, his feeble muse inspire,
Who tells the world in many a mournful number
   He mourns the incompleteness of his lyre.

He tunes his lyre where busy wheels are grinding,
   And flying straps are never, never still;
Where rigid toil the buoyant limbs is binding
   That fain would wander from the dusty mill.
He hears the carol of the country maiden —
   Oh, welcome fancy! real–like and sweet! —
The children bound, with trailing grasses laden,
   And fling their treasures at the rhymester's feet!

And while their eyes grow round with baby wonder
   His toil-stained fingers 'mongst their tresses stray;
But, lo! the engine booms like angry thunder,
   And frights the sympathetic band away!

Spindle and bobbin fill their vacant places,
    And o'er great looms slight figures lowly stoop,
And weary shadows cross the girlish faces
    That like frail flowers o'er stagnant waters droop.

Toil, toil to-day, and toil again tomorrow;
    Some weave their warp to reach a pauper grave!
Naught of romance doth gild their *common* sorrow;
    Yet ne'er were heroines more strong, more brave.
Poor common herd! they never dream of glory!
    This is their work — to *live* is its reward.
Ah! when they end their sad but common story,
    Will the great God such *common souls regard*?

Yes, yes, however menial be the duty,
    He deems it noble, if 'tis nobly done;
The lowliest soul contains the highest beauty,
In its resemblance to that humble one
Who came, not where the kings of earth assembled
    To pay their homage to the Royal Child,
But where the lowliest bent the knee and trembled
    As the blest Babe His sweet approval smiled.

He tunes his lyre in sickly court and alley,
    Where the caged lark, though captive, boldly sings,
As if, above some pleasant country valley,
    He bore the sunbeams on his buoyant wings:
The seamstress hears, and lo! the weary fingers,
    'Mid front and wristband, white and listless lie;
And though his glance upon the gusset lingers,
    No thought of scanty wage nor toil is nigh.

Long e'er she knows her crystal tears are dripping
    O'er the dead bouquet on her window sill —
Her loving lips among the grasses dripping,
    To show, though faded, they are precious still —
Her grateful heart is tenderly recalling
    The sweet, sweet, longing that their perfume made;
And hallowed tears, with withered leaves, are falling:
    She mourns their blight, even while herself does fade.

He tunes his lyre within the garret lonely,
    Where kindly priest in muffled whisper speaks
(Where weary, weary eyes are watching only
    The hectic flush upon the hollow cheeks
Of him who raves of labour long neglected,
    Of children starving and reproaching him).
Oh, God! hath he their piteous prayers rejected?
    The flush dies out, his haggard eyes grow dim.

'Mine, only mine, to toil for and to cherish!
    Lay your cool hand, sweet Mary, on my brow!
Children, plead more, they must not, shall not perish!
    There, do not hold me — I am stronger now!
I've much to do, and precious time is fleeting.'
    The priest bends lower o'er the ragged bed —
No banner waves, nor muffled drum is beating;
    Yet, 'tis a hero that lies still and dead.

He tunes his lyre, in humble chapel kneeling,
    And every note contains some pure desire —
Yea, angel forms, through floating incense stealing,
    Seem breathing benedictions on his lyre.
The great may flaunt their pampered bards above him,
    But when *their* laurels shall be sere and brown,
Kind heaven will grant, because the lowliest love him,
    To the poor rhymester an *eternal crown*.

John L. Owen
THE CITY SINGERS

From *Ben Brierley's Journal* (September 1873), 241. Number III in a
series called 'Manchester Idyls'.

So, each with special burdens, we poor singers
    In company, yet parted, jog along;
And, as the unseen halo round us lingers,
    Beguile the travel with our simple song . . .

This dower of song is manna to the city,
    It is the dew upon a crowded field;
Broadcast it scatters life, and love, and pity,
    And e'en the reapers cannot tell the yield.

The country hath its gardens, lanes, and bowers,
    Its orchards, and its pastures fresh and fair;
While naught but belching chimneys and bald towers
    Point heavenwards above this human lair.

He who can tune his reed to woodland ditties,
    Calm sitting where the brook and river meet,
Knows little of the pulse of mighty cities,
    Dream life as limpid as waves at his feet:

Knows nothing of its intermittent fever —
    How it is lashed into a fitful heat,
How it is crushed and bruised by the lever
    With which the strong press out the tender feet;

In this strange world's wild hurry and confusion
    A song becomes a sermon if it saves,
And teaches that which is not all delusion,
    But which may brighten e'en the brink of graves.

Then louder, louder, sing on, oh, my brothers!
    There is no surfeit in the realms of song:
Let gifts, God-given, be a bliss to others,
    And let your purpose steady be, and strong.

So shall street children, playing in the gutter,
    And toilers sweating at the busy loom,
Instinctively your lyric-lesson utter
    While they shall steal like fragrance through the room . . .

William Billington

SALFORD BRIDGE — That popular resort of the great unwashed

From *Sheen and Shade: Lyrical Poems* (Blackburn, J. H. Haworth, 1861), 146.

> Blakewater hath a broad bridge stretched across
> It, consecrated to the goddess Sloth;
> There may be seen the vulgar, vile, and gross,
> The lame and lazy — rich and ragged, both;
> And many a greasy fop in threadbare cloth;
> The idle huxter and slink butcher too;
> Men that do nought, and men with nought to do;
> The Monday-lurking tailor, smith, and snob;
> 'Jours,' tramps, and scamps, and beggars out of job,
> And vagabonds whose names the muse would loathe
> Pronounce lest they pollute the listener's ear;
> By ignorance urged on, with many an oath,
> Some graceless ragamuffin in the rear
> Insults the passer-by with shocking jibe and jeer.

Dedicatory, Celebratory, and Memorial Poems

Just as poems about writing poems or about being a poet were a central interest for self-taught writers, so were poems about, or dedicated to, other writers. In the numerous poems addressed to other writers, the self-taught poets sought to re-assert their own contribution to cultural and artistic life, as well as to celebrate the endeavours of a fellow poet. The double focus of so much self-taught writing is again apparent. At one level the dedicatory poem sought to abolish social and cultural distinctions by asserting the affinity between *all* writers regardless of class or education. Dedicatory poems were a further effort towards setting up a classless, universal discourse for working people, in which their precise social affiliations would cease to matter through being submerged in a wider artistic endeavour. At another level, the dedicatory poem was often used to assert the separateness of self-taught poets as a distinctive social group, and to assert the comradeship and self-interest of such a group, often in a tone of slightly intimidating jocularity or chumminess. On many occasions, dedicatory poems are both inclusive and exclusive at the same time, pointing both to the universal discourse of all readers and writers of poetry and to the closed world of the local bardic circle.

Dedicatory poems had a further purpose in attempting to define a poetic tradition, or rather a version of the poetic tradition which re-inforced the values of self-taught writers often at the expense of current critical orthodoxies. The artisan writers were surprisingly ungenerous to those eighteenth-century writers who, on the evidence of autobiographies and reminiscences as well as the poetry, provided their early reading and constant poetic models: Goldsmith, Thompson, Gray, and even Pope. Instead, the self-taught writers preferred to write dedicatory poems to those writers whose political awareness might be read as being progressive or sympathetic to popular progress (Milton, Crabbe, Byron, and Shelley in particular), to writers who could claim humble origins or authentic working-class sympathies (Bloomfield, Elliott, and, overwhelmingly, Burns) and to local bards and friendly fellow poets. If the resultant traditions of poetic influence and homage look somewhat eclectic and contradictory to modern readers, it is none the less necessary to recognize how important it was for self-taught writers to be able to appropriate those elements in bourgeois writing which best suited their own poetic purposes — to have available as models, for example, the social indignation of Crabbe without his persistent moralism, or the energy of Shelley without his patrician disdain. In trying to forge a poetic tradition from such disparate writers with evidently differing levels of poetic skill and achievement, self-taught writers opened themselves to the ridicule of educated critics both for their presumption and for their lack of discrimination. Yet the re-reading of the whole range of British poetry was the only education many self-taught poets ever had. Given their differing poetic intentions, it was not necessarily stupid to number Gerald Massey confidently alongside Milton, or Ebenezer Elliott alongside Burns, in a poetic pantheon.

The dedicatory poems below show these various intentions. The first poem, originally declaimed at a meeting of the Manchester 'Sun Inn group' of poets, was reprinted in a broadside format before its volume appearance in *The Festive Wreath*. The poem suggests the intimacy and exclusiveness of local bardic groupings, as well as providing a useful introductory list of local self-taught writers of the 1840s. The joviality of the poem and its strenuous claims for the range and achievements of the 'Sun Inn' writers is rather offset by the need for explanatory footnotes — fame was a fragile local awareness rather than a place in the universal discourse of poetry. The next group of poems suggest an interesting pattern of aspiration through association: Burns is celebrated by Massey, Massey by William Billington, William Billington by George Hull. The decline from great poet to local bard barely known outside Blackburn may be seen in the quality of the verse, but the chain of dedicatory association does assert a continuity and community created by the act of writing poetry. More than this, the importance of *reading* is also recognized — the acknowledgement of poetic achievement else-where is an essential part of the writer's own conception of his role and purpose. The final poem is the acknowledgement by one Sheffield poet of another: Richard Furness's apocalyptic vision of Elliott's power and influence underlines yet again the tremendous claims made by self-taught writers for the status of poetry as a moral and intellectual force in society.

Alexander Wilson
THE POET'S CORNER

Sung at the second meeting of the Lancashire Poetical Soirée held at the sign of the Sun, Long Millgate, 24 March 1842. This poem was reprinted as a broadside, and then appeared in *The Festive Wreath* (ed. J. B. Rogerson, Manchester, Bradshaw and Blacklock, 1843), a volume which reprinted the original contributions to the evening's entertainment with some additional material. This text is taken from the broadside copy annotated by the novelist Isabella Banks (*née* Varley), who as a young aspiring writer had known most of the Sun Inn writers.

Where the SUN shines so brightly, both daily and nightly,
And glasses drink lightly 'mid poesy and glee.
We sign and we laugh it, and merrily quaff it,
For sons of bright Phoebus and Momus are we;
Then empty the bottle, and moisten your throttle,
Till *Mind* and *not* mottle appears to the view;
The rosy god o'er us, choice *spirits* before us,
Come join me in chorus ye kindred crew.

       Then fill up a thumper, a classical Bumper,
       To Tragedy, Comedy, BYRON, and BURNS;
       To MILTON and MOORE, to their genius and lore,
       To the ever-green laurels entwining their urns.

The SUN is a SCHOOL, where the wit or the fool
May improve him by rule both by night and by morn;
Lit up by a BAMFORD, (1) the *Radical gas*-light,
Whose *flame* will shed lustre on ages unborn.
There's ELIJAH (2) the Bellman, who, self-taught, and well, man, —
I'm happy to tell, man, hath courted the muse;
He'll quote and recite for a day and a night,
From Tim Bobbin or Shakespeare, at 'Owd Willey Booth's.'

    CHORUS

Our Scholars are sons, too, of all the great guns, too, —
We've three of WILL'S-SONS — (3) but they're not very tall; —
We've ROGER'S-SON (4) Chairman, and RICHARD'S-SON, (5)
  there, man, —
And JOHN DICKIN'S-SON, (6) who binds books for us all.
Our host (7) drinks your health, your good fortune and wealth, —
We've a whole host of others, including an elf
Who sings, plays, and writes — paints and acts Taglioni, —
The gay MOSES MILLS — a whole host in himself.

      CHORUS

Mr WACK, (8) the schoolmaster, is no poetaster,
And none teaches faster, and then he's so kind,
That happen what may, come desert or disaster,
You've food for the body as well as the mind.
We've a ROSE, (9) from whose prose even poetry flows,
We have Rhyme and Romance, and we've Reverie and all,
And then through the season this fine feast of reason
Is graced by a learned and poetical BALL (10).

      CHORUS

We've publicans, sinners, CORK CUTTERS (11) and dinners;
A HARPER (12) who tunes, a REPEALER IN CORN;*
With lawyers (13) and PROCTERS, (14) Engravers (15) and Doctors,
And a PRINCE (16) of *more worth* than the prince lately born:
We've a beautiful SWAIN (17) as e're traversed the plain,
We've Rogerson's *Fiddle* his *Harp*, and his *Lute*,
With whig agitators, and tory debaters,
A SCULLY, (18) a STOTT (19) and TIM BOBBIN (20) to boot.

      CHORUS

They tell of a corner and little Jack Horner,
And Bell's noted corner for fistics and fun,
Whose glories so shorn are, whose pages forlorn are,
The great 'POET'S CORNER's the sign of the Sun!'
We have Bards of all colours, *Blues*, *Reds*, and *Black-yellows*,
The best of good fellows you'll know by his fleece;

Though not quite so fair, he's a second Lord Byron,
He's never content but in *Turkey* and *grease*.

CHORUS

We've GASPEY, (21) who first eulogises Sir Robert,
Then melodies gives on *Sir Robert's* poor law.
And SCHOLES (22) with his subjects *remarkably touching*,
Especially *that* on a bailiff's dread paw:
We've songs by a STOREY, (23) who sings like a tory
A TAYLOR (24) so warm and so wanton it seems,
He admires all the *Maidens* he meets in a Snow-drift,
And takes the advantage of *Girls* in their *Dreams*.

CHORUS

We've a HOWARD, (25) whose name for philanthropy passes,
A LORD (26) who despises the follies of France,
And a HILL (27) that is worthy as that of Parnassus,
Who fosters the genius of art or romance:
We've pipes and we've PORTER, (28) we've brandy and water,
We've wine from the vine, and we've Woodville cigars;
You must travel, and soon, like the man in the MOON,
To the SUN, if you wish to commune with the STARS.

>   Then fill up a thumper, a classical bumper,
>   To Tragedy, Comedy, BYRON and BURNS;
>   To MILTON and MOORE, to their genius and lore,
>   To the ever-green Laurels entwining their urns.
>   Let us claim your alliance, or tell us for why hence,
>   We place our reliance on friends for a call;
>   Come visit and try hence, our new HALL OF SCIENCE,
>   And Add to the GEMS of the SOCIALISTS' ALL.

(1) Mr Samuel Bamford, Author of Hours with the Muses, Life of
     a Radical, &c.
(2) Mr Elijah Ridings, Author of the Village Muse, &c.
(3) The Wilsons Authors of Songs &c., Greece, Malta, and the
     Ionian Isles, &c.
(4) Mr J. B. Rogerson, Author of Rhyme, Romance and Reverie,
     and a Voice from the Town.

(5) Mr George Richardson, Author of the Patriot's Appeal and other Poems.

(6) Mr John Dickinson, Bookbinder, Angel Court.

(7) Mr William Earnshaw, Landlord of the Sun.

(8) The Host.

(9) Mr Robert Rose, the Bard of Colour.

(10) Mr John Ball, of Seacombe School, a Poet.

(11) Mr James Boyle, a Poet.

(12) Mr William Harper, Author of Genius and other Poems.

(13) I. T. Brandwood Halstead, Esq., an Admirer.

(14) Mr Procter, Poet and Author of Reminiscences of a Barber's clerk.

(15) Mr Horsfield, and Mr Parry, Admirers.

(16) Mr John Critchley Prince, Author of Hours with the Muses, &c.

(17) Mr Charles Swain, Author of The Mind and other poems.

(18) P. D. Scully, a Poet.

(19) Mr Benjamin Stott, a Poet.

(20) One of the Wilsons.

(21) Mr William Gaspey, Author of Poor Law Melodies and other Poems.

(22) Mr John Scholes, Author of a Touching Scene and many Poems.

(23) Mr Robert Storey, Author of Conservative Songs, &c.

(24) Mr William Taylor, Author of the Maiden of the Snow, the Dreaming Girl, &c.

(25) John Howard, Esq., an Admirer.

(26) James Lord, Esq., an Admirer.

(27) John Hill, Esq., an Admirer.

(28) Mr William Eamer, Porter Agent, an Admirer.
　　　　　*Mr John Rawsthorne, an Admirer.

Gerald Massey
From ROBIN BURNS

From *Havelock's March* (London, Trubner & Co., 1861), 125–29. The Preface to the volume suggests that 'Robin Burns' had previously been published as a separate pamphlet.

I

A hundred years ago this morn,
   He came to walk our human way;
And we would change the Crown of Thorn
   For healing leaves To-day.

But we can only hang our wreath
   Upon the cold white marble's brow;
Tho' loud we speak, or low we breathe,
   We cannot reach him now.

He loved us all! he loved so much!
   His heart of love the world could hold;
And now the whole wide world, with such
   A love, would round him fold.

'Tis long and late before it wakes
   So kindly, — yet a true world still;
It hath a heart so large, it takes
   A Century to fill.

II

Aye, tell the wondrous tale to-day,
   When songs are sung, and warm words said;
Tell how he wore the hodden gray,
   And won the oaten bread.

With wintry welcome at the door,
   Did Nature greet him to his lot;
Our royal Minstrel of the Poor
   Hid in an old clay Cot.

167

There in the bonny Bairn-time dawn,
   He nestled at his Mother's knee,
With such a face as might have drawn
   The Angels down to see

A rosy Innocent at prayer, —
   So pure and ready for the hand
Of Her who is Guardian Spirit where
   Babes sleep in Silent Land.

There young love slily came to bring
   Rare balms that will bewitch the blood
To dance, while happy spirits sing,
   With life in hey-day flood:

And there she found her darling Child,
   The robust Muse of sun-browned health,
Who nurst him up into the wild
   Young heir of all her wealth.

And there she rockt his infant thought
   Asleep with visions glorious,
That hallow now the Poor Man's Cot.
   For evermore to us.

Disguised Angelic playmates are
   Those still ideal dreams of Youth,
That draw it on to Greatness; there
   We find them shaped in truth.

Yes, there he learned the touch that thrills
   Right to the natural heart of things;
Struck rootage down to where Life heals
   At the eternal springs.

Before the lords of earth there stood
   A Man by Nature born and bred,
To show us on what simple food
   A hero may be fed.

No gifts of gold for him; no crown
  Of Fortune waiting for his brow!
But wrestling strength to earn his own:
  It shines in glory now!

Wild music on lone shingly shores, —
  Wild winds that break in seas of sound;
Sad gloamings eerie on the moors;
  The murdered Martyr's mound;

Wan awful Shadows, trailing like
  The great skirts of the hurrying Storm;
Bronzed purple thunder-lights that strike
  The woodlands wet and warm;

Meek glimpses of peculiar grace,
  Where Beauty lyeth, in undress,
Asleep in secret hiding place,
  Out in the wilderness:

Those glorious Sunsets, God's good-night,
  Is smiled thro' to our world, and felt;
All, all enrich his ear and sight, —
  Thro' all his being melt.

He rose up in a dawn of light
  That burst upon the olden day;
Many weird voices of the night
  In his music passed away!

He caught them, Witch and Warlock, ere
  They vanisht; all the revelry
Of wizard wonder, we must wear
  The mask of Sleep to see!

Droll Humours came for him to paint
  Their pictures; straight his merry eye
Had taken them, so queer and quaint,
  We laugh until we cry.

William Billington
GERALD MASSEY

From *Sheen and Shade — Lyrical Poems* (Blackburn, John Neville Howarth, 1861), 141.

Sweet-numbered poet, proudly we thy name
Behold among the British bards inscribed,
In golden letters, on the List of Fame!
A second Burns, that never could be bribed,
By Fear or Favour, to forsake the class
Whence thou didst spring — the lowly labouring mass,
Whose feelings, fears, and hopes have tipped with flame
Thy potent pen! Let not occasion pass —
Portray their wrongs, regardless of the blame
Which Cant may cast on thee, in hope to tame
Thy scathing indignation! Let thy tongue
Be ever heard in humble Worth's defence,
And may the Muses still inspire thy song
With truth, and love, and life-instilling eloquence!

George Hull
TO THE MEMORY OF WILLIAM BILLINGTON
(who died January 3rd 1884)

From *The Heroes of the Heart and other Lyrical Poems* (Preston, J. H. Platt, 1894), 64.

The Singer has departed; and no more
   Is heard his voice, so strong and clear and sweet,
   Cheering the crowds, in factory and in street,
With melody, as in the days of yore.

His was a master-mind; and 'twill be long
   Before old Blackburn, through the smoke and gloom
   That gather round the busy lathe and loom,
Shall see another half so bright in song.

He needs no lays to blazon forth his name, —
  His *own* will bear it o'er the sea of time!
Yet I, a child of song, to whom he came
  With friendship true and counsel most sublime,
Would to his memory dedicate this stave,
And lay my simple wreath upon his grave.

Richard Furness

TO THE MEMORY OF EBENEZER ELLIOTT,
THE CORN-LAW RHYMER

From *The Poetical Works of the late Richard Furness* (ed. G. Calvert Holland,
London, Partridge & Co., 1858), 240.

Since first the breast glowed with celestial fire,
Of all the bards that waked the immortal lyre,
From Homer down to modern days we find
But few have sung to benefit mankind;
Their songs are writ in blood, and scattered wide
To praise false honour, or to flatter pride.
This did not he, who for my children sung,
And from the iron grip of ruin wrung
The staff of life.
Oh! if his ear incline,
I thank him deeply for myself and mine,
Yet not to me and mine his strains belong,
Millions now feel the sunshine of his song.

  Can Burnard's skill, however true or just,
Add honour to his name or lifeless dust?
No! mountains, rocks, vales, streams, with these were blent
His soul, and these shall be his monument!
On Winhill's summit, still he sits alone —
Still hears the floods roar round his granite throne,
King o'er the fierce, and lord o'er all the proud,
He speaks — his lightnings strike protection's crowd.
Firm in the storm, he grasps his thunders blue,
And shakes his Aegis o'er the banded few;

Clad in immortal mail — truth-tempered meet,
He strikes the iron bondage from our feet.
'Loose them, and let them go,' he cries in ire.
Loose them! cries Kinder from a cloud of fire;
Free! echo all — the rocks the words rehearse,
And love-tongued Liberty repeats the verse!

Genius and Intemperance

'Genius and Intemperance' is the title of a long and ambitious poem by the Airedale poet John Nicholson. It is not clear how fully Nicholson understood the complex and highly Romantic associations of his title, but the simple irony in the poem is immediately obvious on reading John James's introductory 'Life' of Nicholson. James begins his 'Life' with a characteristically abstract account of 'weakness of character' and 'misfortune' as widespread failings among self-taught poets, and only later translates these abstractions into social realities by apologetically recounting the story of Nicholson's arrest in London for drunkenness. Lithgow's *Life of J. C. Prince* conceals a similar tale under a veneer of euphemisms, and you do not have to read many lives of self-taught poets to recognize that heavy drinking was, if not characteristic, then at least commonplace among poor writers. A charitable critic might put this down to the deeply felt social ambiguities and dislocations inevitably experienced as a consequence of becoming a working-class or self-taught writer. Clare was not alone in making a fool of himself through drink when faced with the social awkwardnesses of a London literary soirée — many self-taught writers found even the local vicar or squire beyond the range of their normal manners. Yet, of course, many self-taught writers were drinkers before they were writers, and many others remained teetotal all their lives. A more revealing connection between writing and drink is suggested rather by the title of Nicholson's poem than his life. If intemperance was not the direct product of genius, still the relentless ambitions, self-analyses, and intensity which the self-taught writers derived from the Romantic model of creativity, did give a certain encouragement to personal excesses. The connection between talent and personal indulgence was not merely an aesthetic one. It could be translated promptly and simply into social values and moral judgements. John James does exactly this in his account of Nicholson: 'The reason of this almost universal wretchedness attendant upon poetic pursuits seems evident. For the possessors of poetic genius being ever of strong passions, ardent imagination, and exquisite sensibility, which indeed seems the first requisite of a poet, are naturally disposed to indulge in day dreams of gay hope, and disregard until too late, the stern monitions of prudence.'

Given the chance of illustrating these interesting equations between poetry and excess, it may seem perverse to devote a section of this anthology to temperance poems. However, rhetorical excess is well enough represented elsewhere. Without wanting to reinforce James's moralism, I think that the persistent equation between verbal energy and social or moral menace is the creation of a predominant middle-class perception of self-taught writers, filtered through Wordsworth and Shelley, which owes more to class interest than to historical accuracy. The image of the drunken genius was as useful to middle-class critics as a warning as it was attractive to socially uncertain and semi-talented writers as a romantic possibility.

There are poems in this anthology in praise of conviviality. Alexander Wilson's 'The Poet's Corner', with its 'classical Bumper' is an obvious example. There are many others in praise of community, fellowship, and gathering. There are still others which celebrate solitary walks, introversion, and which accept alienation and isolation as a poetic necessity. Given these variations in emphasis (variations which have been used to structure this anthology), it seems proper to represent the 'respectable' working class defence of temperance and prudence, even when it manifests itself in an intemperately ambitious poetic guise. In fact a considerable number of temperance poems by self-taught writers show distinct formal ingenuity and often surprising skill at avoiding the sententiousness, melodrama, and banality which might seem to be inherent in the whole genre. I hope the three poems reprinted here reflect this unexpected energy. Thomas Nicholson was a Manchester poet who was, by his own admission, 'humble and obscure', but not afraid, as he states in the Preface to *A Peal for the People* (1849), to offer poems which 'should convey a moral' and 'be instructive, as well as amusing'. In another of Nicholson's volumes, *The Warehouse Boy of Manchester* (1852) the title poem is a simple narrative tale written to denounce the pernicious effects of gambling and 'low company'. 'The Sabbath Peal', a typically Parnassian meditative and moral poem in Spenserian stanza form, links temperance firmly to a vision of quiet, self-reliant cultural progress within and by the working classes. The optimistic account offered here of industrial and mechanical progress belongs more usually to broadsides than to more ambitious contemplative verse. Cornelius McManus, a Blackburn essayist, story-writer, and occasional poet, offsets his staunchly teetotal message against a humorous dialect mode which alludes heavily to traditional archetypes and folk-lore motifs.

John Nicholson's 'Genius and Intemperance' is in the elevated neo-classical mode which gained him the title of 'The Airedale Bard'. The poem, after opening with a solemn declaration of its theme — 'two friends by wine untimely slain' — describes the poetic education of the sensibilities, the travels, and the eventual decline through drink of an historical and allegorical painter ('Paros') and a Romantic poet ('Philo'). Paros's death is described with an interesting emphasis on the bottle as a source of both inspiration and decay, an ambiguous version of the influence of drink which runs through the poem. Philo only fades away after declaiming an extensive — and surprisingly powerful — evocation of genius in distress. Philo's poetic list of poverty-stricken bards recalls Cooper's *Purgatory of Suicides*. The effect of 'Genius and Intemperance' ought to be that of bathetic, even ludicrous, melodrama, but to my mind Nicholson manages to dignify his subject rather than belittle it. The poem ends with a moment of self-reproach which is rescued from banality by its tragic applicability. The large pretensions of the poem collapse into an uncomfortably confessional and direct piece of self-recrimination.

Thomas Nicholson
THE SABBATH PEAL; or, PAST, PRESENT, AND FUTURE. A MORAL ESSAY

From *A Peal for the People, with sundry changes. A Poetical Miscellany* (Manchester, Galt & Co., 1849), 17. 'The Sabbath Peal' is bound in in my copy as a supplement to *A Peal for the People*, with separate pagination, so it may well have been issued in separate pamphlet form.

Who can divine what the dim future holds
In store for those poor dwellers of the cot?

Undream'd of mysteries Old Time unfolds,
To change the features of a frowning lot.
What great results have patient toil begot!
Who gains true eminence, must climb the hill,
Nor cease to strive, till he has reached the spot,
Where he, with ease, can contemplate at will
His former toils, nor fear to fall by adverse ill.

Perhaps the embryo philosopher
Here walks, with stoical indifference,
In clotted clogs: one that may minister
To science, and, with penetrating glance,
Her mysteries abstruse to light advance.
The soul of Newton may he not possess,
And give to order what was claim'd by chance?
Or, with a Locke's or Bacon's truthfulness
The human mind's great capabilities express.

Perhaps some youthful poet ranges in
Those rustic ranks, whose genius may frame
A harp, whose lofty tones may win
For him a Milton's or a Dryden's name
Recorded in the dooms-day book of Fame,
And echo'd through admiring lands, as wide
And universal as the sun's bright flame;
And he, like them, might be a nation's pride,
Acknowledg'd most when the poor mortal part had died.

In this young gathering may we not behold
The future Patriot, of dauntless zeal;
The senator, whose wisdom might unfold
Means of salvation to the public weal;
Or, with persuasive eloquence, might heal
The widening breach, that party feud had made,
And e'en avert the use of slaughtering steel,
'Twixt hostile nations, in war's deadly trade:
The field where patriotic zeal is best display'd.

Perhaps some artist saunters in this row,
Whose name shall yet be dear to art and fame:

Whose skill may bid the unconscious canvas glow,
Truthful to nature's animated flame.
Or he, the painter's sister art might claim
To Angelo, Canova, or our own
Fam'd self-taught Chantry's, bring a rival name; —
But who might reach the former, in renown,
Who bade the marble speak, his master-piece to crown?

Let learning's friends the generous impulse give,
To bring the latent principle to birth:
If there the seeds of greatness do not live,
The better germs of goodness may put forth,
And yield a harvest of far greater worth. —
The human capabilities are great;
Witness the modern miracles on earth:
'Impossibilities' have met defeat,
'Cannot be done,' is now fast going out of date.

What magic pow'r those wonders has achiev'd?
Our modern truth is far more strange
Than ancient fiction that no man believ'd:
We, for 'the wondrous horse of brass,' exchange
Our 'horse of iron,' with a mighty range
Of chariots, whirl'd on with rapid wing,
O'er public city, or secluded grange! —
Ajax, of old, defied the blue lightning: —
We make it run our errands on a metal string.

I will maintain, too, that 'tis better sped:
A heaven-born messenger, of less delay,
Than Mercury, though wing'd both heel and head:
Ours is, *de facto*, working, every day;
Theirs, but a vain poetical display.
The ancients gave their lightning to their god,
To thunder 'gainst them in war's dread array;
But, we give ours to a conducting rod,
That leads it down, and buries it beneath the sod.

Then if the mind, from its exhaustless store,
Those ever varying treasures can unfold,

177

Should we not seek its regions to explore,
For gems so rare, of greater worth than gold? —
For rich Peru, false Spain her honour sold,
And Mexico with streams of blood she bought;
Yet Spain grew poor, amidst her wealth untold!
England thy mind's great enterprise hath wrought
A *substance*, and a *name*, all else have vainly sought.

The field expands. More honours must be won,
No nation can be free, and yet be blind:
A mighty work remains, yet, to be done,
To break the stubborn bondage that doth bind,
In darkest ignorance, the human mind.
Men physically blind can have no aim:
They jostle on; yet none the road can find,
While each for blindness all the other blame;
And ignorance still blunders on, and doubts, the same.

Ye labouring millions, whose incessant toil
Pours wealth into the coffers of the state!
Seize the brief intervals from worldly moil,
And strive — oh strive! yourselves to elevate.
Hang not upon the favours of the great, —
Would you in real independence live,
Work out your own salvation, and create
A thriving weal. — Yes! from yourselves receive
The precious boon, no other earthly pow'r could give.

To that great end, be Temperance your star:
Your constant guide, through perils that surround,
As the lone mariner views, from afar,
The light that points where rocks and shoals abound:
His constant care the varying deep to sound,
And watch his onward course with vigilance
Till his good ship is safe in harbour bound. —
What obstacles will not sound common sense
O'ercome, led on by self-denying abstinence?

The loud, admonitory bells now cease,
Their last, faint echo dies in air away;

But other notes, peal upon peal, increase:
The strong, deep organ bursts, in solemn sway,
A swelling chorus to the psalmist's lay;
And the exalted soul, on buoyant wing,
Into the awful future bears straightway,
Which, by anticipation, seems to cling
To Immortality and heaven's Eternal King.

Cornelius McManus

JOHN BARLEYCORN'S DIARY: AN UNCOLOURED PICTURE

From George Hull ed., *Poets and Poetry of Blackburn* (Blackburn,
J & G Toulmin, 1902), 425–427.

John Barleycorn walked eawt one morn,
While th' dew clung weet to th' ripenin' corn;
He sang reet cheerily, dud John,
An' fooak o wondered wod were on.
One says to him, 'Thae'rt early eawt;
'It's soon for thee to be abeawt.'
'The birds come eawt ere th' worms be gone,
Aw'm gooin' a-huntin foo's,' says John.

An' deawn bi th' wood walked Harry Hood;
Nooan liked ale moor than Harry dud;
But neaw he'd settles deawn to wark,
He sung as merry as a lark.
He'd med a vow he'd drink no moor,
Nor be the foo' he'd bin befoor.
'Just wait till we pass th' 'Public' yon;
Aw think aw've fun' a mate,' says John.

'Here, Harry, let's co' here an' sup,
A drop ov ale 'll set tho up.'
'O reet,' said Harry, 'as it's thee;
To tell tho th' truth aw do feel dree.'
They supped a while, an' John says, 'Well,

179

Tha'll never leove mo to misel''
'Nowe,' Harry says, 'Aw'll werk to-morn,
Thae'rt a rare owd friend, John Barleycorn.'

Hood sheawts 'Hurray' — he feels so gay
At sich a lucky holiday;
John Barleycorn fotched him a cleawt
As med Hood's senses reel quite eawt.
'Ged hooam, tha drunken foo'!' says he,
'There's nowt but pigs'll stop wi' thee.
Thi heyd'll werch reel weel i' th' morn,
Tha'll remember owd John Barleycorn.'

John went eawt, an' looked abeawt;
He sped a farmer, hale an' steawt.
He'd done a rare good trade thad day
I' horses, cattle, ooats an' hay.
'Here,' says the tempter, 'come wi' me,
We'll hev a day o' mirth an' glee;
Moor than tha's hed sin' tha were born;
Come, sit deawn wi' John Barleycorn!'

Wi' no alarm at ony harm
This victim took his tempter's arm.
He went away so drunk thad day,
Th'owd farmer could'nd see his way.
John Barleycorn laughed at his plight;
He laughed so leawd 'at th' hoss took fright.
Id' maister were fun killed i' th' morn;
He were murdered bi John Barleycorn.

He'd bait to draw booath heigh an' low, —
He tackled th' better end an' o, —
Wi' costly wines he started th' game,
Then robbed their money an' good name.
Fro' palaces he took his slaves,
Then landed 'm in pauper's graves.
That's one day's werk; one page aw've torn
Fro' th' diary o' John Barleycorn.

John Nicholson
GENIUS AND INTEMPERANCE

From *Poems by John Nicholson, The Airedale Poet* (London, Longman; Bradford, Charles Stanfield, 1844), 48–83.

On the broad canvas Paros had pourtray'd
The varying glances of each shining blade,
Left all descriptive poetry behind,
And stamp'd at once the battle on the mind;
But close behind him was the bottle hung —
He drank when faint, then painted as he sung;
But when the cheering draught had lost its head,
His pencil shook, and all his fancy fled.
When warm'd with wine, his airy thoughts brought home
The paintings, statues, and the scenes of Rome;
Columns of ev'ry order, laid on earth,
Where Desolation frolick'd in her mirth;
All Nature roll'd before his strong ideas —
The land, the skies, the cities, and the seas;
But soon his pulses in quick motions beat,
His ruin'd appetite enjoys no meat,
His frame decays, the mind is weaker made,
He starts in dreams — his bosom's sore afraid.
No pleasure can his weeping Anna give;
To him 'tis now no happiness to live;
He values not the bubble of a name,
Nor prides himself in vain posthumous fame.
When his bright eyes grew dim, and fancy fled,
Bound to the confines of a dying bed,
The pleasing landscape could no longer cheer;
His mind was weak, his dissolution near,
When his pale cheek was laid on Anna's breast,
And his cold hand by her he lov'd was press'd.
What weeping then! — no language now can tell
How tears were rain'd when such a genius fell.
Then was destroy'd a gen'rous noble mind,
While the destroyer lurk'd in shades behind.
Dreadful Intemperance! thy tempting snare
Holds while thou slayest, O, father of Despair!

There lay the artist, ready for the tomb,
His valued paintings hung around the room . . .

Thro' ev'ry stage of life he strove to pass,
Resolv'd to see how varied Nature was:
But here the youth was foolish, learn'd, and vain,
His genius drowned in the bright champagne;
Wisdom departed, riot took her place,
And led young Philo into deep disgrace.
The scene must drop, and hide him from our sight,
With all the follies of a drunkard's night.
Learning is not true wisdom. — Youths may be
Refin'd and polish'd to a high degree;
Genius may mark the scholar for her own,
Yet by her brightest sons is often shown
Minds that can soar in rapture to the skies,
On Learning's wings — feel noblest ecstacies,
Then sink to earth; and, mixing with the throng.
In Folly's path with drunkards roll along.
With best of resolutions Philo came,
And deeply sigh'd, through grief and inward shame.
Oppress'd with sickness, his ideas fled,
His memory weaken'd, and an aching head;
A ruin'd appetite, a trembling hand,
His pen obeying not his mind's command.
To drive away the melancholy train
Of dark ideas, he flew to wine again;
And ecstasy he felt in getting drunk —
To what a depth his learned mind was sunk!

Then horror seiz'd him, and his eyes rain'd tears,
That all the learning of his youthful years,
With which his father hop'd to make him bless'd,
Should only leave his bosom more oppress'd,
Oft would his mind upon the Muses' wings
Soar to the skies, and leave all earthly things;
Beyond mortality were Philo's strains
Tun'd to the orbs that deck the heavenly plains.
He sung not love's soft passion, lovers' care,
His theme the heavens, the ocean, earth, and air;

In deepest bursts of passion he could shine,
And power and harmony fill'd every line.
With thoughts original, with words at will,
His verses made his readers' blood run chill,
But not with horror, — mid the stars he trod,
And sung th' omnipotence of Nature's God . . .

At intervals, the Muse of Philo sung
In strains like these, then silent was her tongue,
The hand that holds the fatal potion shakes,
Invention's fled, the nervous feeling wakes;
His eyes have lost their fire, his falt'ring tongue
Speaks not in sentences so firm and strong,
His memory's fled, invention laid at rest —
His heart-strings quiver in his weaken'd breast;
But still the thoughts of other bards' despair,
The sons of misery and rankling care,
Prompted a last, though enervated lay,
And this the substance of his weak essay: —

'Where merit lives the greatest sorrow swells,
'Fortune forsakes the spot where anguish dwells;
'Obscure in life the man of letters mourns,
'While hope, and care, and sorrow came by turns;
'Or if his reputation widely spread,
'Oft has he starv'd, and even wanted bread,
'Perish'd in poverty, of little note,
'While others profited by what he wrote.
    'Poor blind Homer, the noblest bard of all . . .
'But poets seldom rise while here they live,
'The critics break their hearts, and then a stone they give.'

Philo irresolute, is still led on,
Till health, and genius, and his strength are gone.
The rosy cheek is pale, the manly face,
Where Health had stamp'd her own strong masc'line grace,
Fast shrinks away, and difficult the breath —
He feels the woeful harbingers of death.
Fain would he turn to his once healthful food,
But nought he sees can do the smallest good.

Life would die out as tapers do expire,
Did not strong spirits keep alive the fire.
His old companions, true to him when young,
Come to inquire, but when he hears each tongue,
Oh, how he weeps! — he knows what is the cause
Of his strong system making such a pause,
Wishes that all the spirits e'er he drunk,
Had deep within the mighty ocean sunk.
I leave the thoughts that press upon his mind,
When he must leave his dearest love behind.
The cares of earth with him will soon be o'er,
But what a boundless ocean lies before! . . .

Oh! could I write that myself could save
From this one curse, this sure untimely grave,
This endless want, that soon must stop my breath,
These flaming draughts, which bring the surest death,
Then should my Muse upon her wings advance,
And Genius triumph o'er Intemperance.
I know there's mirth, and there's a flash of joy,
When friends with friends a social hour employ,
When the full bowl is circled all around,
And not a single jarring string is found;
But truest wisdom of a young man's heart,
Is well to know the moment to depart.
Thousands of hopeful youths, who first begin
To mix with friends in this bewitching sin,
Soon lose their resolution, and what then?
Their privilege is gone to other men,
Their wealth has wasted, and the landlord, where
They seem'd so happy with his social cheer,
When all is spent, and all resources o'er,
Soon kicks the starving wretches out of door.
I could employ my pen for weeks, for years,
Write on this subject, wet it with my tears;
For spacious as the ocean is the scope,
For drinking downs all genius, wealth, and hope,
Lies best of characters below the dust,
And fills connections with a deep distrust.
But in weak verse the ills can ne'er be told —

Eternity alone can these unfold.
That I may know these ills, and stop in time,
Is my last wish, as thus I end the rhyme.

The Subject of Poetry:
poetry and working-class aspirations

If the countryside was the most common subject matter for working-class writers, poetry itself came a close second. Often, as in Prince's 'The Poet's Sabbath' or Skipsey's 'The Brooklet' in the following section, the two subjects became metaphors for each other in a single poem. The view of poetry expressed in such verse will come as no surprise to anyone who has read this chapter. Poetry was generally regarded by self-taught writers both as a personally redeeming force for the individual poet, offering consolation, self-expression, the possibility of fame (or, as was sometimes preferred, that of unjustified neglect), or social status, or forgetfulness of pressing material circumstances, *and* as an important social force, heightening moral and aesthetic awareness, spirituality, brotherhood, and love. Often there appears to be a tension between overwhelming individual therapeutic need and an aspiration towards a kind of poetry which stepped beyond the here and now into a trans-historical, impersonal discourse on 'higher things'. Such a tension between the 'personal' and the 'universal' is, given the circumstances under which self-taught poets wrote, inevitable, as is their adoption of a Romantic, Shelleyan account of their own poetic purposes. The seriousness and often moving intensity with which these writers strove to improve their fellows' intellectual and spiritual awareness is only partially undercut by the obvious individual needs, aspirations, and self-doubts which prompted such ambitions. It is easy now to see the Parnassian endeavour by self-taught writers as politically diversionary, as an absurd misreading of the cultural and political needs of the emergent working classes. Yet as this anthology clearly shows, the 'appropriate' or 'alternative' modes which might have arisen from a coherent working-class view of the changes taking place in early industrial Britain were not easily to be found.

Most of the writers represented in this section have already contributed to the anthology. Rogerson, Prince, Massey, Ernest Jones, and Skipsey were among the best-known self-taught writers, owing their prominence partly to the quality of their work, partly to their exemplary lives which represented varying kinds of cultural and social achievement in the face of adverse circumstances, and partly to their friendships and contacts among the culturally and politically active middle classes. The views of poetry expressed here, while not unanimous, together form a paradigm of the possibilities available to ambitious self-taught writers without specific political affiliations or intentions.

In 'The Minstrel's Lot' Rogerson broods on the hardships of unrecognized genius with apparent bitterness, but actually with some enthusiasm for the notion of present neglect shading into retrospective fame. Prince's two poems. 'To Poesy' and 'The Poet's Sabbath' are strong expressions of the ways in which poetry might be used to console, or even redeem, the harassed industrial writer by opposing solitary, rural 'intellectual ecstasy' to the realities of urban working life. Jones, Waddington, and Skipsey all concentrate on the idea of the poet as bard and on poetry as an important moral and intellectual force within society, without ever abandoning their belief in literature as an act of personal consolation. Waddington was an employee at Sir Titus Salt's model factory at Saltaire, and his works were published posthumously in collected form after having enjoyed some measure of local celebrity as newspaper and magazine contributions. Similar themes are put forward by the prose apologies for poetry. Prince concentrates again on the capacity of poetry to transform individual hardship and suffering into celebration and solace. His essay stands in interesting contrast to Massey's direct and powerful 'Preface', which maintains that poetry should have its origins in perceptions of social injustice and oppression. Poetry, he argues, is important not primarily for its capacity to reform its author's consciousness but rather for its influence on the attitudes of the mass of people. Massey's stubborn refusal to celebrate his own works, seeing them rather as the compulsive outcome of poverty and injustice, is a strongly alternative view to most of those expressed in this chapter. Janet Hamilton's extraordinary literary career might have been expected to have made her sympathetic to Massey's point of view. A shoe-maker's wife who had been taught to read at her mother's knee, using the Bible as her only text, Janet Hamilton brought up her large family before turning to her literary ambitions when she reached late middle age. To do this she had to teach herself to write. Despite this career of exemplary literary hardship, Mrs Hamilton's writings remain a compendium of ferociously conservative attitudes, which include this utterly untroubled celebration of the pleasures of reading. Skipsey's essays, first published in the unlikely setting of *Igdrasil*, the Ruskin Reading Guild Journal, are unremarkable both in their defence of 'genius', or the transforming power of poetic inspiration, and in their rhapsodic and half-mystical mode. But Skipsey's poems — reticent, pointed, poignant lyrics — show little of the gushing Romanticism of his prose. The difficulties of finding a *prose* style suitable for self-taught writers seem to have been just as great as those of finding an appropriate poetic voice — perhaps, given the scarce opportunities for publishing prose, even greater.

John Bolton Rogerson
THE MINSTREL'S LOT

From J. B. Rogerson ed., *The Festive Wreath* (Manchester, Bradshaw and Blacklock, 1842), 18–22.

What is the minstrel's lot upon the earth?
　　It is to nourish unsubstantial dreams;
It is to feel within his soul the birth
　　Of lofty thoughts and heaven-created gleams;
It is to feel of sympathy the dearth,
　　And seek companions in the woods and streams;
'Tis to endure the worldling's bitter spurns,
And bear the fire that in his bosom burns.

The Minstrel mingles with the busy throng,
　　Yet knows himself no kin unto the men
Who pass with haste and care-worn brows along,
　　And spend their days in money-getting den,
Scorning alike the poet and his song —
　　They cannot feel the magic of his pen,
The thirst for wealth hath wither'd up their veins —
They toil, and grasp, and — die amid their gains.

What though the Minstrel hath no lordly hall,
    What though he boast not of his gardens fair,
And mingleth not in courtly festival,
    Nor banqueteth on viands rich and rare —
The encircling sky to him seems palace-wall,
    The fields a garden free and fresh as air;
With thankful heart he eats his homely meal,
And feels sweet thoughts like incense round him steal.

When by his glimmering lamp in lonely room,
    He holds commune with the undying dead,
Gone like a shadow is each thought of gloom,
    And all the cares that gird his fate seem fled;
Bright flowers of intellect around him bloom,
    The light of mind is o'er his chamber shed;
Shapes fancy-born spring up before his eyes,
And bath'd in bliss his tranquil spirit lies.

Then to him comes the poet's golden hour,
    When all his soul runs riot through his veins;
Rich thoughts drop from him as a summer-shower,
    His spirit pants as though 'twould burst its chains,
He feels that his is an immortal dower,
    And soareth far above this world of pains,
Treading with fearless steps amid the skies,
And drinking in the light of angel eyes.

He roameth forth at breath of early morn,
    When the lark singeth in the sun-rays bright,
And silver crystals, hanging on the thorn,
    Seem priceless jewels to his raptur'd sight;
By him the breeze with odours sweet is borne,
    Like Nature sighing in her own delight:
The sky above, the lake below him clear —
All make to him both earth and heaven more dear.

The lowliest flower that smiles upon the ground,
    The tiniest insect fluttering on the wing —
He findeth pleasure in each sight and sound,
    He seeth beauty in the lowliest thing;

He knoweth God is watching all around,
    And his heart swells with silent worshipping:
No blossom will he pluck, but onwards pass
Nor harm the daisy peeping from the grass.

He seeks again the ever-trodden street,
    And marks the earthly pass him heedless by —
Well-garb'd and proud, they will not deign to greet
    The humble bard with recognizing eye:
With glance awry, and quicker-hurrying feet,
    Eager again to Mammon's haunts they fly,
As though they thought their heaps of glittering gold
Would buy an entrance to the heavenly fold.

The poet dies, the rich man fades away —
    The one reposes in a lowly bed —
Above the other's undeserving clay
    A stately cenotaph erects its head,
And lines of virtue, penn'd for hireling's pay,
    Upon the costly monument are read:
The gazer views the cold unblushing stone,
Wondering such deeds were all before unknown.

Why do the strangers mark that humble spot?
    Why on that grave their reverent glances bend?
He who sleeps there in life was honour'd not,
    And unto him did wealth no influence lend;
His was a friendless and unpitied lot —
    No mourning crowds did at his couch attend;
Say, why are men with pilgrim-homage there,
Deigning no look on marble scutcheon fair?

Such is the Minstrel's lot — in life unknown,
    Unpitied and uncar'd for by the crowd;
When from the earth the soul of song hath flown,
    The nation's voice is rais'd in accents loud,
And myriads flock to gaze upon the stone
    Which covers only coffin, clay, and shroud:
E'en be it so — so let the Minstrel fall,
An age of fame is earn'd by life of thrall.

John Critchley Prince
TO POESY

From *Hours With The Muses* (Sixth edition, Manchester, Abel Heywood, 1857), 53–5. First published in 1841.

Best solace of my lonely hours!
  Whose tones can never tire,
Oh, how I thrill beneath thy powers, —
  Sweet Spirit of the Lyre!
On streamlet's marge, or mountain's steep,
In wild, umbrageous forests deep,
  Or by my midnight fire, —
Where'er my vagrant footsteps be,
My soul can find a spell in thee!

Thy home is in the human mind,
  And in the human breast,
With thoughts unfettered as the wind,
  And feelings unexpressed;
With joys and griefs, with hopes and fears,
With pleasure's smiles, with sorrow's tears,
  Thou art a constant guest:
And oh, how many feel thy flame,
Without a knowledge of thy name!

Beauty and grandeur give thee birth,
  And echo in thy strain —
The stars of heaven, the flowers of earth,
  The wild and wondrous main:
With nature thou art always found
In every shape, in every sound,
  Calm, tempest, sun, and rain; —
Yes! thou hast ever been to me
An intellectual ecstasy!

When Poverty's dark pennons wave
  Exulting o'er my head, —
When Hope's best efforts fail to save
  My soul from inward dread, —

When woman's soothing voice no more
Can charm with fondness that before
   Such joyous comfort shed;
Thy smile can mitigate my doom
And fling a ray athwart the gloom.

When sickness bends my spirit low,
   And dims my sunken eye,
And, wrestling with my subtle foe,
   I breathe the bitter sigh; —
Again I seek thee — once again,
To weave a meek, imploring strain
   To Mercy's source on high:
And — oh, the magic of thy tone!
I feel as though my pangs were gone!

When light on expectation's wing
   My joyous thoughts arise,
Elate with thee I soar, and sing,
   And seem to sweep the skies:
Though disappointment's voice of fear
Sternly arrests my wild career,
   And expectation dies;
Yet thou, unchanged, art with me still,
Wreathing with flowers the thorns of ill.

Misfortune's blighting breath may kill
   Hope's blossoms on the tree;
Mild sorceress! it cannot chill
   My cherished love for thee!
When Death put forth his withering hand,
And snatched, of my domestic band,
   The darling from my knee,
Thou didst not fail to breathe a lay
Of sorrow o'er its sinless clay.

I loved thee when a very child —
   For every song was dear;
In youth, when Shakespeare's 'wood-notes wild'
   First charmed my ravish'd ear;

In manhood, too, when Byron's hand
Swept the deep chords, and every land
   Enraptured turned to hear;
And oh, when age hath touched my brow,
Still may I cling to thee, as now!

The lonely swan's expiring breath
   In mournful music flows;
He sings his requiem of death
   Though racked with painful throes;
Sweet Poesy! let such be mine, —
The calm, harmonious decline
   To earth's serene repose!
May thy last murmurs still be there,
And tremble through my dying prayer!

From THE POET'S SABBATH

From *Hours With The Muses*, 36–8.

Blest hour of Peace, of Poetry, and Love!
Spell-breathing season — care-subduing time!
Dim emanation of a world above,
Hallowed and still, soft, soothing, and sublime!
My heaven-aspiring spirit seems to climb
Nearer to God, whose all-protecting wing
Shadows the universe; my feelings chime
In unison with every holy thing,
That memory can give, or meditation bring!

The voice of Nature is a voice of power,
More eloquent than mortal lips can make;
And even now in this most solemn hour,
She bids my noblest sympathies awake.
Nature! I love all creatures for thy sake,
But chiefly man, who is estranged from thee!
Oh! would that he would turn from strife, and take
Sweet lessons from thy love, and learn to be
Submissive to thy laws, wise, happy, good, and free!

Now the lone twilight, like a widowed maiden,
Pale, pure, and pensive, steals along the skies;
With dewy tears the sleeping flowers are laden —
The leaves are stirred with spiritual sighs;
The stars are looking down with radiant eyes,
Like hosts of watchful Cherubim, that guard
A wide and weary world; the glow worm lies,
A living gem upon the grassy sward,
Uncared for and unsought, save by the wandering bard.

Now 'tis the trysting time, when lovers walk
By many a wild and solitary way,
Winging the moments with enraptured talk —
Breaking the silence with some plaintive lay:
Hushed be the tongue that flatters to betray
Confiding Woman in the tender hour;
Sad be the heart, that will not own the sway
Of her ennobling, soul-refining power, —
She, of life's stormy wild the only constant flower.

I journey homeward; for the taper's light
Gleams from the scattered dwellings of the poor,
Down the steep valleys, up the mountain's height,
And o'er the barren surface of the moor;
Shadows are round me as I tread the floor
Of balmy breathing fields; my weary feet
Bear me right onward to my cottage door; —
I cross my threshold — take my accustomed seat,
And feel, as I have always felt, that home is sweet!

My wife receives me with a quiet smile,
Gentle and kind as wife should ever be;
My joyous little ones press round the while,
And take their wonted places on my knee:
Now with my chosen friends, sincere and free,
I pass the remnant of the night away;
Temper grave converse with becoming glee —
Wear in my face a heart serenely gay,
And wish that human life were one long Sabbath-day.

Some poet's song inspiring hope and gladness,
    Gives to my social joys a sweeter zest;
Some tale of human suffering and sadness
    Brings out the deeper feelings of my breast.
Sad for the millions stricken and oppressed,
    My cheeks with tears of sympathy impearled,
I urge my little household unto rest,
    Till morn her rosy banner hath unfurl'd
And care shall call me forth to battle with the world.

Blest Sabbath time! on life's tempestuous ocean,
    The poor man's only haven of repose —
Oh, thou hast wakened many a sweet emotion,
    Since morning's sun upon thy being rose!
Now thou art wearing gently to a close —
    Thy starry pinions are prepared for flight —
A dim forgetfulness within me grows —
    External things are stealing from my sight —
Good night! departing Sabbath of my soul — good night!

Ernest Jones
THE POET'S MISSION

From *The Battle Day and Other Poems* (London, G. Routledge, 1855),
121–122. This poem is part of a short sequence called 'The Poet'.

Who is it rivets broken bands
    And stranger-hearts together,
And builds with fast-decaying hands
    A home to last for ever?

From thunder-clouds compels the light,
    And casts the bolt away,
Upluring from the soulless night
    The soul's returning day?

Who is it calls up glories past
    From tombs of churches old?

And proudly bids the hero last,
  Tho' fades his grassy mould?

Who is it, with age-vanquished form,
  Treads death's ascending path;
Yet stronger than the fiery storm
  Of tyrants in their wrath?

Whose voice, so low to human ears,
  Has still the strength sublime
To ring thro' the advancing years —
  And history — and time?

Who is it, in love's servitude,
  Devotes his generous life,
And measures by his own heart's good
  A world with evil rife?

The Bard — who walks earth's lonely length
  Till all his gifts are given;
Makes others strong with his own strength,
  And then fleets back to Heaven.

James Waddington
SONNET TO POESY

From *Flowers From the Glen* (Bradford, Abraham Holroyd, 1862), 147.

I felt thy touch divine, rapt Poesy,
  When boyhood wandered through enchanted dreams,
  And, sauntering o'er the moss of prattling streams,
In search of feather'd nest and velvet bee,
It heard thy harp Aeolian in the tree;
  And when a youth and Love's celestial light
  Made earth elysium to my raptured sight
What honied rhymes I sung as taught by thee!
Now close immured within the city's heart,
  A nightly toiler in the round of trade,

196

Thou com'st to bid my weariness depart,
With all the sweetness of a Sabbath dawn,
  Wafting me back where long ago I played
Amid the clover on my native lawn.

GENIUS

From *Flowers From the Glen*, 153.

The Bard is Nature's favourite. She has made
  His soul partaker of her secret love;
  And to his ravished eye her boundless store
Of matchless grace and beauty stand array'd.
All things to him, from sun to tiny blade
  Wear deep significance; the flowers and birds
  To him speak audibly sublimest words;
And man's deep heart to him is all displayed.
His soul can scale the sky or wander down
  The deep of Hell. Though Fortune try to warp
His seraph wing, he scorns her envious frown;
  Even bent beneath her stroke, give him his harp
And let his muse inspire his soul with song —
He towers above his cares, sublime and strong.

Joseph Skipsey
THE BROOKLET

From *Songs and Lyrics* (London, Walter Scott, 1892), 38.

A little brooklet trilled a song
As merry as the day was long,
To which a music-hater stung
To frenzy said 'I'll bind thy tongue,
And quell thy merriment:' That night
A dam check'd babbler's song and flight;
But blind are ever hate and spite!
And so it fell, the brook did swell —
Ah, truth to say, ere dawn of day,

197

Had grown a sea, unquelled would be,
And soon with ruin, down the dell,
Dashed with a fierce triumphant yell;
And cried, 'Ha, ha! ho. ho! oh, la!
Where now thy skill, my voice to still? —
Ah, dost thou find that he who'd bind
The tongue, e'en of a rillet, may
Be doomed to hear instead, one day,
What shall with terror seize, control,
And wring with agony his soul? —
In very deed then, reck the rede!'
Thus roared the flood and onward swept;
And music-hater heard and wept:
And so weep all who'd try, or long,
To render dumb the child of song.

THE MINSTREL

From *Songs and Lyrics*, 83.

Ah, deem not when thy minstrel tunes
　　His harp to hours and glories vanished,
His star of stars, his moon of moons,
　　Can ever from his heart be banish'd.

Each tune he wakes, each note that takes
　　And charms the heart, Love's arrow woundeth,
But flows from strings she only rings,
　　And from a Deep she only soundeth.

John Critchley Prince
RANDOM THOUGHTS ON POETRY

From an essay prefatory to *Hours With The Muses*, first published in 1841
and then reprinted in subsequent editions of the book.

It is almost impossible to take too extended a view of the nature and
characters of Poetry. All the strange vicissitudes of human life, — all
the harmonious beauty of the Universe, — all the incomprehensible

sublimity of the Supreme Being is Poetry in the widest and most significant sense of the word. Whatever excites our wonder and admiration, awakes our best sympathies, and stirs up the hidden depths of our passions, is Poetry; inasmuch as it brings into exercise the moral and intellectual faculties of the mind. Nature is the grand Temple of Poetry, and that man who hath received the celestial fire of inspiration, is the chosen High Priest of her rites. He expounds her sacred mysteries; he points out her ineffable beauties. In fancy his feet are planted from mountain to mountain; his face is lifted towards heaven; he opens his mouth, and in the language of angels, he moves, raises, and refines myriads of human hearts. He is all eye, all ear, and almost all soul; for the strong wing of his imagination soars through the uttermost regions of Time and Space, — pierces the veil of Eternity, and even attempts to penetrate into the holy sanctuary of the Invisible himself. . . .

It is true that the greater portion of the people, the poor and the uneducated, can neither understand nor appreciate the higher principles of Poetry; but while they can be cheered by a simple air, and melted by a pathetic ballad, — while they have joys and griefs, hopes and fears, feelings and affections in common with all mankind, they cannot be said to be entirely unmoved by its influence. The spirit of poetry is within them, and only requires the quickening breath of moral and mental culture to give it a more permanent and elevated character. I think that a day will come, and I look forward to it with the cheerfulness of constant hope, when the sayings and sentiments, beauties and truths, of the master-minds of every age and clime, shall become 'familiar as household words'; — when the Poet shall be looked up to as a being sent by Providence for a special and benevolent purpose, as the favoured interpreter of all that is good and true, all that is lovely and sublime, all that is wonderful and harmonious in universal things: when he shall be loved and revered while living, honoured and mourned when dead, and his name enshrined in the hearts and memories of myriads of his fellow creatures.

It is almost impossible to imagine a more exalted character than that of a man possessed of great mental powers and indomitable moral courage; — a man dignified in manners, winning and eloquent in speech, prompt and decisive in action; a man just, brave, benevolent, pure, and serenely virtuous; in private, gentle and affectionate as a child, — in public, upright and awful as a sage. But, if in addition to these rare qualities, he were gifted with a Poet's inspiration — that holy fire which gives light to thought, and warmth to feeling — his pre-eminence would be greater still. Above all, if he had the will to devote his God-like energies to the good of his fellow-men, his existence would be a blessing and a benefit to the age in which he lived, and his name a beacon of glory to succeeding generations. A few such mighty spirits would effectively regenerate the human race, and raise it to a state of perfection 'little lower than the angels.' It is gratifying to believe — and this is a faith from which I cannot willingly swerve — that such men will rise up in after times, whose purifying powers shall banish from the earth selfishness, superstition, ignorance, and crime; and make their fellow-mortals more worthy of the beautiful world in which it has pleased God to place them.

It is a lamentable fact — and one that almost appears an anomaly in nature — that the divine gift of Poesy has been made subservient to the basest of purposes; by pandering to licentious passions, — promulgating dangerous doctrines, and giving false and distorted views of men and things. . . . There was another sad perversion of this great gift, which, thanks to reason and truth, is now becoming obsolete; namely the practice of singing in praise of war and the wine-cup . . . It is, however, consoling to know that a few Master-Spirits of the Lyre have soared above these ignoble themes, and vindicated the high character of the Muse, by singing *as* men *to* men capable of every virtue here, and born for immortality hereafter . . .

To many these 'Random Thoughts' may appear false and extravagant; but, as I do not dogmatically assert them to be correct, I may, at least, be allowed to flatter myself with the hope that they are so. My enthusiastic love of Poesy may have led me to view it through a too-highly coloured medium; for I cannot express how much I have been indebted to Poetry, as a source of intellectual enjoyment, during years of many sorrows, many baffled hopes, and many vain endeavours to rise above the evils of my condition. Yes, Poetry has been the star of my adoration, affording me a serene and steady light through the darkest portion of my existence; — a flower of exquisite beauty and perfume, blooming amid a wilderness of weeds, — a fountain of never-failing freshness, gushing forth in an arid desert, — a strain of witching and ever-varying melody, which so softens my heart with sympathy, and strengthens my heart with fortitude that I bless God for having made me susceptible to feelings so elevating, so humanising, so divine.

Gerald Massey
PREFACE

From the Third Edition of *The Ballad of Babe Christabel*, and reprinted in most subsequent editions of Massey's *Poems*. This Preface was first published in 1854.

. . . I have been blamed for the rebellious feelings to which the political pieces give utterance; but they were perfectly natural under the circumstances. Indeed, I look upon these same rebellious feelings as my very deliverance from a fatal slough. There are conditions in which many of the poor exist, where humanity must be either rebel or slave. For the slave, degradation and moral death are certain; but for the rebel there is always a chance of becoming conqueror; and the force to resist is far better than the faculty to succumb.

It is not that I seek to sow dissension between class and class, or fling firebrands among the combustibles of society; for when I smite the hearts of my fellows, I would rather they should gush with the healing waters of love, than with the fearful fires of hatred. I yearn to raise them into loveable beings. I would kindle in the hearts of the masses a sense of the beauty and grandeur of the universe, call forth the lineaments of Divinity in their poor worn faces, give them glimpses of the grace and glory of Love and the marvellous significance of Life, and elevate the standard of Humanity for all. But strange wrongs are daily done in the land, bitter feelings are felt, and wild words will be spoken. It was not for myself alone that I wrote these things: it was always the condition of others that so often made the mist rise up and cloud my vision. Nor was it for myself that I have uncurtained some scenes of my life to the public gaze, but as an illustration of the lives of others, who suffer and toil on, 'die, and make no sign;' and because one's own personal experience is of more value than that of others taken upon hearsay. . . .

I have been congratulated by some correspondents on the uses of suffering, and the riches I have wrung from Poverty; as though it were a blessed thing to be born in the condition in which I was, and surrounded with untoward circumstances as I have been. My experience tells me that Poverty is inimical to the development of Humanity's noblest attributes. Poverty is a never-ceasing struggle for the means of living, and it makes one hard and selfish. To be sure, noble lives have been wrought out in the sternest poverty. Many such are being wrought out now, by the unknown Heroes and Martyrs of the Poor. I have known men and women in the very worst circumstances, to whom heroism seemed a heritage, and to be noble a natural way of living. But they were so in spite of their poverty, and not because of it. What they might have done if the world had done better by them, I cannot tell; but if their minds had been enriched by culture, the world had been the gainer. . . . The beauty of Suffering is not to be read in the face of Hunger.

Above all Poverty is a cold place to write poetry in. It is not attractive to poetical influences. The Muses do not like entertainment which is not fit for man or beast. Nor do the best fruits of Poetry ripen in the rain, and shade, and wind alone; they want sunshine, warmth, and the open sky. And should the heart of a poor man break into song, it is likely that his poverty may turn into hailstones that which might have fallen on the world in fructifying rain. A poor man, fighting his battle of life, has little time for the rapture of repose which Poetry demands. He cannot take Poetry like a Bride to his heart and home, and devote a life to her service. He can only keep some innermost chamber of his heart sacred for her, from whence he gets occasional glimpses of her wondrous beauty, when he can steal away from the outward strife, like some child who has found a treasure, and steals aside to look on it in secret and alone, lest rude and importunate companions should snatch it from the possessor's hands. Considering all things, it may appear madness for a poor man to attempt Poetry in the face of the barriers which surround him. So many hearts have been broken, so many lives have been wasted, so many lions are in the way of the Gate Beautiful, and so many wrecks lie by the path! And so it is, — a diseased madness, or a divine one. If the disease, then there is no help for a man: if the divine, then there is no hindrance for him. . . .

Had I known, when I began to write verses, what I know now, I think I should have been intimidated, and not have begun at all. So many and so glorious are the luminaries already up and shining, that one would pause before lighting a rushlight. But I was ignorant of these things. And as I have begun, and conquered some preliminary difficulties, — as I have been sweated down to a proper jockey weight at which I can ride Pegasus with little danger of spraining his wings, — and as a purpose has gradually and unconsciously grown upon me, — I dare say I shall go on, making the best of my limited materials, with the view of writing some songs that may become dear to the hearts of the people, cheering them in their sorrows, voicing their aspirations, lighting them on the way up which they are groping darkly after better things, and saluting their triumphs with hymns of victory!

Janet Hamilton
From THE USES AND PLEASURES OF POETRY FOR THE WORKING CLASSES

From *Poems and Essays* (Glasgow, Thomas Murray, 1863), 187–89.

I have often thought and felt it to be a matter of deep regret that working-men and women, in consequence of their social position, and the want of means and leisure, are to a great extent debarred from the attainment of the elegant tastes and refined perceptions acquired by those on whom the gifts of fortune, and a desire of improving and adorning their minds, have conferred the high advantages of a liberal and finished education. Still, the working-man who is a good English reader, and possessed of an intellectual cast of mind, seasoned with a dash of fancy and feeling — although he may never have offered up his personal devotions at the shrine of the Muses, nor ever essayed to 'build the lofty rhyme,' thanks to the facilities afforded by cheap literature! — may yet indulge a taste for the sublime and beautiful, and be quite as capable of appreciating the treasures contained in the rich and varied stores of the higher walks of the best poets, as if he had ascended through all the gradations of learning from the parish school to the finale of a classical education in the patrician halls of Oxford and Cambridge. The workman may never be able to 'tread the classic shores of Italy;' he may never feast his eyes on the glorious monuments of antiquity which surround the eternal city; he may never roam the sunny land of Greece,

> 'Land of the Muses and of mighty men;'

nor glide with oar and sail over the gorgeous waters of the golden Horn; nor wander over

> 'Syria's land of roses'

and feel

> 'The light wings of zephyr, oppressed with perfume,'

fanning his cheek amid the roses of Sharon in the Holy Land.

No; the workman, as such, will probably never see, except in dreams, these lands of song and story, not gaze upon the glowing scenes where all that is grand and beautiful in nature and art combine to trance the soul in admiration; but still he can, when the toils of the day are ended, retire to his home, and having performed his ablutions, and solaced himself with

'the cup which cheers but not inebriates'
he then,

'when worldly crowds retire to revel or to rest,'
can

'trim his little fire,'
or light his frugal taper; and while holding communion with the spirits of the mighty masters of song in their immortal pages, may feel every noble principle of his mind strengthened, every emotion of his heart warmed and purified, and every feeling refined and elevated.

Joseph Skipsey
THE POET, AS SEER AND SINGER

From a series of three essays published in *Igdrasil — Journal of the Ruskin Reading Guild*, Vol. 1 (1890), 69–76, 136–141, and 182–189. The following paragraph is the conclusion of the final essay.

And now, in conclusion, for a word or two as to the development of these gifts: how is that to be best effected? In what way? By the poet taking himself away from the concerns and out of the haunts of men, and shutting himself up in a cave or a cot or a hall among lonely hills and dells and lakes, there to spend his days in the mere contemplation of trees and flowers and water and sky — the ripples on the lake and the variety and form of the colour of the clouds? By no means. Retirement and study of all this may be useful to his art; but the poet who would do what I have said — and what Chaucer and Shakespeare and Milton and Burns and Hood and our ballad writers have done — the poet who would sing his thoughts into the hearts and souls of his fellow-men, must to some extent live the lives of these men, and must essentially have a deep sympathy with whatever concerns their highest weal. Like the most prosaic of these, he will have his ups and downs in the great battle of human life, and, like them, he will have its manifold duties to perform; for though he is born with a golden bell in his soul, he may not be born with a silver spoon in his mouth; and, to his solace, in so doing he finds he is storing up ambrosia and nectar for the Muse; and when he has retired from the hubbub and distractions of the world, then, it may be, in the dead hour of the night, and 'when drowsiness has locked up mortal sense,' by some secret power a peal from the golden bell within is rung, and lo! at the first tone the broken angles and curves and the harsh and painful hues and sounds which he may have been *struck* with in his daily round of toil become as if possessed, and while the clear, sweet, rich bell within continues to ring, they become vital, meet, mix, unite; and from this operation results an image, a picture of human action, from which a second image is evolved, and from this a third; and so proceeds the mystic dance of evolution, till the soul itself is half startled and exults in a result which is the fulfilment of an oracle that is now perceived was written on every feature of the first image; and so a WHOLE has been conceived which, once in some adequate way expressed, another jewel has been brought to the light of day that in due time will take its place as a factor among those stars in the literary heavens which are ordained to illumine, to elevate, and fill with delight the soul of man, till —

> 'The cloud-capped towers, the gorgeous palaces,
> The solemn temples — the great globe itself —
> Yea, all that it inherits, hath dissolved,
> And, like the baseless fabric of a vision,
> Left not a rack behind!'

Chapter Three

LOWLY BARDS AND HOMELY RHYMERS

Alexander Anderson ('Surfaceman')

The title of this chapter — 'Lowly Bards and Homely Rhymers' — sounds dismissive. Yet the two phrases are taken from poems by authors represented here who were not at all ashamed or deferential about their poetic intentions. Fanny Forrester's 'The Lowly Bard' can be found in Chapter 2; Samuel Bamford's volume *Homely Rhymes, Poems, and Reminiscences* which provides several of the poems in this chapter, includes poems called, without any apparent embarrassment over their limited aspirations, 'Homely Advice to the Unemployed', 'Rhymes for the Times', and 'What! Another Cracked Poet!'. One of Laycock's volumes is called *Warblings from an Old Songster*. In short, the evidence for the limited literary aspirations of the poems here can be found by looking no farther than the titles. I have some sympathy with any reader who might feel that 'Homely Rhymers' are merely failed 'Parnassians', the casualties of artisan pretensions, the walking wounded in the cultural struggles within Victorian Britain. Certainly, the general level of poetic ambition and achievement in this chapter is probably lower than anywhere else in the anthology. The work, for instance, of the Penge potato-salesman Joseph Gwyer, while extending the range of trades practised by self-taught writers, offers little beyond doggerel platitudes, and even the relatively skilful poems included here seem unadventurous in their literary methods and social attitudes. Yet it is important to make a distinction within artisan poetry between verse directed upwards in society, towards a middle class or even aristocratic audience, and that directed outwards or sideways towards a predominantly working-class readership. Just as Chapter 2 acknowledged the cultural aspirations of working-class authors, so this chapter attempts to give a sense of that poetry written by artisans *for* artisans.

Interestingly enough, it was as hard, if not harder for artisan authors to find a readership amongst their own class as it was for them to find interest and enthusiasm among the middle classes. This apparent anomaly has much to do with 'the difficulties of appearing in print' described in Chapter 5, and with the lack of an immediately obvious working class literary genre outside the specifically political mode presupposed by Chartist poetry. In order to find an artisan readership, self-taught authors either had to operate at an entirely local level, and so abandon their metropolitan ambitions and lose the chance of a sophisticated and appreciative middle-class readership, or else publish their work in those more metropolitan literary journals where their work could be returned to an artisan readership through the mediation of the London journals of popular progress. In the first case the author was dependent upon the maintenance of subscription publishing, newspapers, patronage, pamphlet and broadside outlets within the immediate neighbourhood. In the latter case, he or she was dependent on the approval of sympathetic editors, and on success in open competition with metropolitan journalists and experienced hack writers. Neither solution was entirely satisfactory, and this introduction should be read alongside that to Chapter 5 in order to give some sense of the inhibitions created by the nature of access to print for poor and inexperienced authors.

The poems in this chapter seek to illustrate these two specific sets of literary relationships by reprinting a selection of poems from one of the London journals (*The People's Journal*) written by some of its most persistent artisan contributors, as well as representing work by essentially 'local' authors who never sought to speak beyond their locality or, indeed, beyond their social class. Despite these severely circumscribed literary ambitions, the resultant poems are not necessarily trivial or uninformative. While these poems may be found over-simple in their poetical ambitions and in their social analysis, this very simplicity poses certain questions about their authenticity and representativeness as class statements. It might be possible to argue that these modest poets, slightly more articulate than their neighbours, jotting down the commonplace experiences, the catchpenny anecdotes, the homely truisms, by which working-class experience was made explicable and tolerable, might represent 'authentic' working class attitudes more accurately than the Chartists or the Parnassians, whose political and cultural ambitions inevitably distinguished them from the mass of ordinary working people. Does the account of a stoical, wry, friendly, parochial, God-fearing, patriotic, respectable, cohesive, enduring 'class' of working people posited by writers like Edwin Waugh or Samuel Laycock not offer a legitimate counter-blast to seekers, like Martha Vicinus or myself, for a complex, increasingly self-aware and contradictory, literary vision of cultural progress and class development in Victorian

210

artisan writing? Put simply, is not the least sophisticated poetry likely to offer the most accurate (because least pre-meditated or self-conscious) account of working-class ideology?

The argument is a tempting one, and it is clear that more study needs to be made of, for example, the yearning for pre- or just-industrial community in Brierley or Waugh, and of the precise cultural referents of apparently naïve dialect vocabulary. The relationship between dialect poetry and the speech patterns of industrial workers remains unexplored in a literary context. Yet this argument for 'revealing simplicity', underscored by the continued local popularity of much Victorian dialect poetry, has to be pushed beyond an acceptance of meaning in poetry produced almost entirely at the level of transparent ideological statement. This book has chosen to structure its account of Victorian artisan literature largely by concentrating on the issues of literary mode and of literary production, both seen as dynamic and changing aspects of class relationships. The apparent simplicity of many of the poems in this section should not conceal the complexities of literary mediation, of audience, of the whole nature of 'local' culture which Martha Vicinus began to explore in *The Industrial Muse*. These poems may be simple at the level of apparent statement, but in so far as they belong to complex discourse produced by the emergent industrial city, they are not simple at all.

This chapter is almost inevitably the least 'representative' of any in this book. In order to select at all I have had to use a number of structural units which are in no way subtle or wide-ranging enough for their purposes. I have also drawn largely on material close to hand in Manchester at the evident expense of other regions. However this anthology seeks to understand the whole range of artisan literary production, and it is, for understandable reasons, the local writing which has both survived most vividly and been given the most attention. I am not afraid of those Lancashire readers who may feel aggrieved at the omission of their local favourite. Indeed, I would turn them round and point them to chapters 1 and 2. The local can only be understood alongside the contemporaneous aspirations to the national and to the universal. The reader must still make his or her own choice as to which of these forms of identity seems most crucial.

Poems from The People's Journal

The developments in mass journalism dating from the 1840s were an essential element for the growth of artisan literary ambitions. Although 'the difficulties of appearing in print' still remained formidable for self-taught writers, access to publication was substantially improved, both by the emergence of cheap magazines aimed at artisan readers and by the entrepreneurial interest of the liberal middle-classes in the cultural progress of the artisans. Chapter 5 offers a more detailed account of these possibilities, but in seeking for representative poems by artisan writers it seems essential to turn to those artisan magazines produced in London by cultural impresarios from, or sympathetic to, the artisan classes, and aimed at the double readership of both those middle-class sympathizers who wished to understand (and usually to applaud) developments within artisan culture more fully, and at the artisans themselves. I have explored this double sense of address more fully elsewhere (see bibliography) but I think that this dual sense of audience, as well as the specific formats of the magazines, are crucial determinants of the kinds of poems which artisan writers submitted to the magazines of popular progress. On the one hand, magazines like *Tait's, Eliza Cook's, Howitt's,* and *The People's*, did offer artisan writers a metropolitan outlet, and (usually — see p. 48) undifferentiated and unannotated publication alongside authors of the stature of Smiles or Reach. But the double audience, the insecurity of the authors themselves, and the limited space and function of the 'poetry slot' in the magazine tended to push authors towards short lyric poems on the commonplace subjects of artisan writing: patient suffering, spiritual consolation, the rewards of family life, the pleasures of reading. It is difficult to tell how such poems were read: were they understood primarily as gentle assertions of the artisan cultural presence, or did they offer serious ideological comment, reinforcing widely held social values? The poems are certainly deferential in their use of commonplace literary mode, diction, and verse form. Yet so also are the poems contributed to *The People's Journal* or *Tait's* by authors who elsewhere wrote in much more radical or complex ways. Ebenezer Elliott, W. J. Linton, and Goodwyn Barmby, all leading figures in a variety of political contexts, are among the contributors to *The People's Journal*, yet their poems give little sense of their wider commitment to radical causes. Barmby, whose communistic and millenarian writings show an extraordinary stylistic energy and promote an extreme and eccentric literary diction, none the less wrote entirely conventional lyrics for the journals of popular progress. The same goes for Elliott or Linton. It is hard to find the authors of 'The Black Hole of Calcutta' or 'Bob Thin' in the commonplace magazine verse found in *The People's Journal*.

The purpose, then, of this kind of artisan writing remains open to doubt. At one level it registers the artisan cultural presence, and, without fuss or overt challenge, points a wide variety of readers to the growing articulacy and confidence of the working classes. Yet the poetry largely denies any distinctive artisan point of view by its deference to the poetic traditions and social commonplaces of magazine verse. At another level, it might be argued that, commonplace as their social vision might be, such poems do state and reinforce the widely held ideological beliefs of the respectable artisans largely because they are so simple and direct. I am always doubtful whether literature does express ideology in such a direct and purposeful way, and it is certainly necessary to offset ideological statement against an acute awareness of literary tradition. One way of reading the following poems might be to see them as the lowest common denominator, or even as the highest common factor, of respectable artisan belief.

In order to find a way of representing this mass of ordinary and relatively similar verse, I have restricted my choice in this section to a single journal, *The People's Journal*, which, in its eleven half-yearly volumes, spanned the years 1846 to 1851, and survived a brief merger with *Howitt's Journal*. The editors were first John Saunders, and then William and Mary Howitt, three authors who had emerged from artisan backgrounds into the lower reaches of metropolitan literary entrepreneurship. The magazine is untypical largely because of generosity in space and attention to artisan contributors, although its blend of literary, topographical, informative, and analytical articles was characterstic of the whole genre of artisan magazines. Despite the large number of artisan contributors, *The People's*

Journal was largely sustained by professional journalists, albeit those of liberal or progressive sympathies.

I have further selected contributors with known backgrounds. Many of the poems published in *The People's Journal* are by authors so obscure that it is impossible to deduce whether they belong in this anthology or not. I have chosen one poem by Ebenezer Elliott to dramatize the contrasts in mode within Elliott's work, which is represented in the three main chapters of this anthology. I have chosen another poem, that by G. R. Emerson, for its subject matter rather than for the origins of its author. The other eight poems in this section are by three barely recoverable artisan writers: Henry F. Lott, a carpenter whose 1850 volume *One Hundred Sonnets* was loyally and extensively reviewed in *The People's Journal* (vol. 10, 43–45) and also noticed by *Eliza Cook's Journal* (vol. 2, 414); 'Marie', a Chorley factory operative who, as far as I can tell, never published in volume form but who was a regular contributor to *The People's Journal* over a number of years; and John Dacres Devlin, a London working man who corresponded with Dickens, and whose single contribution to *The People's Journal* is this poem. I have also grouped these poems to some extent by subject matter, choosing lyrics which have the nature of artisan life as their theme. It would have been equally easy to identify a group of poems about family, or a selection of pastoral poems, or a collection of simple love lyrics.

These writers, then, represent that mass of artisan writing which is, in the 1840s, just emerging from the pages of local journals into something approaching national consciousness. Undistinguished as these poems may be in their mode or voice, none the less the recognition of their origin and cultural significance was out of all proportion to their poetic achievement.

Henry F. Lott

SONNETS

From *The People's Journal* vol. 5 (1848), 266, 328.

O! how my Poet's-spirit doth it vex,
That I must still be told, by cautious men,

'Beware the muse! A *Fatuus* o'er a few,
That will your step mislead, your mind perplex.'
Why, worldlings, I'm as proud to wield the axe,
As I am happy I can guide the pen
To frame a sonnet — and return again
To a day's toil, that would disjoint the necks
Of half your dandy poets. Out! Away!
Throw not your scandal on the holy muse.
Hers is a sacred mission to infuse
The thoughts that elevate: and this my lay,
Conjoined with daily toil, may disabuse
The world's first notion that she leads astray.

I

Dream not, poor poet, that th' ephemeral breath
    Thy brain-creation draws from out the Press
    Shall save thee from the struggler's sure distress
Or snatch thee from oblivion's cold dark death:
Bleed will thy temples with a thorny wreath
    Just as thou deem'st the laurels of success
    Should have adorned them; — disappointment's stress
Will, in the end, thy spirit crush beneath.
The social mind is of material class,
    And flowers of song — the beautiful, the pure,
Strewn by your hand upon the leaden mass —
    Is held a paltry, fading garniture;
Unvalued by the sordid crowds that pass,
    Intent alone to keep their footsteps sure.

II

If 'twere not for the dignity inborn,
    That grows and strengthens in his high pursuit,
    How many a humble poet's heart were mute,
Chill'd by indifference or subdued by scorn!
Not more fair blossoms opening to the morn
    Perish untimely, though they promise fruit,
    Than do the strains of many a lonely lute,
Though they might purify, exalt, adorn.
But though the 'genial current of the soul'

Is checked and frozen, wheresoe'er it turns;
　Still ever and anon, bursting control —
　　Urged by 'the thought that breathes, the
　　　word that burns'
It reaches, in impetuous flow, the goal
　For which its elevated essence yearns.

SONNET — MY FRIEND'S LIBRARY

From *The People's Journal* vol. 6 (1848), 238.

Oh! What a precious casket hast thou there
　Fill'd with the brilliant gems of human thought!
　All Song has breathed of — all that Truth has taught,
Selected with judicious taste and care:
Mind-lightnings from brave bold men who dare
　Rend off the veil by ignorance darkly wrought
　O'er Reason's vision — thunders that have brought
On tyrants' cheeks the pallor of despair.
When from the daily world whose grovellings damp
　Thine ardent spirit, sad thou turn'st away
To grieve how gold pollutes, how fetters cramp
　Body and soul, as if God held no sway,
Here thou reviv'st thy hopes, while gleams thy lamp
　O'er page of moralist or poet's lay.

John Dacres Devlin
THE NOVEMBER PRIMROSE

From *The People's Journal* vol. 6 (1848), 316.

Written on seeing one, on the 17th of the month, on the hill of
Church Hougham, near Dover.

Late or soon, which is it, lonely flower?
　That thus thou comest here to glad mine eye,
Smiling beneath the clouds that gloomy lower,
　As thickly charged with dark futurity —

Portents of winter ill?
Late or soon, which is it, sweetest thing?
Or what the tidings which thou now dost bring,
                Young charmer of the hill?

Quick, and the last month of the year will come,
    And yet thou buddest forth, serenely gay,
As thou would'st triumph o'er each frail thing's tomb.
    Creations which have gone to their decay,
                Crushed by the season's chill;
O'er leafless shrub and wild flower's perished hue,
Till even the very fields are blank to view —
                So peep'st thou from the hill!

Or com'st the waning year in love to greet,
    That it might die in thankfulness to thee —
Now, when the dull hours move with leaden feet,
    And the fond bird but moans its misery.
                Oh! what would'st thou instil,
Affection lingering round the happy past,
For flowers and sunbeams which were not to last?
                Say, stranger of the hill?

On mission blessed thou surely art, thy smile
    So redolent of chastened charm appears;
A saint-like thing, homed in a rugged soil,
    A gentle queller of unholy fears,
                Such as the heart might kill;
All this thou surely art, or else why now,
When even lordly man wears sullen brow,
                Tak'st station on the hill?

Welcome! then, let me welcome thee, sweet flower,
    And draw rich stores of comfort from thy look;
So may I o'er this being's cares up-tower,
    As one who finds high good in Nature's book,
                Such as should guide us still:
Yea! thousand welcomes I would free bestow,
Upon the very earth where thou dost grow,
                Sweet Primrose of the Hill.

'Marie'
FELLOW WORKERS

From *The People's Journal* vol. 3 (1847), 21.

From the crevice of a cloudlet,
    In the eastern grey,
Came a beauteous Beam of lightness,
    Leading in the Day.
Flowrets woke up as she softly
    Stole upon the lands;
Joyfully the leaves and grasses
    Clapp'd their dew-wet hands!
Over field, and over forest,
    Silently she went,
Like a messenger in earnest,
    On some mercy bent.

By a quiet, shady hedgerow,
    In a sheltered nook,
Where we love to linger, reading
    In God's leafy book;
There a tender Shoot of greenness
    Claimed earth's needful care,
And the Beam, so soft and gentle,
    Was beside it there;
And, with streaming hands of silver,
    Bent she down in prayer,
While a murmur, indistinctly,
    Rose upon the air:

'Oh, behold this germ of beauty
    Pressing into life;
Come, thou golden god of noontide,
    Help it in this strife!
I will tint its slender leaflet
    And its fragile flower;
Ray of sunshine — Fellow-worker —
    Help me with thy power!'
Light and Heat were fellow-workers,

And God bless'd the deed;
For the flower was passing lovely,
    Though a simple weed!

There are many germs of goodness
    Dormant in each breast,
Lying there in sad half-slumber
    And unquiet rest.
Fain they would both bud and blossom,
    But within the soul,
Prison'd are they — nothing nearer
    To the distant goal.

Come, oh, silvery Beam of Knowledge!
    Turn the dumb intent
To a speaking, healthy action, —
    For this wert thou sent.
Be thou, too, a fellow-worker,
    Glowing Ray of Love;
Pierce within the sheltered hedgerow,
    Draw the germ above:
Souls that else were poor and lifeless
    Shall evolve new powers —
Weeds upon the wayside worthless
    Shall be God's bless'd Flowers!

Chorley, Nov. 1846

HEROISMS

From *The People's Journal* vol. 3 (1847), 163.

With this trusty sword and shield
Rides the warrior to the field: —
    For his bleeding country's wrongs,
        Valiantly he goes:
    Daring danger — braving death,
        Midst her tyrant-foes.
    If he fall — some pilgrim-feet,
        To his lonely grave,

Will in reverence come and bend —
    Worshipping the brave:
If victorious — he will win
    Laurel-wreaths of fame,
While applauding multitudes
    Shout the hero's name!
So, with trusty sword and shield,
Rides the warrior to the field.

With the homely spade and hoe,
To the fields the labourers go: —
    For their hungry families
        They bestir betimes;
    Digging on from early dawn
        To the latest chimes.
    Should they rear them honestly, —
        When the battle's won,
    Unconcernedly they're told,
        ' 'Tis *but duty* done.'
    Should health fail, and pinching want
        Send them to our door,
    Seldom do we stop to read
        The history of the poor.
Yet, with homely spade and hoe,
To the fields the labourers go.

By a dying brother's bed
Sits a maid, and sews for bread: —
    When the lark's first silver note
        Comes upon the air;
    And when tolls the midnight bell,
        Ever sits she there —
    Watching him, and speaking hope,
        Tho' her soul is sad —
    Dropping tears upon her task,
        Yet appearing glad;
    Grudging every moment's rest,
        Every sleepy hour —
    Yet will wander miles away
        For a wayside flower!

Few know this — yet by this bed
Sits the maid, and sews for bread.

God! who seest not in parts,
Strengthen those heroic hearts!
   Those who, with a strong endeavour,
     Win the noblest fight,
   Conquering *self* — and yet all lowly
     Bend them in Thy sight.
   Those who by the sacred hearth-stone,
     Where great trials come,
   Yet with peace, and gentle voices,
     Make it truly *home*:
   Those encased in Love's strong armour,
     Doing valiant deeds:
   For all such *true* heroism
     Our poor praying pleads.
Strengthen those heroic hearts,
God, who seest not in parts!

LABOUR

From *The People's Journal* vol. 10 (1850), 62.

Calm and solemn is the midnight!
   Nothing do I hear
But my heart's dull measur'd beating
   Throbbing in mine ear:
Beating! beating! still repeating —
   'Listen, wakeful soul,
For every beat but brings thy feet
   Onward to the goal!
Spend not, then, the starry midnight
   In a useless sorrow,
But go rest thee, and upnerve thee
   For the working morrow.'
Blessed warning! New religion!
   And if e'er again
To my idol-grief returning,

Utter, clear and plain —
    'Hark, hark, to the live heart beating;
      Life is on the wing;
    Labour is the truest worship
      Any soul can bring.'

Thou who toilest, bless thy toiling!
  Not all nature sings
Nobler anthem, than the music
  When the hammer rings!
Every stroke of spade or hatchet,
  Crieth out aloud, —
'Man is valiant in labour,
  And may well be proud.'
Stroke by stroke, glad time he keepeth
  To his leaping heart;
Who shall, scorning, call him '*poor* man',
  Having this rich part?
He can boldly look existence
  In the very eye;
Nor needs tremble when night whispers
  'Neath the starlit sky —
    'Hark, hark, to the live heart beating;
      Life is on the wing;
    Labour is the truest worship
      Any soul can bring.'

Thou who idlest, quit thy idling,
  'Tis not meet to be
Dumb and voiceless 'midst the chorus
  Of God's melody!
Wind and wave are join'd in labour,
  And the very flowers
Add a beauty to creation,
  Scenting all her bowers.
Do some act that waits the doing —
  Speak some living word —
Lead some soul to cleansing waters
  By good angels stirr'd;
And the morn shall smiling wake thee

With the dawn's grey light,
And in softest, gentlest cadence
    Thus shall sing the night —
            'Hark, hark, to the live heart beating;
                Life is on the wing;
            Labour is the truest worship
                Any soul can bring.'

When great nature, in sore travail,
    Bringeth forth her child —
Some old nation in convulsion,
    With new freedom wild! —
Some long-borne and huge injustice,
    That in dumbness stood,
Pouring out its new-born utt'rance
    In a jargon flood! —
Be thou calm and unaffrighted,
    'Tis but nature's heart
Beating in her children's bosom,
    Bidding wrong depart.
Ages are her fleeting moments, —
    World-times are her years —
In immensity she singeth
    'Mid the shining spheres —
            'Hark, hark, to God's heart beating;
                Time is on the wing,
            Labour is the only worship
                Any soul can bring!'

Ebenezer Elliott
THE PEOPLE'S SABBATH PRAYER

From *The People's Journal* vol. 3 (1847), 25.

From an Unpublished Lyric entitled 'Life According to Law'

Again, oh Lord! we humbly pray
    That thou wilt guide our steps aright:
Bless here, this day, tir'd labour's day!

Oh, fill our souls with love and light!
For failing food, six days in seven
   We till the black town's dust and gloom;
But here we drink the breath of heav'n,
   And here to pray the poor have room.
The stately temple, built with hands,
   Throws wide its door to pomp and pride;
But in the porch their beadle stands,
   And thrusts the child of toil aside,
Therefore, we seek the daisied plain,
   Or climb the hills to touch thy feet;
Here, far from splendour's city fane,
   Thy weary sons and daughters meet.
Is it a crime to tell thee here,
   That here the sorely-tried are met,
To seek thy face, and find thee near,
   And on thy rock our feet to set?
Where, wheeling wide, the plover flies,
   Where sings the wood-lark on the tree,
Beneath the music of thy skies,
   Is it a crime to worship thee?
'We waited long, and sought thee, Lord,'
   Content to toil, but not to pine;
And with the weapons of thy word
   Alone, assail'd our foes and thine.
Thy truth and thee we bade them fear;
   They spurn thy truth and mock our groan!
'Thy counsels, Lord, they *will* not hear,
   And thou hast left them to their own.'

G. R. Emerson
THE DREAM OF THE ARTISAN

From *The People's Journal* vol. 10 (1850), p. 74.

Oh, I have dream'd a pleasant dream of sunny spots and dells,
Of overhanging forest trees, and clear and sparkling wells;

Of sunny skies, of rivers wide, of gently swelling hills,
The song of birds, the voice of herds, and ever-murmuring rills.

Of hawthorn-scented country lanes, and many a pleasant scene,
Of spreading fields, of shady nooks, and cheerful village green;
The oak, slow bending to decay where ages it had stood,
And the shadow-kissing willow, the Narcissus of the wood.

And I heard the voice of children in merry little bands,
As to and fro they ran and leapt, and clapped their tiny hands;
And carolled free as joyous birds beneath the morning skies,
With health upon their sunburnt brows and laughter in their eyes.

I sat down on a fallen tree and watched them in their sports,
I sat me down all silently, communing with my thoughts;
Amidst their glee I felt myself a little one again,
And the legends of my childhood rushed like fresh blood to my brain.

I dreamed , too, of old churchyards, and antique sacred piles,
Of legends quaint on tombs of brass in monumental aisles;
Of effigies of valorous knights, and shrines of ancient dames,
Recorded faith and pious hopes of now-forgotten names;

And of a lone old manor house, with bleak and empty halls,
The court-yard overgrown with weeds, and ivy on the walls;
Its stately avenue of elms and herald-sculptured gate,
The fast-decaying relics of its once manorial state.

I stood on the heathery hill-side, on the golden-flowered ground,
When the ruddy hue of early morn was cast on all around,
And I gazed on the slumbering city, with its pent-up strength of woe,
That lay like a sullen giant in the misty vale below.

I felt myself as one renewed, as I breathed the clear pure air,
And my fresh-born spirit cast away its heavy load of care,
Oh, how I laved in the silver stream, beneath the hanging trees,
And listened to the murmuring sounds that floated in the breeze.

'Twas but a dream! 'twas *but* a dream! grim daylight brought the truth
And I woke from the trance of happiness and the visions of my youth —

I woke to the squalid city, and the strong heart–rending strife
Of wrestling with a weary world for the bitter gift of life.

'We Are Low' Poems

'We are low' poems form almost a sub-genre in working class literary culture, and this anthology contains three, one by Ernest Jones, which appears in the Chartists and Radicals section, and the following two, Robert Nicoll's 'We Are Lowly' and Thomas Blackah's 'We May Be Low'. The three form a paradigm for both the political potential of artisan verse and for its denial. Jones turns his refrains — 'We're low, — we're low, — we're very, very low' and 'a miserable lot are we' — into an oral opportunity for political threat, using gleeful irony to turn mock humility into an assertion of collective strength and purpose. Jones throws the middle-class perceptions of the 'lowly' state of the working classes back at their originators; he accepts the definition 'lowly' largely for its ironic potential. Though working people might properly be described as 'miserable', Jones argues, misery might be a source of political energy, and so the derogatory intention of the word is collapsed into a more appropriate political reality. Jones's clever refrains resulted in lengthy and wide-spread popularity for his poem. In trying to use a similar mode, Nicoll becomes much more literary, and much more earnest, and in the process changes potential threat or complaint into a defence of stoicism and the consolations of working-class life. Working people, he argues, still have their sensitivity, their inner moral and aesthetic strength, to offer as consolation for being the 'afflicted poor'. Lowliness is not necessarily an accurate measure of character, he insists. Thus, through a typical poetic strategy, Nicoll dissolves unhappiness and oppression into celebratory pastoral, with the countryside acting as an ever-present manifestation of God's bounty. Blackah, a Yorkshire miner, uses the dialect to fulfil the process begun by Nicoll, so that his poem becomes an untroubled celebration of the moral rewards of labour. Through another typical poetic manouevre, social tension is here dispersed by the invocation of the pleasures of domesticity. The way in which Nicoll and Blackah's poems begin from a disruptive perception of class difference, and then work out lyrically towards traditional poetic resolutions shows both the strengths and weaknesses of homely rhyming: a warm sense of shared hardships and rewards, a hard-won sense of equilibrium, is gained through simple retaining poetic strategies, and only at the expense of a direct political focus.

Robert Nicoll
WE ARE LOWLY

From *The Poems of Robert Nicoll* (Second Edition, Edinburgh, William Tait, 1842), 108–110.

> We are lowly — very lowly,
>   Misfortune is our crime;
> We have been trodden under foot
>   From all recorded time.
> A yoke upon our necks is laid,
>   A burden to endure;
> To suffer is our legacy,
>   The portion of the poor!
>
> We are lowly — very lowly,
>   And scorned from day to day;
> Yet we have something of our own
>   Power cannot take away.
> By tyrants we are toiled to death —
>   By cold and hunger killed;
> But peace is in our hearts, it speaks
>   Of duties all fulfilled!
>
> We are lowly — very lowly,
>   And yet the fairest flowers
> That by the wayside raise their eyes, —
>   Thank God they still are ours!
> Ours is the streamlet's mellow voice,
>   And ours the common dew;

We still dare gaze on hill and plain,
    And field and meadow too!

We are lowly — very lowly, —
    But when the cheerful Spring
Comes forth with flowers on her feet
    To hear the throstle sing,
Although we dare not seek the shade
    Where haunt the forest deer —
The waving leaves we still can see,
    The hymning birds can hear!

We are lowly — very lowly,
    Our hedgerow paths are gone
Where woodbines laid their fairy hands
    The hawthorn's breast upon.
Yet slender mercies still are left, —
    And heaven doth endure,
And hears the prayers that upward rise
    From the afflicted poor!

Thomas Blackah
WE MAY BE LO', WE MAY BE POOR

From *Dialect Poems and Prose by Thomas Blackah*
(York, Waddington, n.d.), 17.

We may be lo', we may be poor,
An' hev' hard an' lang to toil,
Contented still we jog along,
An' we'y pleasure till the soil.
The rich may romp and roose away,
An' be spending heaps o' treasure;
The gay their gaudy duds display,
When they 'er oot for pleasure.
            Bud we are lo', an' we are poor,
            An' hev' hard an' lang to toil,
            Contented still we jog along,
            An' we'y pleasure till the soil.

229

The bee may labour all't day lang,
An' be bent o'githering honey;
The miser neet an' day be thrang,
We'y his glittering piles of money;
The soldier in the field of strife,
He may hack an' hew his foes
Then draw a pension all his life,
An' seea dwell in sweet repose.
            Bud we are lo', an' we are poor,
            An' hev' hard an' lang to toil,
            Contented still we jog along,
            An' we'y pleasure till the soil.

We like to see wer barns at neet,
We'y ther mothers — smile an' greet us;
We hear we'y joy their pattering feet,
Cumin' on the rooad ta meet us;
We hit in peace wer humble fare,
Produced by honest labour,
Unawed an' free fra' cankering care,
We're at peace we'y friend an' neeber.
            Bud we are lo', an' we are poor,
            An' hev' hard and lang to toil,
            Contented still we jog along,
            An' we'y pleasure till the soil.

Lancashire Bards

The best known self-taught writers in Victorian Lancashire — Samuel Bamford, Elijah Ridings, Samuel Laycock, Edwin Waugh, and Ben Brierley — enjoyed, and continue to enjoy, a local celebrity out of proportion to their literary achievements. Of the many explanations for their popularity, the most plausible have to do with their strong sense of local community, their ability to celebrate the resilience and endurance of working people without rancour, and their acknowledgement of a political and economic context for working-class life which is seldom developed into an overtly political analysis. The yearning for 'community' in their poems is largely a search for a lost 'history' of ordinary people, most usually associated in their work with a rural/industrial village life which just pre-dates urbanization and the factory system. It seemed proper to acknowledge the Lancashire tradition in this anthology rather than those of, say, Tyneside or the West Midlands, partly because of my own connections with Lancashire and partly because the Lancashire writers penetrated furthest into national consciousness. Faced with a vast range of local writing, I have opted for a group of the best known authors, leaving the reader to consult Brian Hollingworth's *Songs of the People* for a much more comprehensive account of dialect literature, and Martha Vicinus's *The Industrial Muse* for a detailed description of the context and development of Lancashire writing. Further information can be found in Vicinus's essay in Dyos and Wolff's *The Victorian City* and in several of the essays in Kidd and Roberts *City, Class and Culture* (see the bibliography). Readers living in Lancashire will be aware of the numerous pamphlets, reprints and local studies which maintain the presence of the Victorian bardic tradition even into post-industrial Manchester.

Samuel Bamford
HOMELY RHYMES ON BAD TIMES

From *Homely Rhymes, Poems, and Reminiscences* (London, Simpkin Marshall; Manchester, A. Ireland. Revised and enlarged second edition), 1864. This volume is reprint of an 1843 edition of Bamford's poems with a considerable number of new poems.

Samuel Bamford (1788–1872), best known for his autobiographical *Passages in the Life of a Radical*, has a claim to be included in all of the first three chapters of this anthology. As an active radical, several times imprisoned for his political activities, his ideological stance, though personal, would qualify him as a 'Chartist or Radical'. Equally, his poetic ambitions and competence distinguish him from the mass of self-taught rhymesters in the Victorian period. His political intelligence is seldom far from the poems, and his anti-physical-force Chartist poem 'La Lyonnaise' might well have found a place among the Parnassians, despite its ostensibly political purpose. None the less, as the title of his collected poems suggests, the discourse used by Bamford remained determinedly popular and accessible, and his ideological position included many moderate and conciliatory elements despite his constant outspokenness on behalf of justice, liberty, and moral responsibility. Bamford's own career, with his spell as a civil servant in London, his Government pension, and his choice of Manchester as a place of retirement, all point to the contradictions and tensions which his work seeks to resolve. Many of his poems, both by political opinion and by mode (for example 'The Patriot's Hymn') belong to the tradition of oral radical poetry but I have placed Bamford's work in this chapter, accepting his own accounts of the modesty of his poetic intentions and as a way of showing how the various definitions adopted in this anthology's structure need to be treated with considerable caution. Bamford's poems were written in the years of Peterloo and the Napoleonic wars, but their continuing relevance to the working-class movement is suggested by the 1843 and 1864 reprintings. 'Homely Rhymes', written in 1817, typically adopts a double address to those in power and to struggling working people. The verse form, tone, and address however align this poem more with local bardic verse than with the wider ambitions of much Chartist and Parnassian verse. 'Here' in stanza five means Lincoln Castle.

232

Erewhile I sang of courtly dame,
With eyes divine and tresses fair,
And look'd, and look'd until there came
Creeping around my heart a snare;
But hitherto we've been aware
In time to shun all sinfulness;
Besides my wife is passing fair,
And doth with true affection bless,
Sufficient then my happiness.

And I have sung about the War
Which swept my countrymen away,
Scattering their mangled bodies far,
From Belgium to Corunna's Bay.
Oh! then the wolf had glorious prey;
Daily he walk'd forth to dine
And lapp'd the warm blood merrily,
As the blithe tippler takes his wine,
That kings might reign by right divine.

And I awake a fearless strain,
About the rulers of our land;
These limbs have borne their heavy chain,
Their fetters too have galled my hand,
And twice accused did I stand
Of treason 'gainst a hated king;
Lo! falsehood fails, and I demand
Justice for my imprisoning —
Justice! Ah, there was no such thing.

E'en now in prison do I write,
This is the sixth in which I've lain,
Not for infringing any right,
Not life nor property I've ta'en.
Ask you the reason, then; 'tis plain —
I made escape upon that day
When many of my friends were slain,
And many sorely wounded lay
Gasping in their strong agony.

And so the fools have sent me here,
'Tis for my benefit no doubt,
To pass my three and thirtieth year
In study and in sober thought.
And feeling grateful as I ought,
How can I less than sing a lay,
The memorable deeds about,
Of Hulton and of Parson Hay,
And that fam'd corps of yeomanry.

Now the long war was o'er at last,
And there arose a shout of joy;
Napoleon, in his prison fast,
No longer could our peace destroy.
And, whilst on pudding, beef, and pie,
The people pleased did regale,
Monarchs were meeting, snug and sly,
And planning how they might prevail
To keep the human mind in jail.

Ah! little thought our workers then
That dire distress would come so soon,
Nor dream't our merry gentlemen
That night would overtake their noon,
A fearful night without a moon,
Or solitary star to light,
When Canning, orator, buffoon,
Should prophesy of daggers bright
Groping for murder in that night.

But thus it was, the Cotton trade
Was presently thrown all aback,
And some who mighty sums had made
Began to feel their credit slack;
And then there came a thundering crack,
Which made the men of straw to stare,
Whilst 'Church and King' look'd densely black,
Saint Chapel man betook to prayer,
Though sometimes he would almost swear.

For was it not perversely strange,
That in a time of peace profound,
Should come so terrible a change
And press them to the very ground,
The rates were almost pound for pound.
While keen taxation still did fleece,
At length some 'sons of Gotham' found
'Twas sudden change from war to peace
That caused our commerce to decrease.

This was indeed a lucky thought,
For though it mended not the case,
A sudden gleam of hope it brought
To cheer that woful length of face
So gravely worn i'th' market place.
Oh! had but Hogarth lived to see
Those signs of 'penitential grace,'
He would have smil'd as well as me
At such grotesque humility.

Clinging to that fallacious hope,
They sank into a blind repose,
Nor did they once their eyelids ope
To take a peep beyond their nose,
Else they had seen how it arose
That commerce lingered more and more,
That tax on bread did interpose
A barrier at the merchant's store,
Or rudely warn'd him from our shore.

Now will I draw the veil aside
And workman's sad condition show;
Come hither, daughters, sons of pride,
And ponder on this scene of woe.
Behold him through the wintry snow
All faint, and slowly take his way,
Whilst the cold wind doth on him blow,
His mournful eyes stare haggardly,
He hath not tasted food to-day.

And he hath been to yonder town
To try if he could work obtain;
Not work he got, but many a frown,
And word of slight, that gave him pain;
And some there were who did complain
Of losses by their 'stock on hand;'
And some did blame the King of Spain,
The 'well-beloved Ferdinand,'
And some the rulers of the land.

And when again he reaches home,
His little ones around him press;
And some do shout for joy, and some
Climb to his knees with eagerness.
Whilst others their 'dear father' bless,
And ask if he hath brought a cake,
When, starting from forgetfulness,
He looketh upward to the flake, —
No bread, for love or pity's sake!

Where is the partner of his care?
Behold her on a wretched bed;
Up bore she long as she could bear,
Then sank at length all famished.
And now he binds her weary head,
Her throbbing temples pain her so;
And now the children cry for bread,
And parents bitter tears do flow,
That twain of hearts, how deep their woe!

Another group are sat to dine,
Behold how greedily they eat;
Sure they have got a proud sirloin
Their hunger keen to satiate.
Nay, not one taste of butcher's meat,
That is a dish they seldom see;
Potatoes garnish every plate,
And if a herring there should be,
'Tis tasted as a luxury.

For supper, father, mother, child,
Are often forced to regale,
Upon a mess of water boil'd,
And sprinkled with a little meal;
And if this homely potage fail,
Call'd by the weavers 'Creep o'er stile,'
All silent to their rest they steal
And slumber until morning's smile
Awakes to further want and toil.

And being pinched thus for food,
How doth their winter clothing go?
Why gents and ladies who are good
Will give a cast-off thing or so,
But not to 'Radicals', oh, no!
'They must not have encouragement,
They want our property, you know,
And to subvert the Government,
Such people never are content.'

Oh! ye who live in wealth and state,
Deem not this colouring too high;
Nothing would I extenuate,
Nor yet attempt to magnify;
Nor is it possible that I
Could half the dire affliction show,
Imagination will supply,
If it with sympathy doth glow,
Omissions in this scene of woe.

Nor would I wound your feelings fine,
Dear ladies, I revere you well;
But ah, those eyes look most divine
When they with tender pity swell,
Then do not the poor soul repel
Who cometh shiv'ring to your hall,
For he will of your goodness tell,
And blessings on your bounty call,
Though his word-loyalty be small.

May He who rules the stormy blast,
That howls amid yon wintry sky,
Protect thee, even to the last,
Wife, sister of mine enemy,
Whom I defied, and still defy,
And though a Radical I be,
Whom they have hunted to destroy,
For all their wrongs to mine and me,
Lady, I would not injure thee.

THE BARD'S REFORMATION

From *Homely Rhymes, Poems, and Reminiscences* (1864), 181–83.

Adieu to the Alehouse, where pounds I have spent,
For drinkin' and smokin' bring little content,
    Where laughin' an' grinnin',
    An' bettin' an' winnin',
    Cause sorrowful sinnin',
    The roar and the rant,
A better beginnin' is now my intent.

Adieu to the fiddle, the dance, an' the song,
To the lads an' the lasses I've trip't it among,
    Adieu unto Johnny,
    Who dances so bonny,
    The tightest of ony;
    Yon flag it can tell
The weight of his steps, an' he timeth them well.

Adieu to the glance of the love-lookin' e'e,
To the lip that is sweet as the mel of the bee;
    The waist that is charmin'
    The movement so warmin',
    The purpose disarmin',
    Of mortals like me;
An' prudence alarmin' commands me to flee.

Adieu to the lads, who are dons in the fray,
I've borne their sore bruises for mony a day;
    There's Darby an' Dobbin',
    Mad Ab' an' Rough Robin,
    For kickin' or nobin'
    Do carry the bay,
There's no country gobbin can bear it away.

Farewell to the lads who love frolic an' fun.
An' gayly support it when once 'tis begun;
    There's Dick, Ned, an' Simon,
    True lovers of joy, mon.
    I ne'er found them coy, mon,
    At fuddle or spree;
The tear an' the sigh, mon, before 'em will flee.

Farewell to the Doctor, whose wit is as bright
As the glim of the glow-worm on grey summer's night;
    His cordial, delicious,
    His green peas for issues,
    Pills, plasters, and washes,
    Are flitted to Lees,
The sick of the village to free from disease.

'The Gentleman's' company I must refrain,
Although the denial may cost me much pain;
    He singeth so sweetly,
    He diddles so neatly,
    With snuff he will treat ye,
    Ay, 'honour' he will;
The toper of topers is 'Gentleman Sprill.'

So now to my own little nook I'll retire,
I'll bar out the storm, an' trim up the fire,
    The witchery breakin',
    All folly forsakin',
    To study betakin',
    My mind to improve;
My muse ever wakin' to freedom an' love.

FAREWELL TO MY COTTAGE

From *Homely Rhymes, Poems, and Reminiscences* (1864), 120–22.

Farewell to my cottage, that stands on the hill,
To valleys and fields where I wander'd at will,
And met early spring with her buskin of dew,
As o'er the wild heather a joyance she threw;
'Mid fitful sun beamings, with bosom snow-fair,
And showers in the gleamings, and wind-beaten hair,
She smil'd on my cottage, and buddings of green
On elder and hawthorn and woodbine were seen —
The crocus came forth with its lilac and gold,
And fair maiden snowdrop stood pale in the cold —
The primrose peep'd coyly from under the thorn,
And blithe look'd my cottage on that happy morn.
But spring pass'd away, and the pleasure was o'er,
And I left my cottage to claim it no more,
Farewell to my cottage — afar must I roam,
No longer a cottage, no longer a home.

For bread must be earned, though my cot I resign,
Since what I enjoy shall with honour be mine;
So up to the great city I must depart,
With boding of mind and a pang at my heart.
Here all seemeth strange, as if foreign the land,
A place and a people I don't understand;
And as from the latter I turn me away,
I think of old neighbours now lost, well-a-day,
I think of my cottage full many a time,
A nest among flowers at midsummer prime;
With sweet pink, and white rock, and bonny rose bower,
And honeybine garland o'er window and door;
As prim as a bride ere the revels begin,
And white as a lily without and within.
Could I but have tarried, contented I'd been,
Nor envied the palace of lady the queen.
And oft at my gate happy children would play,
Or sent on an errand well pleased were they;
A pitcher of water to fetch from the spring,

Or wind-broken wood from my garden to bring;
On any commission they'd hasten with glee,
Delighted when serving dear Ima or me —
For I was their 'uncle', and 'gronny' was she.
And then as a recompense sure if not soon,
They'd get a sweet posy on Sunday forenoon,
Or handful of fruit would their willing hearts cheer;
I miss the dear children — none like them are here,
Though offspring as lovely as mother e'er bore
At eve in the park I can count by the score.
But these are not ours — of a stranger they're shy,
So I can but bless them as passing them by;
When ceasing their play my emotion to scan,
I dare say they wonder 'what moves the old man.'

Of ours, some have gone in their white coffin shroud,
And some have been lost in the world and its crowd;
One only remains, the last bird in the nest,
Our own little grandchild, the dearest and best.
But vain to regret, though we cannot subdue
The feelings to nature and sympathy true,
Endurance with patience must bear the strong part —
Sustain when they cannot give peace to the heart;
Till life with its yearnings and struggles is o'er,
And I shall remember my cottage no more.

THE LANDOWNER

From *Homely Rhymes, Poems, and Reminiscences* (1864), 78–9.

This poem, in Bamford's more satiric radical manner, has been
included partly for the interesting comparison it forms with W. J.
Linton's 'Revenge' from Chapter 1. Lacking Linton's pathos, Bamford's
sly monologue none the less uses to good effect a form and idiom
made approachable by being drawn from a popular song. 'The
Landlord' is a poem which makes a political point without threatening
or challenging its reader with overt radicalism.

There was a famous landowner
  In Inglondshire, d'ye see,
He was a 'graidly gentleman,'
  A jolly old buck was he;
And thus he sang where'er he sung,
  And sing full oft would he;
I care for nobody, no not I,
  Though many have care for me.

My cattle roam a thousand hills,
  For miles of land are mine;
My valleys, with their teeming rills,
  Yield butter, corn, and wine;
The fish, the game, I also claim;
  I'll have them too, by G.
I care for nobody, no not I,
  Though many have care for me.

One son commands a regiment,
  Another hath a See;
My daughter to the palace went,
  A pension soon had she;
To leave behind good things we find,
  Is sin of high degree,
I'll sin for nobody, no not I,
  Whoever may sin for me.

'Tis thus, the army's on my side,
  The church's prayers are mine;
With one I drink, at tother wink,
  When pottle deep in wine;
And whilst we sing God save the King,
  Or Queen, when Queen there be,
I care for nobody, not not I,
  Though many have care for me.

Elijah Ridings
SIMPLE MINSTRELSY

From *The Village Muse* (Third edition, Macclesfield, Thomas Stubbs, 1854), 403–406.

Elijah Ridings (1802–72) is described by Martha Vicinus as an ex-silk hand-loom weaver turned jack-of-all-trades. She includes him among her group of 'major' working-class poets who all 'shared the same definition of poetry, its powers and the role of the poet in society'. But Ridings is interesting as a writer of considerable technical accomplishment and, on occasions, considerable poetic ambitions, who deliberately maintained a local audience and a 'bardic', unpretentious conception of poetry. Such tensions between possibility and performance were underlined by the ideological tensions in his work between a largely progressive view of the cultural and political progress of the working classes, combined with a vigorous defence of the conservative values of family, country, and temperance. Both the title of this book (in fact a collected edition of Riding's work), and this poem point to the deliberate way in which Ridings pitched his work at a working-class readership. However, his poetry has many classical allusions, and even a poem as simple as 'Simple Minstrelsy' develops a series of important historical analogies which presuppose the ability to think in the analogical and historical ways usually associated with poems written for more sophisticated readers. The sense of poetry as an important social influence on working-class conduct is set against a more allusive, more challenging poetic conception. 'My Uncle Tum' moves out from a similarly unpretentious, almost *faux naïf*, domestic celebration into a more complex sense of national identity linked to an emblematic individual. The poem's celebration steps beyond the parochial into an attempt to locate Northern artisan culture in a wider cultural perspective, so that the rather mannered and sentimental stereotype of 'My Uncle Tum' can be evaluated in both a domestic and a national context. The result is surprisingly sophisticated and complex.

> A simple song, perchance may tell
> A simple, humble truth;
> To break the foul inebriate's spell,
> The spell of age and youth:
> For, in this mis-directed sphere,
> Amid the dull and cold,

The cup of Circe is placed near
   The lips of young and old.

I may not tell of war's dread field,
   Nor dreams of old romance;
But I may yet good counsel yield,
   And virtue's cause advance
Thousands, ay, millions, seek the goal,
   Of misery and care;
And from the foul inebriate's bowl
   Quaff waters of despair.

Attend, each youth; attend, each sire,
   To counsel wise and pure;
Touch not the alcoholic fire,
   Make 'surance doubly sure:
With all your fervent heart abhor,
   And loathe with all your mind,
The witch–drink, made for strife, or war,
   And ne'er for peace design'd.

Surely, the evil spirit found
   This fatal drink for man,
Dispers'd it to accurse the ground,
   And thwart vast nature's plan:
Deceiving men with weird drink,
   That charms the sense away;
In poverty and woe they sink,
   And shame the light of day.

Not Athens, in her heathen pride,
   Was half so mad as we;
Though Bacchus there was deified:
   All ancient books agree,
That Apaturian feasts were given
   To Bacchus, god divine;
And warning voices breath'd from Heaven,
   To man, deceived by wine.

The Theban king a law proclaim'd
   Against this furious strife —
A wholesome edict, wisely fram'd,
   Cost him his mortal life;
The madmen dragg'd him from his throne;
   With human blood imbrued
Their cruel hands, that fiends would own,
   In their demoniac mood.

The Roman Coliseum's name,
   Embalm'd in history's page,
Denoteth, now, a place of shame,
   Disgraceful to the age;
Ye, magistrates, and men of might!
   Ye, merchants of renown!
Why slumbers the true legal right,
   To promptly put it down?

O cast the witch-bane to the deep —
   An antidote is found;
Your house and home in order keep,
   The goodly twelve months round:
Then, you will find your simple plan,
   Ne'er maketh you a slave,
Neglecting the pure rights of man,
   To seek a coward's grave.

MY UNCLE TUM

From *The Village Muse* (Third edition, Macclesfield,
Thomas Stubbs, 1854), 39–44.

And hath he finish'd life's brief sum,
And is he dead? poor 'UNCLE TUM.'

A little social man was he,
Remember'd in my infancy;
And often came to see my mother,
And soon I learn'd he was her brother:

How glad I was to see him come,
And always welcome 'UNCLE TUM.'
And when the silk-loom wanted gaiting;
O, then, my anxious mother waiting,
And watching through the window-pane,
To see him coming down the lane,
The while I stood upon a chair,
Regardless of the want and care,
From empty loom and hanging thrum —
O, then, I call'd for 'UNCLE TUM.'

Many a smiling spring pass'd by,
Many a summer's laughing eye,
Many an autumn's golden corn
Was by the reaper's sickle shorn;
Many a winter's snow and frost
Over the Yorkshire moorlands cross'd;
Many a bitter biting blast
By our snug cottage rudely pass'd,
Intervening times beside,
Christmas, Easter, Whitsuntide,
Came as they might, whate'er might come,
O, ever welcome 'UNCLE TUM.'

In gardening delight he took,
And read and studied many a book;
Arithmetic could understand,
And wrote a good old-fashion'd hand;
Oft would discourse of Mother Nature,
And praise her beauty, form, and feature:
And when the festive board was crown'd
The village ale went briskly round,
Loud would he talk of stoic Cato,
And of the transcendental Plato;
Of other names of modern times,
Unsuited to my simple rhymes:
Of battles lost, and battles won,
By Ney, Soult, and Napoleon;
And of the glorious Waterloo,
He'd say, what many count as true,

That Grouchey purposely kept back,
And until Blucher join'd th' attack,
Our greatest Captain cried, *Alack*!
But, if you said the Duke had won it,
He'd swear that British gold had done it.
And who, in all the circle present,
More kindly, cheerful, witty, pleasant,
Laughing, joking, jesting, jibing,
And the home-brew'd ale imbibing,
And, yet, at none would bite his thumb?
The Muse re-echoes 'UNCLE TUM.'

And of *free trade* he'd say 'Egad!
'They must be either drunk or mad,
'Or stricken with *teetotal* blindness,
'Or destitute of human kindness;
'The proudest lords of highest station,
'Starving every one i'th' nation,
'Plunging the country into want,
'Producing nought but dearth and scant,
'Nor caring who was growing thinner,
'Provided they had got their dinner;'
Then, every one within the room,
Cried '*Well done, well done,* UNCLE TUM.'

At learned botanic club, or meeting,
The humble sons of science greeting
Each one the other, in that spirit,
Which truest wisdom does inherit;
Kind, frank, familiar, open, plain,
And never pompous, never vain;
From daily labour stealing hours
Studying nature's varied powers;—
At this great picture language faileth,
And some carping critic raileth; —
Mark where a native plant was found,
Ne'er seen before on English ground,
Note the pure joy, the wond'rous pleasure.
As if each one had found a treasure;
Though some, perchance, might him surpass,

Describing *genus, species, class,*
But, the last to go, and first to come,
Was true and constant 'UNCLE TUM.'

When, mid this life's surrounding shade,
The fondest hopes were doom'd to fade;
When, once, twice, thrice affliction came
And chill'd to clay a living frame;
When, mother's, brother's, sister's breath
Exhal'd in all absorbing death; —
They who had been the village pride,
In death's cold arms lay side by side;
Of three so well-belov'd bereav'd;
E'en Hope's delightful smile deceiv'd;
Our hearth became a scene of gloom,
The dreary darkness of the tomb, —
He was the counsellor and friend
Of each, unto the final end;
He was the comforter, who smil'd
In love, on each surviving child;
And rous'd each drooping heart at last,
To bear resignedly the past,
In decent cheerfulness and hope,
Unlike despairing misanthrope,
Who would let Hope all dormant lie
In heathenish obscurity;
And truth reject, condemn, repel
Unto the old, unfathom'd well;
For, still, this world, with all its gloom,
Had Heaven's own light for 'UNCLE TUM.'

And when, in many after years,
With some of smiles, but more of tears;
When this great goodly frame the earth,
With all its scenes of woe and mirth
With all its pomp and vanity,
And all its sheer inanity,
To me were known; and the remote
And silent ages 'gan to float
Down the eternal stream of mind

In epic, lyric page refin'd:
Old Shakspere, multiform and vast,
And destin'd through all time to last;
Of boundless depth, and many-sided,
By none but senseless fools derided; —
When I would vainly sigh for fame,
And struggle for a deathless name,
Betimes my board with plenty crown'd.
Betimes a scant meal only found;
Who would to me more kindly come,
Than thou, beloved 'UNCLE TUM.'

Alas! tis finished: life's brief dreams
Are over; and to me beseems
More welcome than the first that pass'd
The last brief struggle of the last;
'Tis finished now; and of life's sum
Thou know'st the total, 'UNCLE TUM.'

Edwin Waugh
CULTIVATE YOUR MEN

From *Poems and Lancashire Songs* (Fourth edition, Manchester, Abel Heywood, 1876), 42–44. The publishing history of Waugh's work, which involves broadsides, pamphlets, and books, nearly all of them undated, is extremely complex, and I have contented myself with using the plush 1876 subscription edition, even though the lavish production conceals its purpose as an attempt by Waugh's friends to help the struggling author.

Edwin Waugh (1817–1890) was unusual among Lancashire authors in that he became a full-time writer for the last twenty or more years of his life, after an early career as a bookseller's apprentice and a journeyman printer. Various clerical posts led him out of a poor childhood, but, despite publishing his first book (a series of Lancashire sketches) in 1855, it was not until the early 1860s that the success of his dialect poetry made him a local celebrity. His attempts to exploit this celebrity, and turn fame into an income, are fully described in *The Industrial Muse*, and show Waugh's understanding of the persistent orality of locally based cultural patterns. Waugh became dependent on pensions to sustain himself during a protracted illness, and even his perceptive analysis of local literary enthusiasm was not enough to compensate for the failure of the major provincial cities in developing a professional literary culture. Waugh, in his later years, seems almost the victim of his own success, following, less dramatically and tragically, the frustrated ambitions towards professionalism which had destroyed John Critchley Prince a generation before. The three following poems represent both Waugh's standard English and his dialect idiom, though it was the dialect poems which brought him most recognition.

I

Till as ye ought your barren lands,
    And drain your moss and fen;
Give honest work to willing hands,
    And food to hungry men;
And hearken — all that have an ear —
    To this unhappy cry, —
'Are poor folks' only chances here
    To beg, to thieve, or die?'

II

With kindly guerdon this green earth
    Rewards the tiller's care,
And to the wakening hand gives forth
    The bounty slumbering there;
But there's another, nobler field
    Big with immortal gain, —
The morasses of mind untilled; —
Go, — cultivate your men!

III

Oh, ponder well, ye pompous men,
    With Mammon-blinded eyes,
What means the poverty and pain
    That moaning round you lies:
Go, plough the wastes of human mind
    Where weedy ignorance grows, —
The baleful deserts of mankind
    Would blossom like the rose.

250

IV

But penny-wise, pound-foolish thrift
　　Deludes this venal age;
Blind self's the all-engrossing drift,
　　And pelf, the sovereign rage.
E'en in the Church, the lamp grows dim,
　　That ought to light to heaven,
And that which fed its holy flame,
　　To low ambition's given.

V

Just retribution hovers near
　　This play of pride and tears;
To heaven all worldly cant is clear,
　　Whatever cloak it wears;
And high and low are on one path,
　　Which leads into the grave, —
Where false distinctions flit from death,
　　And tyrant blends with slave.

THE MAN OF THE TIME

From *Poems and Lancashire Songs* (1876), 114–115.

I

He is a sterling nobleman
　　Who lives the truth he knows;
Who dreads the slavery of sin,
　　And fears no other foes.

II

Who scorns the folly of pretence;
　　Whose mind from cant is free;
Who values men for worth and sense,
　　And hates hypocrisy.

III

Who glows with love that's free from taint;
　　Whose heart is kind and brave;

251

Who feels that he was neither meant
    For tyrant nor for slave.

IV

Who loves the ground, where'er he roam,
    That's trod by human feet,
And strives to make the world a home
    Where peace and justice meet.

V

Whose soul to clearer heights can climb,
    Above the shows of things, —
Cleaving the mortal bounds of time,
    On meditative wings.

VI

Malice can never mar his fame;
    A heaven-crowned king is he;
His robe, a pure immortal aim;
    His throne, eternity.

I'VE WORN MY BITS O' SHOON AWAY

From *Poems and Lancashire Songs* (1876), 279–282.

I've worn my bits o' shoon away,
    Wi' roving up an' deawn,
To see yon moorlan' valleys, an'
    Yon little country teawn:
The dule tak shoon, and stockin's too!
    My heart feels hutchin'-fain;
An', if I trudge it bar-fuut, lads,
    I'll see yon teawn again!

It's what care I for cities grand, —
    We never shall agree;
I'd rayther live where th' layrock sings,
    A country teawn for me!

A country teawn, where one can meet
  Wi' friends, an' neighbours known;
Where one can lounge i'th market-place,
  An' see the meadows mown.

Yon moorland hills are bloomin' wild
  At th' endin' o' July;
Yon woodlan' cloofs, an' valleys green, —
  The sweetest under th' sky;
Yon dainty rindles, dancin' deawn
  Fro' th' meawntains into th' plain; —
As soon as th' new moon rises, lads,
  I'm off to th' moors again!

There's hearty lads among yon hills,
  An' in yon country teawn;
They'n far moor sense nor preawder folk, —
  I'll peawnd it for a creawn;
They're wick an' warm at wark an' fun,
  Wherever they may go, —
The primest breed o' lads i'th world, —
  Good luck attend 'em o'!

Last neet I laft the city thrung,
  An' climbed yon hillock green;
An' turned my face to th' moorlan' hills,
  Wi' th' wayter i' my e'en;
Wi' th' wayter wellin' i' my e'en; —
  I'll bundle up, an' go,
An' I'll live an' de' i' my own countrie,
  Where moorlan' breezes blow!

Samuel Laycock
HOMELY ADVICE TO THE UNEMPLOYED

From *The Collected Writings of Samuel Laycock*, ed. George Milner,
(Second edition, Oldham, W. E. Clegg, 1908), 110–12.

Without quite the same success, Laycock's career is directly compar-
able to that of Waugh. His life covered a similar span (1826–93), he

rose from childhood work in the factories to the relatively senior job of cloth looker, but was thrown out of work during the cotton famine in the early 1860s. He then became well-known through a series of poems about the cotton famine, which began as broadsides but which were reprinted in various forms. Then, like Waugh, Laycock retreated to the Lancashire coast, becoming the curator of the Whitworth Institute at Fleetwood. The publication of his works suggests the same kind of pattern as that of Waugh: a range of cheap, accessible, local formats to try to take every advantage of local working-class appeal. Both Waugh and Laycock in a sense became de-classed by their writing, losing contact with the sources of the poetry in later life, but unable to develop their limited skills into professional literary careers.

Tho' unfit to tak' part i' loife's battles
    Or feight wi' th' same pluck as befoor;
As a comrade, an' late brother-toiler,
    Aw feel anxious to help yo' once moor.
Aw've fowt lung an' hard as yo' know, lads;
    But aw'm gettin' near th' end o' mi days;
Aw shall soon have to strip off this armour,
    An' let someb'dy else tak' mi place.

Tak' advice fro' a grey-yeaded comrade,
    Let justice be blended wi' blows:
An' be sure 'at yo' dunnot mak' th' blunder
    O' mistackin' yo'r friends for yo'r foes.
Some o'th' wealthy desarve o they'n getten;
    They'n been workin', an' savin' the'r gowd,
While y'on had y'or honds i' y'or pockets,
    Or, perhaps, played at marbles i'th' fowd.

Tak' an owd friend's advice, an' feight fair, lads;
    Be aware o' what's known as 'bad blood;'
An' whatever yo' do, keep fro' mischief;
    Breakin' windows will do yo' no good.
Yo' do reet to speak eawt when yo'r clemmin',
    An' let o yo'r troubles be known;
But this con be done witheawt threat'nin',
    Or endangerin' th' nation or th' throne.

Lads, aw know what it meons to be pinchin',
    For aw've had a front seat i' that schoo';
Oatcake an' churn milk for a 'baggin' '
    An' a penny red herrin' for two!
It tries a poor starvin' mon's patience,
    An' his feelin's are hardish to quell,
When he sees his rich neighbours are feastin'
    An' he con get nowt nobbut th' smell.

This is one o' thoose wrongs 'at want reightin';
    Ther's a screw loose i'th' job ther's no deawt;
Ther's a foe hangin' reawnd 'at needs feightin';
    Set to work, lads, an' ferret it eawt.
An' while battlin' for th' right, let's be 'jannock';
    Thoose 'at's reet have no need be afraid.
Are these wrongs browt abeawt bi eawr neighbours?
    Or are they — what's likelier — whoam-made?

While th' wealthy are feastin' we're starvin',
    An' for this, lads, ther' must be a cause;
Aw know pratin' Tom ull put this deawn
    To injustice an' th' badness o'th' laws.
Well, ther' may be some truth i' what Tom says,
    But aw know what th' real cause is aw think:
For while Tom's woife an' childer are starvin',
    He's spendin' his earnin's o' drink.

Yo' may prate o'er yo'r wrongs until doomsday,
    An' blame what are coed th' upper class;
But ole yo'r complaints will be useless,
    Till yo'n th' sense to tak' care o' yo'r brass.
Turn o'er a new leaf, fellow-toilers,
    An' let common-sense be yo'r guide;
If ther's one happy spot under heaven,
    Let that spot be yo'r own fireside.

Get a ceaw, if yo' con, an' three acres,
    An' i' future, employ yo'r spare heawers
I' readin' good books; an' yo'r windows,
    Fill these up wi' plants an' wi' fleawers.

Get yo'r wives an' yo'r children areawnd yo',
    Sing an' whistle among 'em loike mad;
An' if this doesn't mak' yo' feel happier,
    Throw th' blame on 'A LANCASHIRE LAD'.

THE SHURAT WEAVER'S SONG

From *Collected Writings* (1908), 15–17.

Confound it! aw ne'er wur so woven afore,
Mi back's welly brocken, mi fingers are sore;
Aw've bin starin' an' rootin' amung this Shurat,
Till aw'm very near getten as bloint as a bat.

Every toime aw go in wi' mi cuts to owd Joe,
He gies mi a cursin', an' bates mi an' o;
Aw've a warp i' one loom wi' booath selvedges marr'd,
An' th' other's as bad for he's dressed it to' hard.

Aw wish aw wur fur enough off, eawt o'th' road,
For o' weavin' this rubbitch aw'm gettin' reet stow'd;
Aw've nowt i' this world to lie deawn on but straw,
For aw've nobbut eight shillin' this fortni't to draw.

Neaw aw haven't mi family under mi hat,
Aw've a woife an' six childer to keep eawt o' that;
Se aw'm rayther amung it at present yo' see,
Iv ever a fellow wur puzzl't, it's me!

Iv one turns eawt to stale, folk'll co me a thief,
An' aw conno' put th' cheek on to ax for relief;
As aw said i' eawr heawse t' other neet to mi woife,
Aw never did nowt o' this sort i' mi loife.

One doesn't like everyone t' know heaw they are,
But we'n suffered so lung thro' this 'Merica war,
'At ther's lots o' poor factory folk getten t' fur end,
An' they'll soon be knocked o'er iv th' toimes dunno mend.

Oh, dear! iv yon Yankees could only just see
Heaw they're clemmin' an' starvin poor weavers loike me,
Aw think they'd soon settle the'r bother, an' strive,
To send us some cotton to keep us alive.

Ther's theawsands o' folk just i'th' best o' the'r days,
Wi' traces o' want plainly seen i' the'r face;
An' a future afore 'em as dreary an' dark,
For when th' cotton gets done we shall o be beawt wark.

We'n bin patient an' quiet as lung as we con;
Th' bits o' things we had by us are welly o gone;
Aw've bin trampin' so lung, mi owd shoon are worn eawt,
An', mi halliday clooas are o on 'em 'up th' speawt'.

It wur nobbut last Monday aw sowd a good bed —
Nay, very near gan it — to get us some bread;
Afore these bad toimes come aw used to be fat,
But neaw, bless yo'r loife, aw'm as thin as a lat!

Mony a toime i' mi loife aw'v seen things lookin' feaw,
But never as awk'ard as what they are neaw;
Iv ther' isn't some help for us factory folk soon,
Aw'm sure we shall o be knocked reet eawt o' tune.

Come, give us a lift, yo' 'at han owt to give,
An' help yo'r poor brothers an' sisters to live;
Be kind, an' be tender to th' needy an' poor,
An' we'll promise when th' toimes mend we'll ax yo' no moor.

BOWTON'S YARD

From *Collected Writings* (1908), 42–44.

At number one, i' Bowton's Yard, mi gronny keeps a skoo,
Hoo hasna' mony scholars yet, hoo's nobbut one or two;
They sen th' owd woman's rayther cross, — well, well, it may be so;
Aw know hoo boxed me rarely once, an' poo'd mi ears an' o.

At number two lives widow Burns, hoo weshes clooas for folk;
The'r Billy, that's her son, get jobs at wheelin' coke;
They sen hoo cooarts wi' Sam-o'-Ned's, 'at lives at number three;
It may be so, aw conno tell, it matters nowt to me.

At number three, reet facin' th' pump, Ned Grimshaw keeps a shop;
He's Eccles-cakes, an' gingerbread, an' traycle beer an' pop;
He sells oat-cakes an' o, does Ned, he 'as boath soft an' hard,
An' everybody buys off him 'at lives i' Bowton's Yard.

At number four Jack Blunderick lives; he goes to th' mill an' wayves;
An' then, at th' week-end, when he's time, he pows a bit an' shaves;
He's badly off, is Jack, poor lad! he's rayther lawm, they sen,
An' his childer keep him down a bit, aw think they'n nine or ten.

At number five aw live misel', wi' owd Susannah Grimes,
But dunno like so very weel, hoo turns me eawt sometimes;
An, when aw'm in ther's ne'er no leet, aw have to ceawer i'th' dark;
Aw conno pay mi lodgin' brass becose aw'm eawt o' wark.

At number six, next door to us, an' close to th' side o'th' speawt,
Owd Susie Collins sells smo' drink, but hoo's welly allus beawt;
An' heaw it is, ut that is so, aw'm sure aw conno' tell,
Hoo happen maks's it very sweet, an' sups it o hersel'.

At number seven ther's nob'dy lives, they laft it yesterday,
Th' bum-baylis coom an' marked the'r things, an' took 'em o' away;
They took 'em in a donkey cart — aw know nowt wheer they went —
Aw reckon they've bin ta'en an' sowd becose they owed some rent.

At number eight — they''re Yawshur folk — ther's only th' mon an'
    th' woife,
Aw think aw ne'er seed nicer folk nor these i' o mi loife!
Yo'll never see e'm foin' eawt, loike lots o' married folk,
They allus seem good-temper't like, an' ready wi' a joke.

At number nine th' owd cobbler lives, th' owd chap ut mends mi
    shoon,
He's gettin' very wake an' done, he'll ha' to leeov us soon;
He reads his Bible every day, an' sings just loike a lark,
He says he's practisin' for heaven — he's welly done his wark.

At number ten James Bowton lives, he's th' noicest heawse i'th' row;
He's allus plenty o' summat t'ate, an' lots o' brass an' o;
An' when he rides or walks abeawt he's dressed up very fine,
But he isn't hawve as near to heaven as him at number nine.

At number 'leven mi uncle lives, aw co him Uncle Tum,
He goes to concerts up an' deawn, an' plays a kettle-drum;
I' bands o music, an' sich things, he seems to tak' a pride,
An' allus mak's as big a noise as o i'th' place beside.

At number twelve, an' th' eend o'th' row, Joe Stiggins deols i ale;
He's sixpenny, an' fourpenny, dark-colour't, an' he's pale;
But aw ne'er touch it, for aw know its ruin't mony a bard,
Aw'm th' only chap as doesn't drink 'at lives i' Bowton's Yard!

An' neaw aw've done, aw'll say good-bye, an leov yo' for awhile;
Aw know aw haven't towd mi tale i' sich a fust-rate style;
But iv yo're pleas't aw'm satisfied, an' ax for no reward
For tellin' who mi neighbours are ut live i' Bowton's Yard.

WHAT! ANOTHER CRACKED POET

From *Collected Writings* (1908), 118– 120.

What! another cracked poet! bi th' mass, Jim, owd lad,
    Aw thowt we'd enoo o' this mack;
An' iv tha'll alleaw me to say what aw think,
    Tha desarves a good stick to thi back.
Aw'll tell thi what lad, tha'll be awfully clemmed
    Iv tha'rt thinkin' to live bi thi pen.
Iv tha wants to get on, get some porritch an' milk,
    An' some good cheese an' bread neaw an' then.

Neaw, aw've had some experience i' this mak' o' wark;
    Aw've bin thirty odd ye'r i' this schoo';
An' what have aw managed to larn, does ta think?
    Well, aw've managed to larn aw'm a foo'!
Tha'll find 'at this scribblin's a very poor trade,
    An' tha'd ger along better bi thi' hawve,

259

Iv tha'd start as a quack, wi' a tapeworm or two,
    Or a few dacent pills an' some sawve.

Iv tha still feels determined to turn eawt as bard,
    Aw'd advise thi to let nob'dy know,
Or tha'll rue it to th' very last day 'at tha lives,
    Tha'll wish tha'd kept quiet — tha will so!
Iv Betty o' Bowsers at th' bottom o'th' lone
    Happens t' lose an' owd favourite cat,
Very loikely th' first body tha chances to meet
    Will ax thi to write abeawt that.

Iv a couple get wed, or a man licks his wife,
    Or some chap in a train steals a kiss,
Aw'll warrant th' first gossip tha meets'll say, 'Jim,
    Tha'll spin us a rhyme abeawt this.'
Tha'll be loikely to feel a bit flattered at first,
    An' think it a stunnin' good trade;
But let me impress just one fact on thi mind,
    It's this, Jim, tha'll never get paid!

Iv tha's ony opinions 'at doesn't just square
    Wi' thoose 'at are held bi thi friends,
They'll look on thi coolly, as iv tha'rn a thief,
    An' turn thi adrift till tha mends.
Iv tha knows heaw to flatter, an' wink at men's wrongs,
    Tha may manage t' get on very weel;   .
But, tackle the'r habits, expose the'r mean tricks,
    An' they'll shun thi as iv tha'rn the de'il!

Well, aw've towd thi mi moind, tha can do what tha loikes,
    Go on rhymin', or let it alone;
Iv th' latter, thi friends may provide thi a fish;
    Iv th' former, they'll give thi a stone.
An' what abeawt sellin' thi poetry, Jim?
    Neaw, tha'll foind that a job, aw can tell;
Iv tha'rt treated loike other poor Lancashire bards,
    Tha'll ha' to go sell 'em thisel'!

Heaw would t' loike goin' reawnd wi' a bag full o' books?
   Heaw would t' loike to go hawkin' thi brains?
Or, when tha's bin tryin' to do some kind act,
   To be towd thar't a foo' for thi pains.
Aw can tell thi this, Jim, it's aboon twenty year',
   Sin' aw wur set deawn as a foo';
An', tho' it's a charge 'at one doesn't loike t' own,
   Aw'm beginnin' to think 'at its true.

Thee stick to recitin', tha'rt clever at that;
   In fact, ther's few loike thee i'th' lond,
An' booath i'th' pathetic an' th' humorous vein
   Tha'rt reckon't a very good hond.
But aw'll drop it, owd friend, for aw'm gradely fagg'd eawt;
   Booath mi brain an' mi hond 'gin to tire;
Iv tha loikes tha can stick these few loines i' thi book;
   Or — iv tha prefers it — i'th' fire.

Joseph Ramsbottom
SORROWIN'

From *Country Words* (Manchester, 17 November 1866), 40.

Although a shadowy figure in the Manchester literary scene, Ramsbottom is widely represented in this anthology, one of the poems from *Phases of Distress* (1864) offering a radical enough perspective to appear in Chapter 1, and his essay on dialect appearing in Chapter 6. The following two poems are in another, less ambitious idiom, yet they show a clear grasp of the dialect mode.

Dunno speak, dunno laugh, Tommy, husht;
   Dunno tell thi tales neaw, stop thi play,
For thi good, doatin' Feyther's just gone,
   An' we'n bwoth lost eawr main prop to-day.
Come an' kiss me, mi lad, for the pain
   An' the sad pressin' weight o' this blow
Makes mi heart closer cling, Tom, to thee,
   'Cose aw'm fyert lest aw losse thee an' o'

In his pain he'r as patient as Job;
　　An' heaw yearnsful he lookt as he lee,
Wi' my hont grippen fast in his two,
　　An' besowt me t' tak great care o' thee.
Tom, he blest thee three times ere he dee'd,
　　An' thi name on his lips hung to th' last;
Heaw aw wish't for thi up at th' bedside,
　　When aw fun ut he'r sinkin' so fast.

What a Feyther he's bin, too, to thee,
　　An' heaw ill thea'll find th' want on him soon;
Heaw he clemm'd an he wove for thoose clogs
　　When thi toes wur'n o' eawt o' thi shoon.
Oft aw've known when we'rn rin to th' last crust,
　　An' it's thoose mak o' times ut thry men,
Ut he's shar'd it between us; an' so,
　　Afther tastin, to th' loom turnt agen.

He wur patient when th' mayl-poke wur low;
　　He wur preawd when 't wur full up to th' neck;
An' o' patience, a wayver's great need,
　　For one gets nowt bi two-an'-two check.
When we'n naygert an' teighlt uppo th' loom,
　　Fro dayleet i th' morn tin t' wur dark,
When aw'r harrisht an' powfagg'd to th' dyeath,
　　Oft to cheer me he'd sing like a lark.

He wur fond of his wife an' his whoam,
　　An' o' th' fondher becose they wur poor;
He'd ha' sheawted an' laugh'd ov a neet,
　　An' ha' marlockt wi' thee uppo th' floor.
If aw'd happent t' be petchin' i'th' nook,
　　An' if quiet no longer thea'd keep,
He'd ha' sung hush-a bee, hush-a-bo,
　　An' ha' rockt till he'd rockt thi asleep.

Then he sometimes 'ud hugg thi i'th' fields,
　　An' he'd get thi a nice hazel bough;
An' a posy bunch tee thi o' th' eend,
　　Made o' daisies an' primroses too.

An he'd bridneeses show thi an' o',
    An' he'd put th' little eggs i' thi brat;
Bo he'd noa let thi break 'em, aw know,
    He wur noane so hard-hearted as that.

Wark had wussent soon afther we'rn wed,
    An' grim Want has knockt oft at eawr dur;
Heaw we'n hop'd 'ut these hard times 'ud mend,
    Bo aw really do think they gwon wur.
Fro pottatoes, an' flesh, an' churn milk,
    To pottatoes, an' saut, an' nowt else,
Is a step not o'er pleasant to tak,
    An' we known what a sad tale it tells.

When thi Feyther sowd th' goods to get mayt,
    An' th' geraniums had t' goo, heaw he soikt;
An' to see him mi heart fill'd so full
    Aw wur like t' goo away while aw skroikt;
For as one afther one they went deawn,
    An' they'rn o' i' sich bonny bloom too,
He'r so back'art ut takkin' up th' brass,
    'Ut what else could a wakely wife do?

Bo it's hard when we'n foughten wi' want,
    As han foughten thi Feyther an' me,
Just at th' time when we feel we con win,
    Ut ther's one sthrucken deawn an' mun dee.
Little rest, heavy care, an' great need.
    Clung abeawt him fro th' heawr of his birth;
Aw should think ut he'll surely go t' heaven,
    For he's bin so ill plagu'd uppo th' earth.

COAXIN'

From *Country Words* (Manchester, 17 November 1866), 25.

Hi thi, Jenny, lyev thi loom,
    Ther's a bonny sky above;
Eawt o' th' days we wortch to live,
    We may tak a day to love.

Wilto stop thi bangin' lathe;
 Come away fro th' neighsy jar;
Let thi shuttle quiet lie,
 For thi bobbins winno mar.

Fling thi clogs an brat aside;
 Let thi treddles rest to-day;
Tee thi napkin o'er thi yead;
 Don thi shoon an' come away.
Everlastin' tugg un teighl,
 If eawr lives mun so be spent,
What's the good o' whistlin' brids?
 Why wur posies ever sent?

Deawn bi th' well, at th' hollow oak,
 Under th' hawthorn blossom sweet.
Wheer a linet sings above,
 An' a rindle runs at th' feet;
An' the red rimm'd daisies look
 Wi' their gowden een int' heaven,
An' eawr gronnies used to tell
 Ut the little fairies liven.

Theer we'll sit, an' talk o' th' time
 Ut we so mich wish ud come,
When we'st find it reet to wed;
 When we'st have a tidy whoam,
Wi' sich lots o' babby smocks,
 An sich rows o' clogs an' shoon,
An' sich breeches, skirts, an' frocks:
 Why — it conno come too soon.

If aw ha t' goo eawt t' mi wark,
 Thea'll noa miss me for a day,
When thea's hauve-a-dozen tongues
 Prattlin' reawnd while aw'm away;
An' a dozen pattherin' feet
 Racin' into th' loane ull come;
They'll be fain to meet their dad
 When they known he's comin' whoam.

O, the skips, the jumps, the romps,
    An' the little songs they'll sing;
Thea'll be th' graceful queen o' th' hearts,
    Lass, an' aw'st be th' jolly king.
So neaw come an' lyev thi loom,
    There's a bonny sky above;
Eawt o' th' days we wortch to live,
    We may tak' one day to love.

Some Other Local Bards

As the heading suggests, this section is a rather miscellaneous one, and perhaps shows the geographical limitations of this anthology as a whole. In trying to represent the metropolitan, the Scottish, the rural, the industrial, and the Lancashire traditions among working-class authors, I recognize that, for example, the North-East is pitifully covered, and the industrial Midlands hardly appear at all. The Scottish and Lancashire authors here reflect the bias of my reading and interpretation. The poems in this section do have defining characteristics however, notably a highly developed sense of localness and a familiar, homely and unpretentious relationship between reader and writer. Localness is here largely, though not entirely, the product of verbal characteristics, of which a dialect vocabulary and colloquial phrasing are the most obvious. The sense is of the poet as a slightly more articulate neighbour, articulating the commonplace experiences and social perspectives of industrial artisan life in a graceful and dignified way. The 'localness' of these poems then is largely defined in terms of shared experiences, whether industrial, geographical, moral, or, occasionally, sectarian. The 'local' society defined by the tone and address of homely rhymers can thus be either very broad indeed ('the dialect-speaking north of England' for example or 'all those engaged in the textile industry'), or very narrow ('those of us who have undergone very hard times recently in Lancashire' or even 'those of us round here who speak like this'). The implication is that shared experiences inevitably lead to shared values, an implication reinforced by the poet's own assumption of ordinariness.

Of the writers reprinted here, Janet Hamilton is described in more detail in Chapter 2, and Ince's own account of himself appears in Chapter 5. Ince, Baron, and Hull form a trio of Blackburn writers, and anyone seeking to study 'localness' in more detail might well begin with Hull's magnificent anthology of *The Poets and Poetry of*

Blackburn (Blackburn, J. and G. Toulmin, 1902), which provides not just a vast range of texts but also plentiful illustrations of the ways in which authors might be 'claimed' for their locality. 'Bill o' th' Hoylus End' represents the Yorkshire dialect bards, while Dawson is something of a rarity — a Lancashire rural labourer poet. Anderson has claims to be in Chapter 2, and provides further evidence of the difficulties of finding a shape and pattern in the vast output of poetry which this anthology seeks to describe.

Janet Hamilton
RHYMES FOR THE TIMES

From *Poems and Essays* (Glasgow, Thomas Murray, 1863), 29–31.

> I've juist been thinkin', neebour Johnie,
> Gif that the warl had mendit ony —
> Since, for the wurkin' man's disasters,
> We've got sae mony sa's an' plaisters.
> I've leukit laigh — I've leukit heigh —
> The gude time comin's unco driegh;
> There's routh o' teachers, schules, an' beuks,
> Chapels an' kirks in a' the neuks,
> Academies an' institutions,
> Wi' scientific contributions,
> On whilk ye may pit a' reliance,
> An' muckle tauk on social science,
> Mechanics, engineerin', minin',
> The gate o' cleanin' an' refinin'
> Oor hooses, streets, oor coorts an' closes,
> An' a' that hurts oor health an' noses;
> 'Bout chemistry, steam, gas, an' win',
> The vera lichtnin's luggit in,
> An' music, paintin', architecture,
> A' weel rede up in mony a lecture.
> We meet tae argue what we think,
> We meet tae cow that horrid drink,
> We meet tae read, recite, an' sing,

An' mony a queer conceitie thing.
Noo, wurkin' men yersel's respec',
Nor leeve in ignorance an' neglec';
Ye've means, but want the wull tae use them.
Ye whiles neglec', an' whiles abuse them;
Ye hae nae time for e'en'in' classes;
Ye've time tae drink, an' see the lasses —
Staun at hoose-en, or change-hoose door,
An' smoke, an' swear, an' raise a splore,
An' play at cards, or fecht wi' dougs,
An' whiles tae clout ilk ither's lugs;
O wad ye no be muckle better,
Tae read a beuk, or write a letter?
Had ye the wull, wi' beuk an' pen,
Ye'd fin' the way tae mak' ye men.
An' mithers, dae ye ken the poo'rs,
The strength for gude or ill, that's yours,
An' that the gabbin', todlin' things,
That's hingin' be yer apron strings,
Wull be a millstane roun' yer neck
Tae droon yer sauls, if ye neglec'
Tae win their hearts, an' train their min'.
In a' that's virtuous, gude, an' kin'?
Yer lassocks, that ye tak' sic pride in,
Hae muckle need o' carefu' guidin';
Mislippent sair they've been, I ween —
They gang ower muckle oot at e'en;
An' fallows are grown sae misleart,
The glaikit things micht weel be feart,
For aften dule an' burnin' shame
Comes poisonin' mony a puir man's hame,
An' gars ye greet, an' rage, an' flyte,
An' the puir faither maist gang gyte;
An' puir aul' Scotlan' hings her heid
An' bids ye leuk tae this wi' speed;
Her bonnie lassocks, bune a' ithers,
She bids you guard — O mithers! mithers!

William Baron
A WARKIN' MON'S REFLECTIONS

From *Bits o' Broad Lancashire* (Blackburn and Manchester,
John Heywood, 1888), 21–23.

Sometimes, when wearied eawt at neet,
   Aw sit me deawn i' th' owd arm cheear,
Bi t' fire 'at bruns so warm an' breet,
   An' think o' t' joy an' comfort theer.
An' strange reflections cross mi mind,
   When studyin' t' ways o' human life;
An' oft, aw try some rooad to find,
   To leeten t' toil an' strife.

Aw think o' fooak 'at fret an' pine,
   An 'uv ther envy mek a show;
Because they corn'd torn eawt as fine
   As somebry else they chance to know.
Wod foo's sich fooak mun be, for sure,
   To sigh for things they corn'd command!
A mon may be, tho' ragged an' poor,
   As good as t' best i' t' land.

A mon 'at's blessed wi' strength an' health,
   To toil an' earn his daily bread,
Should envy nobry o' ther wealth,
   Nor grieve for things 'at he corn'd ged.
Breet gowd con gain respect, aw know,
   While poverty grins deawn on t' poor,
Bur rank an' titles, after o,
   Are empty seawnds — no mooar.

Th' owd squire 'at lives i' th' ho' up yon,
   Surreawnded wi' 'id park an' greawnds;
Con co' o t' land for miles, his own,
   An' gooa eawt huntin' wi' his heawnds.
But when he roams throo' t' meadows green,
   Or throo' his woods, weel stocked wi game;
He con but feeast his een on t' scene,
   An' sooa con aw just t' same.

Because he's deawn i' t' world a bit,
  A mon's no reason to give way;
Be brave i' t' strife, dorn'd mope an' sit,
  For after t' darkness follows t' day.
Cheer up, an' banish care away,
  An' o'er yor troubles gaily sing;
Ther's mony a warkin' mon to-day,
  Far happier than a king.

We've o eawr ups an' deawns to face,
  Sooa buckle to an' mek yor mark;
An' fortune's sun'll shine i' t' place
  O' t' cleawds 'at mek life drear an' dark.
Heawever hard yor lot may be,
  Keep courage, tho' yo chance to fo';
For just look reawnd yo, an' yo'll see
  Ther's plenty woss than yo.

Sooa do yor duty while yo con,
  An' let this be yor daily creed —
To act to every fella mon,
  Wil' truth an' reet, i' word an' deed.
An' aw'll do t' same misel, an' o,
  Until aw tek mi final rest;
An' then when t' judgement comes 'aw know
  Aw'st stan' mi chance wi t' best.

Thomas Ince

THE PEOPLE

From *Beggar Manuscripts* (Blackburn, North East Lancs.
Printing and Publishing Co., 1888), 14–15.

What shall I say to the people?
  How shall I reach to their hearts?
  Had I the wisdom of sages —
  Had I the records of ages —
A clarion tongue from a steeple —
  I lack in enacting my parts.

What can I say to the many,
    That fortune may turn to their good?
        Happy, indeed, to befriend them,
        Gladly my all I would lend them,
For sadly, say I, there's not any
    But better might be if they would.

Why are they always dependent?
    Why ever sad and downcast?
        Why are they browbeat with money?
        Why should the bees have no honey?
For Unity's need each defendant
    Will bleed till salvation is past.

When will the toilers use reason?
    When will they show common-sense?
        Image of God, like the master,
        Travelling Heavenwards faster;
Now is the chance and the season
    To thwart the usurper's pretence.

Then, on to success and renown!
    And forward to freedom and right!
        United your sway shall begin,
        You only need will it and win;
So band yourselves well in each town,
    And organise meetings at night.

A WORKMAN'S HOME

From *Beggar Manuscripts*, 15.

Let lordlings sign, and ladies cling, to wealth, and fame, and place,
Let Handicraft and Science vie, to deck them out in grace;
Amidst a round of gaieties though daily they may roam,
They lack the blessedness within a honest labourer's home.

Besieged with state — betokened great — possessed of wealthy
    hoard —
Surrounded by the flunkeys who attend their bed and board;

271

Yet, though they shine and look so fine, and pleasant seems their lot,
There's a greater charm, and hearts as warm, within a humble cot.

Around the workman's hearth, at night, when daily toil is o'er,
The loved ones sit with spirits light — dull care without the door —
The children's glee is good to see, whilst the elders' happy mien
Excels the studied graces that with affluence are seen.

The schoolboy's task; the baby's care; the dangling father's knee;
The mother's work; the granny's chair (where granny loves to be);
The pleasant chat; the cheerful play; the free and homely joys;
The evening meal; the prayerful kneel of youngest girls and boys.

A later hour — with free power — of devotion fond and true;
Domestic schemes, and loving dreams what Father Time may do;
Perchance some news, awhile amuse in passing night away;
Then off to bed, with reverent head, to rest till coming day.

'Tis little, I know; but who can show a happier lot than this?
Or who could wish for better fare, when such imparts a bliss?
The rich may boast possessions, but contentment beats them all:
So ye who would enjoy the boon, respond to duty's call.

Bill o' th' Hoylus End
THE FACTORY GIRL

From *Poems* (Keighley, John Overend. Revised edition 1891),
34–35.

Shoo stud beside her looms an' watch'd
    The shuttle passin' through,
But yet her soul wur sumweer else,
    'Twor face ta face wi' Joe.
They saw her lips move as in speech,
    Yet none cud hear a word,
An' but fer t' grindin' o' the wheels,
    This language might be heard.

'I't' spite o' all thi treacherous art,
    At length aw breeathe again;
The pityin' stars hes tane mi part,
    An' eas'd a wretch's pain.
An' Oh! aw feel as fra a maze,
    Mi rescued soul is free,
Aw knaw aw do not dream an daze
    I' fancied liberty.

'Extinguish'd nah is ivvery spark,
    No love for thee remains,
Fer heart-felt love i' vain sall strive
    Ta live, when tha disdains.
No longer when thi name I hear,
    Mi conscious colour flies!
No longer when thi face aw see,
    Mi heart's emotions rise.

'Catcht'i' the bird-lime's treacherous twigs,
    Ta wheer he chonc'd ta stray,
The bird his fastened feathers leaves,
    Then gladly flies away.
His shatter'd wings he sooin renews,
    Of traps he is aware;
Fer by experience he is wise,
    An shuns each future snare.

'Awm speikin' nah, an' all mi aim
    Is but ta pleeas mi mind;
An' yet aw care not if mi words
    Wi' thee can credit find.
Ner dew I care if my decease
    Sud be approved bi thee;
Or whether tha wi' equal ease
    Does tawk ageean wi' me.

'But, yet, tha false deceivin' man,
    Tha's lost a heart sincere;
Aw naw net which wants comfort mooast,
    Or which hes t' mooast ta fear.

273

But awm suer a lass more fond an' true
    No lad could ivver find:
But a lad like thee is easily fun —
    False, faithless, and unkind.'

James Dawson
A LABOURER'S SONG

From *Facts and Fancies from the Farm: Lyrical Poems* (London,
John Camden Hotton, 1868), 28–30.

James Dawson is unusual among self-taught working-class writers
only in that he appears to have been an agricultural labourer in an area
(Ashton under Lyne) more usually associated with industrial workmen. His poems follow traditional lyric subjects — dedicatory poems
to Wordsworth, past-oral evocations, and love lyrics. 'A Labourer's
Song' contains a typical mixture of deference and assertion, celebrat-
ing endurance, family, and the possibility of democratic salvation as a
reward for a life of unpretending labour.

I'm a poor working man, and I own it;
    I seek to conceal it from none;
If I *once* had the whim, I've outgrown it,
    And even all trace of it's gone.

I can talk of my trade and my labour
    As proudly (though wanting the gloss)
As my titled omnipotent neighbour
    Dilates on his deeds and his cross.

Though I see many men who grow richer
    Each day and each hour that goes by,
I'm content with my pay as a ditcher,
    That serves my few wants to supply.

With my wife and my children around me, —
    At evening, drawn close to the fire, —
I feel as if Fortune had crowned me
    With all that a man need desire.

And I carol as blithely as any,
    As gay and light-hearted, I trow,
Though grim-looking shadows a many
    Have darkened our threshold ere now.

I consume not my soul with ambition,
    But labour contentedly on;
And though some claim a far higher mission,
    Mine's haply as useful a one.

Ay; and haply, too, when my worn spirit
    Is freed from its casing of clay,
I may vie with the great, and inherit
    As noble a birthright as they.

Alexander Anderson
From A SONG OF LABOUR

From *Songs of the Rail* (Third edition, London, Simpkin Marshall,
1881), 16–19.

Alexander Anderson, who sometimes wrote under the pen name of
'Surfaceman', was an engine driver who published several volumes of
quite ambitious verse, much of which was concerned with industrial
topics. Anderson shows a rather touching enthusiasm for machinery
and the idea of mechanical progress, and with some success he applies
the celebratory instinct more usually associated with pastoral to
industrial subjects. 'A Song of Labour' has characteristics which might
give it a claim on any chapter in this anthology: the celebration of
working community is offset against an ambitious hexameter couplet
form and considerable philosophical ambition, and yet the poem goes
out of its way to deny any great ambition, as the conclusion of this
section shows. Anderson's Preface makes it quite clear that his intended
readership comprises 'fellow-workers on the railway', and suggests that
he saw his purpose and exhortatory energy as more important than any
high degree of poetic accomplishment.

Heart! But this grand world rolls onward through the shadows of
the years
Swift as fell the reckless Phaeton headlong through the startled
spheres;
And along with it we wrestle, shaping bounds we slowly reach,
For this knowledge is a master whose first aim is to unteach.
So, he moves with time and patience, working with a careful heed,
Growing more and more in earnest when he moulds the perfect
deed,
Therefore guide him well, and listen to his slightest spoken word,
For a simple note will sometimes lead us to a fuller chord;
And the finish'd triumph with us shall a hundredfold repay
All the toil, and search, and pantings for the source of purer day.
'But,' says one, who still will murmur in the camp of brotherhood,
'Progress comes with tardy footsteps, and can do the grave no
good.'
There but spoke the cynic, Brothers, curbing down with strongest
steel,
All the width of human purpose, all that brain can do and feel;
Scorning ever outward action, but to wrap himself in toils
Spun to catch the things that wither, spun to catch the dust that soils.
Shame on such! they are not worthy of the common breath they
draw,
Since with it they make existence wither to a narrow law.
Wider range and freer action, nobler maxims for my breath;
I would wish my fellows success from the very jaws of death:
Death! a moment's cunning darkness flung across the trembling eyes
As we flash into the spirit cradled in a wild surprise.
Then what motions come upon us, golden laws of sudden calm,
Raining down eternal silence, raining down eternal balm.
Dare I fix my vision further, deeming that we mould this mind,
But to look in steady splendour on the toiling of our kind?
Heart! but this were something nobler than the poet ever felt
When the fought-for happy laurel clasp'd his forehead like a belt;
When the liquid fire of genius, rainbow colour'd, flash'd and glow'd
All its mighty beams above him with the splendour of a god,
Wider in its stretch and grandeur than the brain could ever dream
To look down upon our fellows from some planet's blinding gleam,
Watching with seraphic vision, grasping with delighted soul,
All the goals to which they hurry as the moments shake and roll,

Linking with an unseen quickness vigour to the tasks they do,
Touching each with fresher impulse as a nobler comes in view.
Then when triumph crowns their striving, start to hear the heaven
    sublime
Fill its azure arch with plaudits echoing from the throat of time;
And to hear the poets singing far above the rush of feet
Epithalamiums of madness when the links of success meet.
This is frenzy, and the overstretching of unhealthy strings,
Let us touch a chord that trembles to the breath of higher things.
Rash in him who sings unworthy, looking not within his heart
For the counsel that should guide him to the honours of his art.
'Sing you thus?' I hear you question, and I answer you again,
I but fit me to that measure chance flings blindly down on men,
Which requires nor heart nor passion, but the will that makes a voice —
Mighty poets sing by impulse, and the lesser but by choice.
'Yet you claim the meed of poet?' and I answer firm and strong,
Count me only as a poet, Brothers, while I sing this song.

Arm to arm, and let the metals into proper range be thrown,
Let us shape the iron pathway for the monster coming on.
What though we be feeble puppets with a little vigour crown'd,
Yet this task is ours, to fence his footsteps into proper bound;
Therefore guide him well, nor tamper with the thread that leads his
    powers,
Since the splendour of his mission flings a dignity on ours.

George Hull
THE TOILER'S WIFE

From *Heroes of the Heart* (Preston, J. & H. Platt, 1894), 57.

My wife looks bright — her heart is light,
    When Fortune's sun is shining;
And in her face I see the grace
    That loves not dull repining.
She gaily sings, and daily brings
    To me a world of gladness;
And drives away, with laughter gay,
    The ghosts of care and sadness.

And so I live, and so I love;
    And though the rich may shine,
Not one, I know, of them can show
    A wife so *blithe* as mine.

But in the hour when life's clouds lower
    Shines forth her virtue's beauty;
For trials serve her soul to nerve,
    And mark the way of duty.
With conscience clear, she conquers fear,
    And yields to no blind sorrow;
But oft will say, 'Though dark to-day,
    The sun will shine to-morrow'.

And so I live, and so I love;
    And though the rich may shine,
Not one, I know, of them can show
    A wife so *true* as mine!

Chapter Four

THE METROPOLITAN RESPONSE

F. Sandys, 'The Old Chartist'

The poetry written by self-taught writers was quickly defined as a movement, or even a phenomenon, by those Victorian social and cultural analysts who were most responsive to signs of class development. One essayist, W. J. Fox, was even prepared to date the origins of this movement very precisely, at the first emergence of Ebenezer Elliott into print, but Fox was not alone in seeing 'industrial' poetry as a sudden new symptom of major changes in the cultural aspirations of the lower orders. Fox, like most other early critics, linked the development of provincial poetry by self-taught writers very closely with the emergence of an identifiable and distinctive industrial urban culture, and his account of Elliott, like those of Carlyle, Gilfillan, and Kingsley, insists on reading self-taught writers through persistent metaphors of industry, labour, sweat, noise, and lurid furnace-smoky skies. The importance and influence of the discussion of self-taught writers is very great, not only because the metropolitan essayists and their work provided clear and influential accounts of what they believed to be the tasks of working-class writing, but also because they show middle-class attitudes and convictions in the process of formulation and dissemination. Interestingly, the metropolitan essayists believed, or said they believed, that they were entering into a 'discourse' with self-taught industrial writers over their work. For the artisan writers themselves the discussions of Carlyle and Kingsley must have seemed like remote and oracular commandments, carrying not just the weight of their authors' literary status and the full powers of their brilliant rhetoric, but also, even more intimidatingly, the dubious benefit of their sympathy and encouragement. Inevitably, given the nature of Victorian literary culture, the main site for this 'discourse' about the nature and status of working-class, industrial, and artisan poetry in a newly industrial society, was in the heavyweight magazines and journals, published in London and Edinburgh, and aimed at the cultured middle-class readership with an interest in social issues and social problems. Some subsidiary essays appeared as Prefaces to editions of poems by self-taught writers, or as other annotations to their work, but the

281

periodicals were the central forum for opinion. One further characteristic of the middle-class account of self-taught poetry needs to be
mentioned here: the metropolitan essayists were as much, if not
more, interested in the *lives* of humbly born poets as in their work,
for there was a crucial link in the middle-class mind between cultural
progress and social or political challenge. Writing poetry was
inevitably read as a symptom of wider, more disruptive aspirations,
which might be identified biographically as well as intellectually. It
is worth looking at the discussions of self-taught writers by the
metropolitan essayists and critics in more detail, for they illustrate
very precisely the ways in which class formation occurs through
cultural debate as well as through economic self-interest.

The key formulations of widespread middle-class attitudes to
self-taught writers were contained in two relatively brief articles in
major periodicals. Thomas Carlyle published 'Corn Law Rhymes'
in *The Edinburgh Review* in 1832, while Kingsley's 'Burns and his
School' appeared in the *North British Review* in 1848. Both were
extensively reprinted. Carlyle's four-volume *Critical and Miscellaneous
Essays* had reached a third edition by 1847, while Kingsley's *Miscellanies*
were constantly in print after their first publication in 1859. Both
books formed part of their authors' collected works and reached
cheap editions in the 1880s. In other words, the essays were in print
and widely known throughout the Victorian period, and in this
respect they make an interesting contrast to artisan writing on the
same themes, which was lucky to survive its original publication as a
Preface to an ephemeral volume or its appearance in a low circulation
local journal or newspaper. Both essays were ostensibly reviews,
but offered wide-ranging and complex responses to the development of a distinctively working-class culture. They are superb
examples of polemical style: Carlyle's dense, jokey, and self-conscious;
Kingsley's urgent, direct, and politically sophisticated. To these
two central essays must be added several others, less positive and
mandarin in their manner, but still influential in expressing widespread anxieties and ambiguities felt by the middle classes at the
appearance of voices from the industrial labouring classes. The
illustrious *Edinburgh* printed a long review of Southey's *Lives of the
Uneducated Poets* written by T. H. Lister in 1831. *The London Review*
published an extensive article by W. J. Fox called 'The Poetry of the
Poor'. As might be expected, the magazines aimed at artisan readers
were also interested in the subject, and *Tait's*, *Jerrold's Shilling*

Magazine, *Eliza Cook's Journal*, and *The Illuminated Magazine* under W. J. Linton included review articles, often with extensive quotation, of books by self-taught authors in the 1840s and 1850s. George Gilfillan's 'Ebenezer Elliott' appeared in his *Gallery of Literary Portraits* (1845), where it is sandwiched between essays on James Montgomery and Allan Cunningham. Another important essay, Mrs Craik's 'A Hedgeside Poet', appeared in the new *Macmillan's Magazine* in 1860. Many other examples could be listed, and some are printed in this chapter. By the 1860s, the phenomenon of self-taught or regional writing had become a stock subject for articles in the London periodicals. Between 1866 and 1881, for example, five metropolitan magazines (*St James's*, *Broadway*, *Temple Bar*, *Dublin University*, and *Fraser's*) published articles on Lancashire writing. Such a concentration of attention on self-taught and regional writing had long been a feature of provincial journalism, but the number and importance of such articles bears striking testimony to the metropolitan awareness of provincial working class culture.

In addition to journalistic interest, the extent of middle-class anxiety about self-taught writing can be seen in the prodigious energy expended on editing, introducing, and annotating the products of obscure self-taught poets. Such an activity seems at first merely an extension of the eighteenth century patronage system, but there are radical differences which are elaborated in the introduction to Chapter 5. The forms of patronage adopted by the sponsors of Victorian self-taught writers are essentially middle class and literary rather than aristocratic; active, even polemical, rather than passive; and have as their source a wide sense of social concern and anxiety which was very different from traditional, settled, feudal ties of obligation. The middle-class presence in self-taught writing is nowhere more apparent than in the mode of patronage which the middle class adopted — direct literary intervention on behalf of the poor poets by editing, introducing, and writing biographical memoirs of their lives and works. The vast majority of volume publications by self-taught writers have some material submitted by a middle class sponsor. In many cases the sponsor's work is lengthier than the poet's. Indeed, it is possible to argue that self-taught writing was generally mediated into public consciousness through its middle-class supporters. Some examples may clarify this process.

Southey's widely known and influential *Lives of the Uneducated Poets* began life in 1831 as an introduction to John Jones's *Attempts in*

Verse. Southey's essay occupies 180 pages of the first edition, Jones's poems 153 pages. As a separate publication, the *Lives* remained in print throughout the century long after Jones's poems had been forgotten. Southey also wrote a Memoir of the Nottinghamshire poet of humble birth, Henry Kirke White, as well as editing his *Remains* in 1807, acts which made Southey prominent in artisan consciousness as a friend to self-taught writers. He maintained this position in spite of the *Lives*, in which he had argued that self-taught writing was invariably bad, but did little general harm while actually bringing pleasure to the author. J. C. Prince, who had died in extreme poverty and neglect in 1867, had his *Life* and *Works* published thirteen years later in the most pretentious provincial manner, with a limited edition in large paper. The editor of this edition was a prominent Scottish doctor, James Lithgow, who exerted every effort in unearthing even Prince's most fugitive pieces. The inappropriateness of such a generous recognition of Prince's talents given the desperate circumstances of his life seems never to have been recognized locally — indeed many other neglected authors underwent similarly retrospective celebration. Furthermore, Lithgow left out all of Prince's important Prefaces, essays, and subscription lists from the *Collected Poems*, making the circumstances and anxieties of the original publications difficult to reconstruct. The wide margins, good print, fancy binding, and generally portentous air of the *Poems* eliminates entirely the sense of difficulty, and of deference, which characterized Prince's original shabby volumes. Lithgow's Prince is much tidier, less tortured than the feckless and misguided suffering individual who emerges from the available letters; Lithgow skilfully manages to disguise Prince's drinking. Many of the memorial volumes of Scottish authors published by Alexander Gardner in Paisley in the 1880s and 1890s exhibit a similar tendency to emphasize achievement rather than suffering, genius rather that personal weakness, and local benevolence rather than general neglect.

Such accounts of the highly annotated nature of the publication or re-publication of the work of self-taught writers could be widely extended, but I hope the main point is clear. Without an attendant middle-class discussion of its significance and merit, self-taught writing remained essentially peripheral to bourgeois culture. Artisan writing would have remained an entirely localized phenomenon dependent on local pride without those middle-class interventions which viewed it as an important cultural and social development, important enough to justify detailed discussion in the prominent publications just described. For various reasons, in pursuit of their own class interests, and motivated by a complex mixture of admiration, guilt, and fear, many well-intentioned members of the middle class did make possible the (usually posthumous) publication of self-taught writers in durable and fairly widely distributed formats. This publication was, however, strictly controlled and annotated by its literary sponsors, and gave rise to a whole series of essays, memoirs, and textual editing which still comprise the main source of information about Victorian self-taught writers. Such incorporation into bourgeois consciousness clearly altered the nature of the ways in which self-taught literary aspirations were perceived. Far from being appalled by the struggles and cultural deprivations apparent in the work of artisan writers, on the whole the middle class found it possible to celebrate the work and the achievements of even the most tragic careers of poor and neglected authors.

There were no separate book-length studies of Victorian self-taught writers, but there were many volumes which celebrated the cultural, political, and technological achievements of the humbly born and poorly educated. On the whole poets do not feature largely in such compendiums, and their authors looked in vain for poets to compare with the likes of George Stephenson and the other self-help heroes celebrated by Smiles and the authors of such books as *Household Names and How They Became So*. It is worth noting, however, that one book in this mode, Joseph Johnson's *Clever Boys and How They Became Famous Men* (Gall and Inglis, c. 1885) contains among its twenty lives three biographies of publishers, all of whom (the Chambers brothers, Abel Heywood, and William Howitt) had risen from humble origins and had developed central roles in the encouragement of artisan writing. But from the mass of Victorian exemplary self-help literature, aimed at increasing industry and fostering high levels of morale among the working population, three books offered major discussion of artisan writing. Edwin Paxton Hood's *The Peerage of Poverty* (1870, but built out of an earlier book published in 1851) is the most important. Hood's book is a huge anthology of brief biographies, loosely grouped by occupation, and interspersed with rousing homilies on the virtue of labour and its rewards, and of the achievements of 'learners and workers in fields, farms, and factories'. Most of Hood's subjects are poets, and he devotes considerable space to Clare, Elliott, Cooper,

John Taylor, Nicoll, Hogg, and Prince. Enough other poets are mentioned to make the book the nearest thing we have to a comprehensive survey of the lives and work of self-taught writers in Victorian Britain. G. L. Craik's *The Pursuit of Knowledge Under Difficulties* (1831) is a similar book to Hood's, but written nearly forty years earlier, and conceived on a more universal scale. Craik was forced to acknowledge the difficulty he had found at this early date in finding adequate poetic biographies to illustrate his Whig propagandist celebration of cultural and social advancement — thirty years later he would have been overladen with poetic examples. William Howitt's *Homes and Haunts of the English Poets* (1847), despite its apparently topographical and anecdotal purpose, is actually a serious introduction to the English poetic tradition for artisan readers, and is important here for its unclouded celebration of the self-taught poets. In their relatively unanxious celebration of the quality and social usefulness of artisan writing, these three books make an interesting contrast to the more troubled and ambiguous response of the metropolitan essayists.

Given this range of middle-class responses to artisan and self-taught writers, is it fair to say that such poetry was largely inhibited or even controlled by middle-class values and ideologies? In general terms, I think the answer is 'yes', although the degree to which this was a conscious process is open to considerable doubt. Yet there are several places where the apparently 'tacit' or 'hidden' ways in which such ideological control operated become obvious. Most obvious of these was the way in which editors actually changed texts, to reduce their level of political awareness, to refine the diction and to tidy up the syntax. Less overtly, pressure was often put on writers to alter texts themselves, and many poets did rewrite their works accordingly. Thirdly, middle-class sponsors often openly encouraged self-taught poets to avoid contentious issues. In a memorably defensive phrase, George Gilfillan advised Ebenezer Elliott to substitute 'Corn Fields' for 'Corn Laws' as a subject for his poems. More subtly, middle-class editors could select and omit poems from collected editions, and two poems in this anthology (J. C. Prince's 'The Death of the Factory Child' and Samuel Laycock's 'What Are We To Do?') despite their evident literary worth were never reprinted as part of their authors' collected works. It is tempting to link this absence to the political outspokenness of both poems, though there is no specific evidence of such a deliberate process of political control. The study of these kinds of evidence would add a great deal of support to a widely-held contention that bourgeois 'control' of working-class writing is most generally evident in the poems which were not written, in the absence of much overtly radical poetry. Although it is true that, with the exceptions of the kinds of poems described in Chapter 1, there are few genuinely radical or oppositional forms available to self-taught writers in the Victorian period, this lack can only partially be explained by pointing to the kinds of middle-class interventions just described. Class awareness within the working class urban groups was not advanced or coherent enough throughout the century to create any original or specifically working-class modes of expression, so that the failure to develop a radical working-class voice cannot be attributed solely to the hegemonic drive of the middle classes. In addition, as chapters 2 and 3 suggest, much literary endeavour within the working classes was aimed not at political opposition, but at respectable and deliberately imitative cultural advancement. All that can be said with certainty is that the presence of the liberal literary establishment in discussions of working-class writing from 1830 onwards does show the speed and intelligence of the bourgeois response to cultural change. In addition, such a presence substantially changed the self-taught writers' perceptions of themselves, and the forms and language in which they wrote. The literary critics and essayists quickly formulated a version of working-class poetry which was politically harmless and culturally ambitious. Yet without the presence of intelligent middle-class criticism and literary patronage, self-taught writing might never have existed at all.

It is possible to generalize a little on the common features of the middle-class response as exemplified in the following extracts and elsewhere. To tackle the subject at all was understood to be an overt act of goodwill towards the working people, an expression of sympathy and concern. Good intentions, even moral courage, were everywhere apparent in the middle-class response. For all the ostensible encouragement represented in these essays, such middle-class criticism was deeply, if subtly, suffused with doubts as to the literary worth or social desirability of self-taught poets. Indeed, middle-class criticism generally made an important connection between literary quality and social function. The social and political threat offered by proletarian or artisan poetic articulacy is constantly glossed over by focusing the discussion on the literary weaknesses apparent in the texts. In other words, the middle-class criticism of self-taught writers is largely an attempt to hold at bay the anxiety generally felt over the social and political challenge of such writing ('the voice of the mob') by diffusing that anxiety into a discussion of the language and formal qualities appropriate for working-class self-expression. Pleased as the liberal critics were at the evidence of the *cultural* advance of the artisans, they were also fearful that it was inextricably linked to *political* challenge. The point at which this anxiety consistently surfaces is in the discussion of the *language* of self-taught writers. Many critics were alarmed at the 'unpoetic' violence in the language of self-taught poets because it threatened poetry itself as a civilized and rational discourse. There was little critical recognition of the achievements in vernacular forms of such poems as Elliott's 'Black Hole of Calcutta' for example, nor of the syntactic originality of Clare's sonnets, nor of the lyrical assurance of Chartist hymns. Instead such original use of available forms and modes was generally regarded as deviance, a straying away from the rules and conventions governing literary discourse, through which sincerity and originality of thought and political conviction actually threatened or even overturned poetry. The urgent voice and ungainly power of self-taught poetry, admirable as evidence of cultural progress, could not be dissociated from mob politics in the liberal literary consciousness. When Carlyle said of self-taught poets 'to which voice, let good ear be given', he recognized both the literary quality *and* the threat represented in the poetry of the 'hitherto inarticulate'. Many intelligent essayists saw Ebenezer Elliott in terms of industrial imagery — for Carlyle he was 'a man who can handle both pen and hammer like a man', while Gilfillan characterized him as 'wielding hammer and pen with little difference in degree of animal exertion and mental fury'. These were of course inaccurate perceptions of Elliott, who was an employer of labour and an entrepreneur rather than a journeyman steelwright. But such images linked related qualities intuitively and collectively perceived by sympathetic metropolitan critics when they looked at the industrial poets: energy, industry, violence, honesty, sincerity, earnestness, threat. The critical resolution of this complex of literary and social perceptions was two-fold. Firstly, many critics aligned poets with the many other examples of cultural advancement within the proletarian and artisan classes, and concentrated on their exemplary biographies rather than on their literary difficulties and achievements. The second strand of discussion focused unremittingly on literary quality, poetic competence, craftsmanship, and 'refinement'. Not surprisingly, self-taught writers were found somewhat wanting in these areas, and their potential as a social and political force was thus diminished or belittled. The following extracts will, I hope, suggest the anxious formulation of the middle class literary awareness of self-taught writers, and point to the subtly inhibiting appeal to literary worth as a dominant criterion. 'Control' was widely perceived in technical rather than political issues.

Lord Byron
ENGLISH BARDS AND SCOTCH REVIEWERS (1809)

Byron's Olympian contempt for the aspiration of amateur and uneducated poets is neo-classical in its formulations and assumptions, brushing aside the rural rhymesters he lists as much by his own literary ease and nonchalance as by his argument. He makes no connection between the poetry of these rural bards and any wider cultural or political challenge beyond poetry — such connections are distinctively the product of the urban and industrial revolutions of the early nineteenth century. Byron can afford to ridicule the technical failures and pretentions of such part-time writers without any sense of anxiety.

> When some brisk youth, the tenant of a stall,
> Employs a pen less pointed than his awl,
> Leaves his snug shop, forsakes his store of shoes,
> St. Crispin quits, and cobbles for the Muse,
> Heavens! how the vulgar stare! how crowds applaud!
> How ladies read, the Literati laud!
> If, 'chance, some wicked wag should pass his jest,
> 'Tis sheer ill-nature — don't the world know best?
> Genius must guide when wits admire the rhyme,
> And CAPEL LOFFT declares 'tis quite sublime.
> Hear, then, ye happy sons of needless trade!
> Swains! quit the plough, resign the useless spade!
> Lo! BURNS and BLOOMFIELD, nay, a greater far,
> GIFFORD was born beneath an adverse star,
> Forsook the labours of a servile state,
> Stemmed the rude storm, and triumphed over Fate:
> Then why no more? If Phoebus smiled on you
> BLOOMFIELD! why not on brother Nathan too?
> Him too the Mania, not the Muse, has seized;
> Not inspiration, but a mind diseased:
> And now no Boor can seek his last abode,
> No common be inclosed without an ode.
> Oh! since increased refinement deigns to smile
> On Britain's sons, and bless our genial Isle,
> Let Poesy go forth, pervade the whole,
> Alike the rustic, and mechanic soul!

Ye tuneful cobblers! still your snores prolong,
Compose at once a slipper and a song;
So shall the fair your handywork peruse,
Your sonnets sure shall please — perhaps your shoes.
May Moorland weavers boast Pindaric skill
And tailors' lays be longer than their bill!
While punctual beaux reward the grateful notes,
And pay for poems — when they pay for coats.

Thomas Carlyle
BURNS

First published in *The Edinburgh Review* 1828 and then reprinted in successive editions of Carlyle's *Critical and Miscellaneous Essays* (vol. 1).

In order to provide comprehensive evidence of the influences on self-taught writers, this anthology would have to contain extensive selections from Romantic accounts of the poet as a major moral force in society, and as an 'unacknowledged legislator' of human conduct and moral aspiration. Such abstract accounts of the poet's elevated functions were well-known to, and admired by, self-taught writers, and they were passed on secondhand through the essays of such cultural polemicists as Carlyle and Kingsley, who shared a basically Romantic perception of the poet's role. Carlyle's essay on Burns, regarded as an heroic example of a self-taught writer, offered a defence of passion and indignation in poetry, a defence which was particularly appropriate to the views of poetry held by artisan and proletarian writers.

But has it not been said . . . that 'Indignation makes verses?' It has been so said, and is true enough: but the contradiction is apparent, not real. The Indignation which makes verses is, properly speaking, an inverted Love; the love of some right, some worth, some goodness, belonging to ourselves or others, which has been injured, and which this tempestuous feeling issues forth to defend and avenge. No selfish fury of heart, existing there as a primary feeling, and without its opposite, ever produced much Poetry: otherwise, we suppose, the Tiger were the most musical of our choristers. Johnson said, he loved a good hater; by which he must have meant, not so much one that hated violently, as one that hated wisely; hated baseness from love of nobleness. However, in spite of Johnson's paradox, tolerable enough for once in speech, but which need not have been so often adopted in print since then, we rather believe that good men deal sparingly in hatred, either wise or unwise: nay, that a 'good' hater is still a desideratum in this world.

For it is not in the favour of the great or of the small, but in a life of truth, and in the inexpugnable citadel of his own soul, that a Byron's or a Burns's strength must lie. Let the great stand aloof from him, or know how to reverence him. Beautiful is the union of wealth with favour and furtherance for literature; like the costliest flower-jar enclosing the lowliest amaranth. Yet let not the relation be mistaken. A true poet is not one whom they can hire by money or flattery to be a minister of their pleasures, their writer of occasional verses, their purveyor of table-wit; he cannot be their menial, he cannot even be their partisan. At the peril of both parties, let no such union be attempted. Will a Courser of the Sun work softly in the harness of a Dray-horse? His hoofs are of fire, and his paths are through the heavens, bringing light to all lands; will he lumber on mud highways, dragging ale for earthly appetites from door to door?

Robert Southey
LIVES AND WORKS OF OUR UNEDUCATED POETS

First published as a prefatory essay to John Jones, *Attempts In Verse* (London, John Murray, 1831) and then separately reprinted on several occasions.

Southey's introductory essay swamped John Jones's book with its extended good intentions, indeed the spine of the first edition carries Southey's name above Jones's. Southey seized the occasion offered by Jones's request for patronage by offering a defence of mediocre or poor poetry on the grounds that its production contributed greatly to the happiness of its authors, a view not borne out by the subsequent history of the humbly born poets. Southey had other motives in mind as well. He attacks vituperative criticism of all kinds while displaying his own critical leniency towards Jones's work. He celebrates the achievements of eighteenth century rural bards. Finally, he clears himself of further responsibility towards all those aspiring writers who were clamouring for his patronage. Southey's essay, then, is easy-going and generous, with lengthy accounts of the lives of John Taylor, Stephen Duck, John Woodhouse, Ann Yearsley, J. F. Bryant, and Jones himself — a good cross section of pre-industrial self-taught authors. Southey's central themes — the warmth and happiness created by primitive rhyming, and the belief that 'uneducated' poets would anyway be a class outmoded by the rapid 'march of intellect' — were generously optimistic, but both widely mistaken.

Upon perusing the poems I wished they had been either better or worse. Had I consulted my own convenience, or been fearful of exposing myself to misrepresentation and censure, I should have told my humble applicant that although his verses contained abundant proof of a talent for poetry, which, if it had been cultivated, might have produced good fruit, they would not be deemed worthy of publication in these times. But on the other hand, there was in them such indications of a kind and happy disposition, so much observation of natural objects, such a relish of the innocent pleasures offered by nature to the eye, and ear, and heart, which are not closed against them, and so pleasing an example of the moral benefit derived from those pleasures, when they are received by a thankful and thoughtful mind, that I persuaded myself that there were many persons who would partake, in perusing them, the same kind of gratification which I had felt. There were many, I thought, who would be pleased at seeing how much intellectual enjoyment had been attained in humble life, and in very unfavourable circumstances; and that this exercise of the mind, instead of rendering the individual discontented with his station, had conduced greatly to his happiness, and if it had not made him a good man, had contributed to keep him so. This pleasure should in itself, methought, be sufficient to content those subscribers who might kindly patronize a little volume of his verses. Moreover, I considered that as the Age of Reason had commenced, and we were advancing with quick step in the March of Intellect, Mr Jones would in all likelihood be the last versifyer of his class; something might properly be said of his predecessors, the poets in low life, who with more or less good fortune had obtained notice in their day; and here would be matter for an introductory essay, not uninteresting in itself, and contributing something towards our literary history. And if I could thus render some little service to a man of more than ordinary worth, (for such upon the best testimony Mr Jones appeared to be), it would be something not to be repented of, even though I should fail in the hope (which failure, however, I did not apprehend) of affording some gratification to 'gentle readers': for readers there still are, who, having escaped the epidemic disease of criticism, are willing to be pleased, and grateful to those from whose writings they derive amusement or instruction.

. . . A newspaper paragraph, which has been inserted in one of the volumes before me, quotes from Sheridan the elder, an ill-natured passage in allusion to the writers who have here been noticed. 'Wonder,' he says, 'usually accompanied by a bad taste, looks only for what is uncommon; and if a work comes out under the name of a thresher, a bricklayer, a milkwoman, or — a lord, it is sure to be eagerly sought after by the million.'

'Persons of quality' require no defence when they appear as authors in these days: and, indeed, as mean a spirit may be shown in traducing a book because it is written by a lord, as in extolling it beyond its deserts for the same reason. But when we are told that the thresher, the milkwoman, and the tobacco-pipe-maker did not deserve the patronage they found, — when it is laid down as a maxim of philosophical criticism that poetry ought never to be encouraged unless it is excellent in its kind, — that it is an art in which inferior execution is not to be tolerated, — a luxury, and must therefore be rejected unless it is of the very best, — such reasoning may be addressed with success to cockeared and sickly intellects, but it will never impose upon a healthy understanding, a generous spirit, or a good heart.

Bad poetry — (if it be harmless in its intent and tendency) — can do no harm, unless it passes for good, becomes fashionable, and so tends to deprave still further a vitiated public taste, and still further to debase a corrupted language. Bad criticism is a much worse thing, because a much more injurious one, both to the self-satisfied writer and the assentient reader; not to mention that without the assistance of bad criticism, bad poetry would but seldom make its way.

The mediocres have long been a numerous and increasing race, and they must necessarily multiply with the progress of civilization. But it would be difficult to say wherefore it should be treated as an offence against the public, to publish verses which no one is obliged either to purchase or to read. Booksellers are not likely to speculate at their own cost in such wares; there is a direct gain to other branches of the trade; employment is given where it is wanted; and if pecuniary loss be a matter of indifference to the author, there is then no injury to himself, and he could not have indulged himself in a more innocent folly, if folly it should deserve to be called. But if he is a good and amiable man, he will be both the better and the happier for writing verses. 'Poetry,' says Landor, 'opens many sources of tenderness, that lie forever in the rock without it.'

. . . It will be seen, from Mr Jones's account of himself, that his opportunities of self-instruction have been even less than were possessed by any of the uneducated aspirants who preceded him. Had it been his fortune to have enjoyed those advantages, of which the great majority of educated persons make no use whatever after they become their own masters, he might in all probability have held more than a respectable place among the poets of his age; and the whole tenor of his conduct shows that he would have done his duty in any station of life to which he might have been called. But except during the time when he had access to Shakespeare's plays, he seems to have read little other poetry than what is occasionally to be found in provincial newspapers. From them he has sometimes copied a pattern, or a tune, — nothing more: he has expressed his own observations, his own fancies, his own feelings, and they are such, though often rudely, unskilfully, and sometimes obscurely expressed, as to show that he has been gifted with the eye, and the ear, and the feeling of a poet: the art is wanting, and it is now too late for him to acquire it.

No other alterations have been made in his pieces than by occasional omissions, sometimes altering a word in such cases for the sake of connection, — and by correcting a very few grammatical errors.

G. L. Craik
THE PURSUIT OF KNOWLEDGE
UNDER DIFFICULTIES

First published in two volumes in 1829 and 1831 under the auspices of the Society for the Diffusion of Useful Knowledge by Charles Knight in his 'Library of Entertaining Knowledge'. Extensively reprinted in single volume format, and often used as a prize or gift book later in the century.

G. L. Craik's *The Pursuit of Knowledge Under Difficulties* is an enormous compilation of examples of self-educated success stories from all ages and cultures. In its relentless accumulation of biographical anecdote, the book is similar in method and effect to Edwin Paxton Hood's *The Peerage of Poverty*. The main readers Craik had in mind were children and artisans, and his aim was to boost their morale and exhort them to greater effort by confronting them with a seemingly inexhaustible list of success gained through will-power and hard work. Such an attempt to belittle the problems of self-education in poverty is not all that common in later accounts. If Craik had been writing twenty years later, poets would have had a more prominent place in his compilation, but in the 1830s, as the following passage suggests, he had few examples to hand: John Taylor, Burns, Kirke White, Bloomfield, and Duck. Craik does make the crucial point, however, that in writing poetry a background of poverty, self-education, and hardship was no asset. Craik later became Professor of English at Belfast and was married to the novelist Diana Mulock, who also wrote on the subject of self-taught poets.

Although he was an extraordinary instance of what the force of native talent will sometimes accomplish, where education has been nearly altogether witheld, yet Bloomfield gave plentiful evidence, especially in his first production, of the disadvantages under which he laboured from the want of early cultivation. A better education in his youth would have saved his homely genius from being misled into affectations uncongenial to its true spirit; and his want of a competent director in his studies exposed his taste to be corrupted by bad examples. It is probably, indeed, a mistake to suppose that the circumstance of an individual having been what is called self-taught, is generally favourable to the originality of his literary productions. There is more reason for suspecting that even those self-taught writers who have displayed most of this highest element of power, would have exhibited it in still greater abundance if they had enjoyed, in addition to their rare gifts of nature, the advantages of a regular education. It is certain, at any rate, that the literary performances of men who have been their own teachers have not, except in a few extraordinary cases, been in any degree peculiarly distinguished by this quality. Of the numerous tribe of self-taught verse-makers especially, the great majority have been the merest imitators. A fair specimen of this race — the individuals of which, although they sometimes excite a temporary attention, generally drop very speedily into oblivion — we have in a writer named Stephen Duck. . . .

Thomas Carlyle
CORN-LAW RHYMES

First published in *The Edinburgh Review* (1832) and then many reprints
in Carlyle's *Critical and Miscellaneous Essays*.

Complex in style, epigrammatic and allusive, Carlyle's review essay
centred on Ebenezer Elliott represents a sophisticated account of
working-class writing. Carlyle takes evident pleasure in teasing the
bourgeoisie with Elliott's savagery and radical reputation, but his
praise for the writer's 'honesty' and clarity of vision is genuine, and
Carlyle's grasp of the way in which self-taught writers might have
something important and different to say is generous. Yet under the
brilliant perception of the potential of self-taught writers, Carlyle
does seem to offer a reductive, even dismissive, view of Elliott. At
times he seems almost the plaything of his own rhetorical skill,
setting fear against praise, gleeful accounts of Elliott's unsettling
radical energy against his 'almost menacing' indiscriminate verbal
clumsiness. This double perception of disconcerting honesty and
unpolished naïve indignation is a paradox which Carlyle seems
unable, or unwilling, to resolve. Certainly, such a double perspective
gives Carlyle's essay an energy and an ambiguity which makes it the
most significant single account of the phenomenon of self-taught
working class authors.

It used to be said that lions do not paint, that poor men do not write;
but the case is altering now. Here is a voice coming from the deep
Cyclopean forges, where Labour, in real soot and sweat, beats with
his thousand hammers 'the red sun of the furnace'; doing personal
battle with Necessity, and her dark brute Powers, to make them
reasonable and serviceable; an intelligible voice from the hitherto
Mute and Irrational, to tell us at first hand how it is with him, what
in very deed is the theorem of the world and of himself, which he, in
those dim depths of his, in that wearied head of his, has put together.
To which voice, in several respects significant enough, let good ear
be given.

Here too be it premised, that nowise under the category of
'Uneducated Poets', or in any fashion of dilettante patronage, can
our Sheffield friend be produced. His position is unsuitable for that:
so is ours. Genius, which the French lady declared to be of no sex, is
much more certainly of no rank. . . . In fact, it now begins to be
suspected here and there, that this same aristocratic recognition

which looks down with an obliging smile from its throne, of bound Volumes and gold Ingots, and admits that it is wonderfully well for one of the uneducated classes, may be getting out of place. There are unhappy times in the world's history, when he that is the least educated will chiefly have to say that he is the least perverted; and with the multitude of eye-glasses, convex, concave, green, even yellow, has not lost the natural use of his eyes. For a generation that reads Cobbett's Prose, and Burns's Poetry, it need be no miracle that here also is a man who can handle both pen and hammer like a man.

. . . However, we are not here to write an Essay on Education, or sing *misereres* over a 'world in its dotage'; but simply to say that our Corn-Law Rhymer, educated or uneducated as Nature and Art have made him, asks not the smallest patronage or compassion for his rhymes, expresses not the smallest contrition for them. Nowise in such attitude does he present himself; not supplicatory, deprecatory, but sturdy, defiant, almost menacing. Wherefore, indeed, should he supplicate or deprecate? It is out of the abundance of the heart that he has spoken: praise or blame cannot make it any truer or falser than it already is. By the grace of God this man is sufficient for himself; by his skill in metallurgy can beat out a toilsome but a manful living, go how it may; has arrived too at that singular audacity of believing what he knows, and acting on it, without leave asked of any one; there shall he stand, and work, with head and hand, for himself and the world; blown about by no wind of doctrine; frightened at no Reviewer's shadow; having, in his time, looked substances enough in the face, and remained unfrightened.

. . . He has turned, as all thinkers up to a very high and rare order in these days must do, into Politics; is a Reformer, at least a stern Complainer, Radical to the core: his poetical melody takes an elegiaco-tragical character; much of him is converted into hostility, and grim, hardly-suppressed indignation, such as right long denied, hope long deferred, may awaken in the kindliest heart. Nor yet as a rebel against anything does he stand; but as a free man, and the spokesman of free men, not far from rebelling against much; with sorrowful appealing dew, yet also with incipient lightning in his eyes; whom it were not desirable to provoke into rebellion. He says in Vulcanic dialect, his feelings have been *hammered* till they are *cold-short*; so they will no longer bend; 'they snap, and fly off', — in the face of the hammer. Not unnatural, though lamentable! Nevertheless, under all disguises of the Radical, the Poet is still recognizable: a certain music breathes through all dissonances, as the prophecy and ground-tone of returning harmony; the man, as we said, is of a poetical nature.

. . . With much merit far from the common in his time, he is not without some of the faults of his time. We praised him for originality; yet there is a certain remainder of imitation in him; a tang of Circulating Libraries; as in Sancho's wine, with its key and thong, there was a tang of iron and leather. To be reminded of Crabbe, with his truthful severity of style, in such a place, we cannot object; but what if there were a slight bravura dash of the fair tuneful Hemans? Still more, what have we to do with Byron, and his fierce vociferous mouthings, whether 'passionate', or not passionate and only theatrical.

. . . We mean no imitation in a bad palpable sense; only that there is a tone of such occasionally audible, which ought to be removed; — of which in any case, we make not much. Imitation is a leaning on something foreign; incompleteness of individual development, defect of free utterance. . . .

. . . As for our stout Corn-Law Rhymer, what can we say by way of valediction but this 'Well done; come again, doing better'? Advices enough there were; but all lie included under one; to keep his eyes open, and do honestly whatsoever his hand shall find to do. We have praised him for sincerity: let him become more and more sincere; casting out all remnants of Hearsay, Imitation, ephemeral Speculation: resolutely *'clearing* his mind of Cant'. We advised a wider course of reading: would he forgive us if we now suggested the question, whether Rhyme is the only dialect he can write in; Whether Rhyme is, after all, the natural and fittest dialect for him? . . . Rhyme has plain advantages; which, however, are often purchased too dear. If the inward thought *can* speak itself, instead of sing itself, let it, especially in these quite unmusical days, do the former! In any case, if the inward Thought do not sing itself, that singing of the outward Phrase is a tender-toned false matter we could well dispense with. Will our Rhymer consider himself, then; and decide for what is actually best? Rhyme, up to this hour, never seems altogether obedient to him; and disobedient Rhyme, — who would ride on *it* that had once learned walking.

George Gilfillan
EBENEZER ELLIOTT

From *A Gallery of Literary Portraits* (First series, Edinburgh, 1845).
Reprinted in the 1856 complete edition of the *Gallery*, volume 1.

Gifillan's essay on Elliott is an extraordinary exercise in feverish
rhetoric, in which the author's exaggerated jocularity gave way to
peevish hostility and bluster when actually confronted with the *Corn
Law Rhymes*. This modulation from ostensible approval to covert
hostility, characteristic of many accounts of self-taught writers, reaches
an almost ludicrous level of ambiguity, which is resolved in an
unconvincing rhetorical flourish in which Gilfillan recommends the
substitution of 'corn fields' for 'Corn Laws' as appropriate for an
aspiring self-taught poet. Gilfillan, less skilfully than Carlyle,
unintentionally reveals terror as well as disdain for an author he is
trying to praise.

. . . And yet the forge had wrought and raged for ages, and amid all
its fiery products reared no poets until it was said, 'Let Ebenezer
Elliott be.' And though he stood forward somewhat ostentatiously
as the self-chosen deputy to Parnassus of the entire manufacturing
class, it is easy to find in the large rough grasp of his intellect, in the
daring of his imagination, in the untameable fire of his uneven yet
nervous line, in his impatient and contemptuous use of language,
traces of the special trade over which he long presided; of the
impression which a constant circle of fire made on his imagination;
and of the savage power which taught him at one time to wield the
hammer and the pen with little difference in degree of animal
exertion and mental fury. We can never divest our minds as we read
him of a grim son of the furnace, black as Erebus, riving, tearing,
and smiting at his reluctant words; storming now and then at the
disobedient ends of sentences; clutching his broad-nibbed quill, and
closing the other and the other paragraph with the flourish of one
who brings down upon the anvil a last sure and successful blow. . . .

So stands, leans, labours, growls and curses at times, not loud but
deep, with foot firmly planted, and down-bent flaming eye, this
'titan of the age of tools.' You see, too, that he has the true vision of
the poet — that mysterious eyesight which sees the spiritual as well
as the material shadow which falls from off all things, and which to
the bard alone is naked and bare. Be this penetrating and incom-

300

municable glance a blessing or a curse; and, as in the case of the second-sight, it is one or the other, according to the objects presented — being, if a genial temperament show the unseen border of beauty which edges and flowers all things, one of the greatest of blessings; but if accident, or position, or a black bilious medium, discover the halo of misery which invisible surrounds every object in this strange world, one of the greatest of curses: be it the one or the other, it has, and for ever, unsealed his eye. You regret to perceive, on more narrow inspection, that he has fixed his piercing eye too much on the dark side of things — that his view is angular, not comprehensive — that passion has given his eye now a portentous squint, now a ferocious glare — that he has seen through 'shams' not in the sense of seeing what even they contain of good and true, but seen through them as through empty spaces into the black, hollow, and hideous night. . . .

. . . And yet, when it chooses him to 'look abroad into universality,' and instead of inveighing against a corn-law to walk forth into the corn-fields; to pierce the shady solitude of the lane; to converse with 'cloud, gorse, and whirlwind on the gorgeous moor;' to spend his solitary Sabbath upon the mountain; to bare his heated brow in the fresh breeze, as an act — as an altar of worship to the poor man's God; — what a delightful companion does the stern iron-worker become!

Friedrich Engels
THE CONDITION OF THE WORKING CLASS IN ENGLAND (1845)

Engels's brief analysis of the reading habits of the working classes in Manchester is significant chiefly for its recognition of the distinctive way in which the literary products of the bourgeoisie were read — and understood — among self-taught writers. A second short comment underlines Engels's recognition of the central role of Shelley in the formation of working-class poetic and political consciousness.

And in how great a measure the English proletariat has succeeded in attaining independent education is shown especially by the fact that the epoch-making products of modern philosophical, political, and poetical literature are read by working-men almost exclusively.

The bourgeois, enslaved by social conditions and the prejudices involved in them, trembles, blesses, and crosses himself before everything which really paves the way for progress; the proletarian has open eyes for it, and studies it with pleasure and success. In this respect the Socialists, especially, have done wonders for the education of the proletariat. They have translated the French materialists, Helvetius, Holbach, Diderot, etc., and disseminated them, with the best English works, in cheap editions. Strauss' *Life of Jesus* and Proudhon's *Property* also circulate among the working-men only. Shelley, the genius, the prophet, Shelley, and Byron, with his glowing sensuality and his bitter satire upon our existing society, find most of their readers in the proletariat; the bourgeoisie owns only castrated editions, family editions, cut down in accordance with the hypocritical morality of today. The two great practical philosophers of latest date, Bentham and Godwin, are, especially the latter, almost exclusively the property of the proletariat; for though Bentham has a school within the Radical bourgeoisie, it is only the proletariat and the Socialists who have succeeded in developing his teachings a step forward. The proletariat has formed upon this basis a literature, which consists chiefly of journals and pamphlets, and is far in advance of the whole bourgeois literature in intrinsic worth.

It was next said that he [Shelley] never could become popular, and therefore the mischief he could do was limited. He *is* become popular, and the good that he is likely to do will be unlimited. The people read him; though we may wonder at it, they comprehend him — at least so far as the principles of freedom and progress are concerned; and in these he will not lead them astray. He is the herald of advance, and every year must fix him more widely and firmly in men's hearts.

William Howitt
HOMES AND HAUNTS OF THE BRITISH POETS

1847. This quotation from the fifth edition (London, Routledge, Warne & Routledge, 1863), 229–230.

Howitt is an important figure in the development of a London-based literature aimed at artisan readers, and poems from his *Journal* appear in chapters 1 and 3. Despite its title, *Homes and Haunts* is more critical and biographical than topographical. Howitt's main intention was to celebrate the richness of the British poetic tradition and the British countryside, but the emphasis of his selection is on the self-taught poets, and the contribution that poets from poor and unlettered backgrounds have made to the literary tradition. This extract from the chapter on Burns offers the least equivocal celebration of artisan writing to be found in Victorian criticism. Submerging political considerations under poetic ones, Howitt successfully avoids the anxiety which characterized most literary support for self-taught writers. The chapters on Elliott and Shelley also have interesting things to say on writers from working class backgrounds. Howitt's often re-issued book offered both artisan and middle-class readers an attractive and unclouded celebration of the virtues of the British poetic tradition.

We come now to the man who is the great representative of a class which is the peculiar glory of Great Britain; that is, to Robert Burns. It is a brilliant feature of English literature, that the people, the mass, the multitude, — call them what you will, — have contributed to it their share, and that share a glorious one. We may look in vain into the literature of every other nation for the like fact. It is true that there may be found in all countries men who, born in the lowest walks of life — orphans, outcasts, slaves even — men labouring under not only all the weight of social prejudices, but also under the curse of personal deformity, have, through some fortunate circumstance, generally the favour of some generous and superior person, risen out of their original position, and through the advantages of academical or artistic education have taken their place amongst the learned and illustrious of their race. We need not turn back to the Aesops and Terences of antiquity for such characters; they are easy to select from the annals of the middle ages, and modern art and learning; but there is a class, and this class is found in Great Britain alone, which, belonging to the body of the people, has caught, as it were passingly, just the quantum of education which had come within the people's reach, and who, on this slender participation of the general intellectual property, have raised for themselves renown, great, glorious, and enduring as that of the most learned or most socially exalted of mankind. These extraordinary individuals, who are found in the literature of all civilized nations, — these men who, admitted from the ranks of the people to the college or the studio, have distinguished themselves in almost every walk of science or letters, — these have vindicated the general intellect of the human race from every possible charge of inequality in its endowments. . . .

In other countries few think; it is a few who are regularly educated, and arrogate the right to think, to write, and govern. If the poor man become an acknowledged genius, it is only through the passage of the high school. The mass is an inert mass; it is a labouring, or at best a singing and dancing multitude. But in Great Britain, there is not a man who does not feel that he is a member of the great thinking, acting, and governing whole. Without books he has often caught the spark of inspiration from his neighbour. In the field, the workshop, the alehouse, the chartist gathering, he has come to the discussion of his rights, and in that discussion all the powers of his spirit have felt the influence of the sea of mind around, that has boiled and heaved from its lowest depths in billows of fire. Under the operation of this oral, and, as it were, forensic education, which has been going on for generations in the British empire, the whole man with all his powers has become wide awake; and it required only the simple powers of writing and reading to enable the peasant or artisan to gather all the knowledge that he needed, and to stand forth a poet, an orator, a scientific inventor, a teacher himself of the nation.

To these circumstances we owe our Burns, Hogg, Bloomfield, Clare, Elliott, Allan Cunningham, Bamford, Nicoll, Thom, Massey; our Thomas Miller, and Thomas Cooper. . . .

It is with pride, and more than pride, that I call the attention of my countrymen to this great and unique section of their country's glorious literature. I look to the future, and see in these men but the forerunners of a numerous race springing from the same soil. They are evidences of the awakened mind of the common people of England. They are pledges that out of that awakened mind there will, as general education advances, spring whole hosts of writers, thinkers, and actors, who shall not merely represent the working classes of our society, but shall point out the people as the grand future source of the enrichment of our literature. They are luminous proofs, and the forerunners of multitudinous proofs of the same kind, that genius is not entirely dependent on art; but can, having once the simple machinery of reading and writing, seize on sufficient art to enable it to exhibit all the nobler forms of intellectual life, and to speak from heart to heart the living language of those passions and emotions, which are the laments of all human exertion after the good and the great, which console in distress, harden to necessary endurance, or fire to the generous rage of conquest over difficulties, and over the enemies of their just rights. These men are the starry lights that glitter on the verge of that dawn in which mankind shall emerge to its true position, — the many being the enlightened spirits, and 'the few the weak exceptions, shrinking like shadows from the noonday of human progress.

Charles Kingsley
BURNS AND HIS SCHOOL

From *The North British Review* 1848. Reprinted in Kingsley's *Miscellanies* (2 vols. 1859 and many subsequent editions).

Kingsley had always shown himself to be alert to the cultural activities of the artisan and proletarian classes, and he became a sympathetic and widely respected commentator on working-class life. His essay on 'Burns and his School' was an early attempt to show the general tendencies apparent in artisan writing by examining poets whom Kingsley saw as Burns's heirs in influencing the moral life of working people. The review article covered works by Elliott, the two Bethunes, William Thom, Thomas Cooper, and Alexander Whitelaw. Regarding these disparate writers as a 'school' gave great emphasis to the self-conscious formulation of a general set of attributes which might be ascribed to self-taught writers, and Kingsley deliberately set out to list what he thought to be the proper characteristics of progressive, but not too challenging, working-class writing. The entire essay is an important one, noticeably accurate, intelligent, and wide ranging in its sympathies. The passages below show Kingsley both praising and criticizing the developments discernible in self-taught writers, but also keeping an eye on the great importance which he ascribed to poetry as a social and moral force among the labouring classes.

The critic, looking calmly on, may indeed question whether this new fashion of verse writing among working men has been always conducive to their own happiness. As for absolute success as poets, that was not to be expected of one in a hundred, so that we must not be disappointed if among the volumes of working men's poetry, of which we give a list at the head of our Article, only two should be found, on perusal, to contain any writing of a very high order, although these volumes form a very small portion of the verses which have been written, during the last forty years, by men engaged in the rudest and most monotonous toil. To every man so writing, the art, doubtless, is an ennobling one. The habit of expressing thought in verse not only indicates culture, but is a culture in itself of a very high order. It teaches the writer to think tersely and definitely; it evokes in him the humanizing sense of grace and melody, not merely by enticing him to study good models, but by the very act of composition. It gives him a vent for sorrows, doubts, and aspirations, which might otherwise fret and canker within, breeding, as they often do in the utterly dumb English peasant, self-devouring meditation, dogged melancholy, and fierce fanaticism. And if the effect of verse writing had stopped there, all had been well; but bad models have their effect as well as good ones, on the half-tutored taste of the working men, and engendered in them but too often a fondness for frothy magniloquence and ferocious raving, neither morally nor aesthetically profitable to themselves or their readers. There are excuses for the fault; the young of all ranks naturally enough mistake noise for awfulness, and violence for strength; and there is generally but too much, in the biographies of these working poets, to explain, if not to excuse, a vein of bitterness, which they certainly did not learn from their master, Burns. But the two poets who have done them most harm, in teaching the evil trick of cursing and swearing, are Shelley and the Corn-Law Rhymer; and one can well imagine how seducing two such models must be, to men struggling to utter their own complaints. . . .

In Great Britain . . . the people have been left to form their own tastes, and choose their own models of utterance, with great results, both for good and evil; and there has sprung up before the new impulse which Burns gave to popular poetry, a considerable literature — considerable not only from its truth and real artistic merit, but far more so from its being addressed principally to the working-classes. Even more important is this people's literature question, in our eyes, than the more palpable factors of the education question, about which we now hear such ado. It does seem to us, that to take every possible precaution about the spiritual truth which children are taught in school, and then leave to chance the more impressive and abiding teaching which popular literature, songs especially, give them out of doors, is as great a niaiserie as that of the Tractarians who insisted on getting into the pulpit in their surplices, as a sign that the clergy only had the right of preaching to the people, while they forgot that, by means of a free press, (of the licence of which they, too, were not slack to avail themselves), every penny-a-liner was preaching to the people daily, and would do so, maugre their surplices, to the end of time. The man who makes the people's songs is a true popular preacher. Whatsoever, true or false, he sends forth, will not be carried home, as a sermon often is, merely in heads, to be forgotten, before the week is out: it will ring in the ears, and cling round the imagination, and follow the pupil to the workshop, and the tavern, and the fireside; even to the deathbed, such power is in the magic of rhyme.

Anonymous
REVIEW OF JOHN EVANS'S
LANCASHIRE AUTHORS AND ORATORS

The absence of women from this anthology both as producers and as consumers of artisan literature is an accurate reflection of my research. Some women authors were contributors to the local periodicals, and a few, like 'Fanny Forester' who is represented in Chapter 3, clearly came from humble working-class backgrounds. Women were present in the London- and Edinburgh-based cheap artisan periodicals as editors (Mary Howitt and Eliza Cook for example), as contributors mainly of fiction (Eliza Meteyard — 'Silverpen' — for instance), and even in one case as owner (Christian Johnson and *Tait's*). But artisan writing remained formidably male in its aspirations and even in its language — 'manly' was a commonly used term of praise in writers like Kingsley and Carlyle, and the violent metaphors used to describe industrial writing generally insist upon it as a form of masculine toil. This absence is rarely a source of comment, so the following remarks from *Eliza Cook's Journal* (probably written by the editor herself) offer a rare chance to assess contemporary explanations of the lack of women writers in industrial working-class communities. The explanations offered here make a powerful distinction between the full contribution made by women to the industrial process and domestic economy, and their literary productivity.

In the midst of all this array of talent, we find the names of only three ladies. That certainly does not represent the fair proportion which the female intellect represents of the talents of this country. We, who know how much literary ability is manifested by the women of England, might well express surprise at the apparent scarcity of it which Lancashire exhibits, but then we must remember that that political and manufacturing activity, which has roused the minds of the men of that county, has not comprehended, at all events to the same extent, its women. The same causes have not had so powerful an operation on the females as upon the males, and that may partly account for the fact. It may not, too, be an incorrect opinion to hazard, that our manufacturing and trading system is unfavourable to the development of the qualities proper to the female mind. It is probable that the true literary sphere of women is poetry, the region of the imagination, the impulses, and the affections. Women, in common with men, exercise their poetic faculties upon the beauties of nature, but they have a dominion of their own where they are supreme. The home is their kingdom. The charm of the domestic hearth, the joys of the family circle — these belong to them, and there their peculiar attributes are best nurtured; but the manufacturing system, where it affects women at all, tends in this respect to unsex them. They leave their beds to answer the factory bell, their children are put out to the day nurse, or their dame school — they are co-workers with the men during their hours of toil; they return at night to the ill-kept, cheerless home, and the poetry of women's nature is too often stifled and deadened. We do not wonder, then, that while Mr Evans records his opinions of sixty-five talented men, ranging in rank from him who wears a coronet to the humble writer or speaker, who scarcely rises above the operative or the peasant, he writes but of three women, and these not belonging to the humbler grades of society.

There would appear, too, if we may judge from Mr Evans's collection, not to be a superabundance of poetic talent among the great men of Lancashire. Possibly some of the causes we have adverted, when speaking of the female celebrities of the county, may have had their effect upon the men. There is mention of something less than a dozen names associated with the poetic world, but few of them have more than a local reputation, chiefly gained through the columns of the newspapers circulating in the districts in which they live — a medium by the way through which the public were first made acquainted with the very sketches which have prompted this notice. These poets are mostly self-educated, comparatively poor men, and though fame does not trumpet their names very loudly, are possessed of considerable natural poetic talent. They are certainly not indebted to the circumstances in which they have been placed, or the associations by which they have been most constantly surrounded, for their ability, but to the natural poetic tendencies of their minds, which were too strong to be crushed out of them even by the most adverse circumstances.

Having said so much of the subject matter, upon which Mr Evans has exercised his mind, we can only say that the sketches themselves are plain, simple, intelligible, and (judging by the characters we are acquainted with), as far as they go, truthful. They bear evident traces of the hurry of a newspaper writer, but they will be welcome to many, as familiar descriptions of the persons and manners of men, who have many followers and admirers, and have acquired a sufficiently elevated present position, to ensure the certainty that posterity will be called upon to pronounce its verdict upon their merits.

F. W. Robertson
TWO LECTURES ON THE INFLUENCE OF POETRY ON THE WORKING CLASSES

From F. W. Robertson's *Lectures, Addresses, and Other Literary Remains* (London, Henry S. King, 1876), *passim*. The two lectures were delivered to Brighton Mechanics' Institute in 1852. Robertson's *Lectures* were still being re-issued as late as 1906.

The Preface to Robertson's *Lectures* stresses two things: that he was an unwavering champion of working class cultural improvement, and that he was a magnificent orator. Certainly his lectures on 'The Influence of Poetry' are an extremely lucid elaboration of Romantic poetic theory, and Robertson's account of the possible social uses of poetry is an intelligent one. Robertson, a Brighton clergyman, typified the enlightened, if still inhibiting and class interested, enthusiasm of the middle-class supporters of working-class progress. As the Preface to the *Lectures* puts it, 'When many of the clergy and richer classes were looking suspiciously at the growing intelligence of working men, and connecting it with revolutionary events then going on in Europe, Mr Robertson threw himself boldly into their cause. . . . In public and

private he ever sought to bring classes together.' I have taken considerable liberties with Robertson's expansive and highly illustrated text in
order to pick out his main arguments, because his list of the uses of
poetry does seem to summarize the conception of poetry held by many
working men writers as well as by middle class literary apologists.

When the old colours of a regiment are worn out, it is sometimes the
custom to burn them, and drink the ashes in wine, with solemn
silence: before the consecration of new colours. Well, that is all we
want. Let old forms and time-honoured words perish with due
honour, and give us fresh symbols and new forms of speech to
express, not what our fathers felt, but what we feel. Goethe says, 'The
spirit-world is not foreclosed. *Thy* senses are dulled; *thy* heart is dead.
Arise, become a learner; and bathe that early breast of thine, unwearied,
in the dew of a fresh morning.'
    And this alone would be enough to show that the Poetry of the
coming age must come from the Working Classes. In the upper
ranks, Poetry, so far at least as it represents their life, has long been
worn out, sickly, and sentimental. Its manhood is effete. Feudal
aristocracy, with its associations, the castle and tournament has
passed away. Its last healthy tones came from the harp of Scott.
Byron sang its funeral dirge. But tenderness, and heroism, and
endurance still want their voice, and it must come from the classes
whose observation is at first hand, and who speak fresh from
nature's heart. What has poetry to do with the Working Classes?
Men of Work! We want our Poetry from you — from men who will
dare to live a brave and true life; not like poor Burns, who was
fevered with flattery, manful as he was, and dazzled by the vulgar
splendours of the life of the great, which he despised and still longed
for; but rather like Ebenezer Elliott, author of the Corn Law
Rhymes. Our soldier ancestors told you the significance of high
devotion and loyalty which lay beneath the smoke of battle-fields.
Now rise and tell us the living meaning there may be in the smoke of
manufactories, and the heroism of perseverance, and the poetry of
invention, and the patience of uncomplaining resignation. . . .
    We proceed to name a few of the modes in which Poetry does
actually influence men.
    First. In the way of giving relief to feeling. It is a law of our nature
that strong feeling, unexpressed in either words or action, becomes
morbid. You need not dread the passionate man, whose wrath vents

310

itself in words: dread the man who grows pale and suppresses the language of his resentment. There is something in him yet to come out. This is the secret of England's freedom from revolution and conspiracies: she has free discussion. Wrongs do not smoulder, silently, to burst forth unexpectedly. . . . In an artificial state of society, perhaps some young, warlike spirit pines for a more dangerous life than our quiet days give. Well, he reads Scott's border raids, or 'Scots wha hae wi' Wallace bled,' or Hohenlinden, and the vivid forms of imagination receive, as it were, his superfluous energies, and the chafing subsides in unreal battle-fields: or some diseased germ of misanthropy is enlarging in his heart — secret discontent with life; disagreement with the world; conflict between his nature and civil regulations. Let him read Byron — a dangerous cure — but in the end a certain one. Byron has said all that can be said upon the subject. What more can be added? There is no restless feeling left behind of something unsaid. Exhaustion follows — then health. For it is a mistake to think that Poetry is only good to nurse feeling. It is good for enabling us to *get rid* of feeling for which there is no available field of action. It is the safety valve to the heart.

It has besides, an elevating influence. It breaks the monotonous flatness of existence by excitement. Its very essence is that it exalts us, and puts us in a higher mood than that in which we live habitually. And this is peculiarly true of modern Poetry. . . . But when we say Poetry elevates, let it not be understood of the improvement of physical comforts. Poetry will not place a man in better circumstances; but it may raise him above his circumstances, and fortify him with inward independence. . . . The tendency, again of Poetry is to unite men together. And this is both indirectly and directly. It has already been said that the highest Poetry is that which represents the most universal feeling, not the most rare . . . Or again, Byron and Shelley — aristocrats both by birth, yet no minions of a caste, nor champions of hereditary privilege — they were men; and their power lay in this, that they were the champions of human rights, as well as utterers of the passion that is in men. So far as they are great, they are universal; so far as they are small or bad, they are narrow and egotistical. . . .

It is thus that poets universalize and unite. 'One touch of nature makes the whole world kin.' And, hence, Poetry has been silently doing a work for the poorer classes when they were not aware of it; for even that Poetry which does not interest them, may be opening the hearts of the richer classes towards them. Did Burns teach the nobles no sympathy with the cares, and the loves, and the trial's of the cotter's life? And when poor Hood wrote the 'Song of the Shirt,' so touchingly expressive of the sorrows of an unknown class, the over-worked needlewoman, and all England thrilled to the appeal . . . and when, in consequence, plan after plan was tried, and investigations instituted, and a kindlier interest evoked to ameliorate their condition, tell us — Had Poetry done nothing for the Working Classes?

. . . Lastly, I name the refining influence of Poetry. We shall confine our proofs to that which it has already done in making men and life less savage, carnal, and mercenary; and this especially in the three departments which were the peculiar sphere of the Poetry which is called romantic. Beneath its influence passion became love; selfishness, honour; and war, chivalry.

Anonymous
A BIOGRAPHICAL SKETCH OF GERALD MASSEY

Originally published in *Eliza Cook's Journal* in 1851, this Sketch — probably by Samuel Smiles — was added to Massey's book of poems *The Ballad of Babe Christabel* (London, David Bogue, 1854) which went through four editions in the year of its publication.

Massey's poems were extremely well received, with the main critical emphasis falling on their passionate youthful intensity and defence of Freedom and Justice. As a review in *The Dundee Advertiser* put it, 'Glasgow, Manchester, Sheffield, Nottingham, Leeds, and London, — tending anxiously their machinery and merchandise, — have all reared poetic children, protesting against the worship of wealth, and hymning the excellence of spiritual nobleness and beauty.' This sense of the abstract nature of self-taught poetry is interestingly aligned with a more specifically political perception of their work in the following account of Massey. A further progressive element in these comments is the recognition that the patronage system had dominated the subject matter of poetry as well as its tone, but that the new industrial writers were beginning to deal with the most appropriate themes, those that touched upon their social and political explanation. While remaining a generous reading of the development of the working class poetic voice, the evidence elsewhere in this anthology does not suggest that self-taught writers did enjoy the freedom and appropriateness of subject matter attributed to them in this article.

You see at once that the writer is a man of vivid genius, and is full of the true poetic fire. Some of his earlier pieces are indignant ex-postulations with society at the wrongs of suffering humanity; passionate protest against those hideous disparities of life which meet our eye on every side; against power wrongfully used; against fraud and oppression in their more rampant forms; mingled with appeals to the higher influence of knowledge, justice, mercy, truth, and love. It is always thus with the poet who has worked his way to the light through darkness, suffering, and toil. Give a poor down-trodden man culture, and, in nine cases out of ten, you only increase his sensitiveness to pain: you agonize him with the sight of pleasures which are to him forbidden; you quicken his sense of despair at the frightful inequalities of the human lot. There are thousands of noble natures, with minds which, under better circumstances, would have blessed and glorified their race, who have been forever blasted — crushed into the mire — or condemned to courses of desperate guilt! — for one who, like Gerald Massey, has nobly risen above his trials and temptations, and triumphed over them. And when such a man does find a voice, surely 'rose-water' verses and 'hot-pressed' sonnets are not to be expected of him; such things are not by any means the natural products of a life of desperate struggling with poverty. When the self-risen and self-educated man speaks and writes now-a-days, it is of the subjects nearest to his heart. Literature is not a mere epicurism with men who have suffered and grown wise, but a real, earnest, passionate, vehement, living thing — a power to move others, a means to elevate themselves, and to emancipate their order. This is a marked peculiarity of our times; knowledge is now more than ever regarded as a power to elevate, not merely indi-viduals, but classes. Hence, the most intelligent working-men at this day are intensely political: we merely state this as *a fact* not to be disputed. In former times, when literature was regarded mainly in the light of a rich man's luxury, poets who rose out of the working-class sung as their patrons wished. Bloomfield and Clare sang of the quiet beauty of rural life, and painted pictures of evening skies, purling brooks, and grassy meads. Burns could with difficulty repress the 'Jacobin' spirit which burned within him; and yet even he was rarely, if ever, political in his tone. His strongest verses, having a political bearing, were those addressed to the Scotch Representatives in reference to the Excise regulations as to the distillation of whiskey. But come down to our own day, and mark the difference: Elliot [sic], Nichol, Bamford, the author of 'Ernest', the Chartist Epic, Davis, the 'Belfast Man,' De Jean, Massey, and many others, are intensely political; and they defend themselves for their selection of subjects as Elliot did, when he said, 'Poetry is impassioned truth; and why should we not utter it in the shape that touches our condition the most closely — the political?'

Diana Mulock
A HEDGE-SIDE POET

From *Macmillan's Magazine* (April 1860), 449.

Diana Mulock's (or Mrs Craik as she was known as a novelist) article was published in an early issue of *Macmillan's Magazine* as an exemplary account of a respectable and neglected local poet, and the hardships which he endured without complaint. James Reynolds Withers was a Cambridgeshire shoemaker, day labourer, and poet. Mrs Craik's account of him is itself exemplary of many widespread middle-class attitudes: Withers 'never pens a verse which a good man might blush to see one of his growing-up daughters read', and he is praised for his 'refinement', but censured for his 'rough' and 'careless' diction. Mrs Craik admits that most of Withers's work is derivative, common-place, and banal, but she discovers occasional felicities which make Withers a 'true poet'. Mrs Craik's essay is almost a footnote to her husband G. L. Craik's *Pursuit of Knowledge Under Difficulties* (see p. 295), analysing the social changes that have taken place to self-taught writers over the thirty years before 1860.

We hear a good deal now of poets of the people. The days are gone by when glorious ploughmen and inspired shepherds were made much of at noblemen's tables, and treated by noblewomen with something of the magnificent protection which the great Glumdalclitch afforded to Lemuel Gulliver. We no longer meet them led about as tame lions by an admiring, yet patronizing host, who hints 'hush' at the least prospect of their roaring; and they are expected to roar always at the keeper's will — never against it. But if in these times they are more independent, they are much less rare and majestic creatures. They haunt every literary drawing-room by twos and threes, — the mud of their aboriginal fields still sticking to their illustrious boots, — pleased, but awkward; trying hard to tone down their native accents, manners, and customs, to the smooth level of what is termed 'good society'. Or else, taking the opposite tack, are forever thrusting forward, with obnoxious ostentation, their 'origin'; forgetting that the delicate inborn refinement which alone can save a nobleman from being a clown is also the only thing which can make a clodhopper into a gentleman. If it have not made him such — in manners as in mind — he may be a poet, but he remains a clodhopper still.

But, happily, many of these poets of the people are likewise of the true 'gentle' blood; and thus, be their birth ever so humble, they rise, step by step, educating themselves — heaven knows how — but they are educated: acquiring, as if by instinct, those small social *bienséances*, which are good as well as pleasant, being the outward indication of far better things. Men such as these, wherever met, are at once easily recognizable, and quickly recognized; society gives them a cordial welcome; they are neither merely tolerated nor insultingly patronized; but take by right their natural place in the world, as its 'best' portion — its truest aristocracy.

There is yet another class of born poets, whom the muse finds at the plough, the loom, the forge, the tailor's board, or the cobbler's stall, — and leaves them there. This, from various causes. First, because genius, or talent — call it which you please — is infinite in its gradations; the same amount of intellectual capacity which, found in an educated person, will enable him to take a very high place among 'the mob of gentlemen who write with ease,' will not enable a common day-labourer to teach himself everything from the alphabet upwards, and raise himself from the plough-tail to the Laureateship. Secondarily, because, almost invariably, the organization, mental and physical, which accompanies the poetic faculty is the one least fitted to that incessant battle with the world, for which a man must arm himself who aims to rise therein. Therefore it is, that while our noble Stephensons, and the like, — men who live poems instead of singing them, — move grandly on

315

through the brave career, which may begin in a hut and end in Westminster Abbey, — those, who may be called our 'hedge-side poets', never rise out of the station in which they were born. Unless some Capel Lofft or Savage Landor should catch them or exhibit them, they probably flutter on through life, singing their harmless songs to themselves, or to a very small audience; far happier in many things, than if they had been set up to plume and strut their little day in the gilded cage of popularity.

Yet, hear them in their native meadows, expecting from them neither epic hymns, nor operatic *fioriture*; and we are often charmed and amazed to find how exquisitely they sing: with a note as sweet and unexpected as a robin's warble out of a yellowing hedge, when leaves are falling and flowers few.

Edwin Paxton Hood
THE PEERAGE OF POVERTY

The *Peerage of Poverty* was a development of Hood's earlier *The Literature of Labour — Illustrious instances of the education of poetry in poverty* (Partridge and Oakey, 1851). Published in two series in 1859 and 1861, *The Peerage of Poverty* reached its final form in the fifth edition (S. W. Partridge, 1870) from which this extract is taken.

Paxton Hood's books are important soures of information about the lives and achievements of self-taught writers. At another level, they reveal a surprisingly optimistic view of the opportunities available to the poorly educated in Victorian England. Hood's list of working class cultural achievements appears to overwhelm his sense of the difficulties in the way of proletarian and artisan self-expression, and this imbalance of evidence leads the author to assert inhibitions as opportunities in an apparently perverse way. While writers like Gerald Massey were arguing that 'Poverty is a cold place to write Poetry in', Hood was arguing that poverty was actually a *source* of poetic power and inspiration. Such attempts to apologise for the cultural deprivations of the poor were apparent enough in middle-class essays, but seldom showed themselves in so transparent a form. Hood was an active Unitarian minister who wrote an astonishing range of educational and biographical works for artisan readers. An important chapter of *The Peerage of Poverty* is devoted to Clare, whom Hood visited on several occasions. B. E. Maidment's 'Popular

Exemplary Biography in the Nineteenth Century — Edwin Paxton
Hood and his Books' (*Prose Studies* vol 7, 2 September 1984, 148–167)
offers a recent account of this interesting writer.

And now, if these be poetry, we may ask what are the circumstances
of the labourer's lot which seem peculiarly to fit him among men to
be the poet, the minister, and instructor of his race? We suppose that
he has had no opportunity of studying in the library. Schools and
colleges have been closed to him; a first glance would lead us to
suppose that he was cut off from leisure; if so, what is there in the
life of this man which makes up for these deficiencies, and tends to
the exaltation of his name? In reply, there are many teachers: Ist. We
may say POVERTY ITSELF IS A TEACHER. Poverty when it comes to
the right man, and the right mind, greatly fits for the message of
instruction: its bleak winds bear seeds to the spirit, and in the right
mind they spring up and bear much fruit. Perhaps it may be said,
that he who has not suffered is unfitted to be a minister to the people.
We are all 'made perfect through suffering', and although there is a
nobler, because a severer kind of suffering than the merely physical,
yet to the poor man, invariably, the sensations of his own poverty
harrow him also with the spectacles of suffering beside his own.
Thus it is that the sympathies of our hearts are unlocked; thus it is
that some of the greatest lessons in our human history are com-
municated to us. There are, of course, many natures not proof
against poverty, and let us not speak too harshly of their failings,
even these are high angels compared with many of the children of
wealth and rank; but there are noble natures whose hearts have
fluttered through the searching fires unscathed; like the Hebrew
children in the fiery furnace, they beheld, and others beheld, 'the
likeness as of the Son of man' in their fire: the fires were fierce, but
they could not scorch away the true affections of their nature; they
contracted no misanthropic hatred of their kind; they did not
blasphemously blame the Father of all good, but looked up with
most reverent eyes to His throne; and so, from that time forth, they
came, harp in hand, qualified to be the ministers and instructors of
their race; nay, sometimes from the very furnace of trial itself there
came forth, as the wail of music, a strong spiritual nature battling
with despair, Light as of old, contending with darkness.

A second source of inspiration is the very fact of LABOUR. A
working man feels his strength, feels his independence, and in that

independence is the soul of all effort. There is no vanity about labour; pride is there, a generous and noble pride. Birth, dress, place, precedence — all these are low and little; but to create good and blessed things from most remote causes, to feel that our own arm bears up state and throne; there is no vanity there. There is poetry, there is inspiration, when there is moral significance; when the spiritual, felt, but unseen, stands behind and invests the real with ideal beauty: there is no true labour but it may become all this, the symbol of a higher life. And the true poet is he, whether he belongs to the working classes or to any other class, who arrives at the moral significance of his being, and of all being; to whom the seen is not the only real, and the useful, in the ordinary sense, not the only object worthy of pursuit.

Another circumstance is, that the working classes are compelled, naturally, to find the principal sources of their enjoyments at HOME. The spreading of our feelings, and fancies, and tastes over an extensive surface of attractions is unfavourable to the development of any feeling in any intensity. Our affections are called into play greatly by the mere fact of companionship, concentration, and association. Our hearts linger; our memories delight to dwell over scenes which we naturally expect during the whole of the day, and poverty only throws around those scenes a more tender and touching character. Our love is deep truly, in proportion as there are few things to claim our love. They must, indeed, be highly healthy natures who, beneath the witchery of palaces, enjoy any comfort in comparison with those which humble cottagers enjoy. If it were not for this fact, it would seem strange that I know none of the Poets of the working class who have not sung of the delights and joys of Home; and I know but few of the other poets who have even condescended to mention so commonplace a theme. But I cannot imagine an intense nature seated by the cheerful fireside without shaping its thoughts and feelings into poems; it may not utter them; but the Power and the Passion are there; there is the school of the soul; there the spots where the holiest feelings and affections are born. Look at it wherever it is, there is the earthly heaven. The man who has not such a shrine is indeed an exile; and the exile who has gathered on the foreign shore two or three hearts around him, and built from the wreck a home there, has vistas of Heaven opening through the darkness to his view.

There is yet one other circumstance more favourably developed to the working classes than to others, or frequently so — NATURE. This was the case with the ploughman and cottars of the ancient days, and it is so in no inconsiderable degree still. It is a great thing to live in the presence of Nature, even though it be in flats, and fens, and dykes. There is an opportunity for the cultivation of an acquaintance with Man, as well as with the details of Nature's life, which does not occur in cities; and it need not be said that from the most ancient time this great lesson came to us — STUDY NATURE; there is no little trivial thing that is not replete with instruction and wisdom. It is good to live in the presence of scenes that perpetually awaken in you the highest and best thoughts. Each season, each month, each day, reveals something new of Nature's economy, turns down some fresh page; we all live too much in the city, too near the works and wonders of Man's hands. It is well, frequently, to lose ourselves in the sense of the sublime and the infinite. Almost every object we can look upon in the World of Nature suggest emotions like these. Almost every work of Man, to the thoughtful mind, ever suggests the idea of the finite and the conceivable; and in the perpetual collision with our race we forget the veneration due to Man; but in the presence of Nature and her sublime works we re-animate and re-invigorate our purposes; our views become wider and more catholic; we drop our conventionalism and our customs, and learn more readily and promptly to Adore. In many of our more eminent poets we seem to see that they followed Nature, at best, afar off. They were not devotees in the highest sense; such can never be the greatest poets; they cannot have much to communicate: for he who has not closely observed the minutiae of Nature in the flower has not closely observed either the minutiae of Nature in the heart. To the poor man Nature opens the only saloon, spreads the only carpet, hangs the only lamps. He is debarred admittance to many temples, to every palace; he cannot tell what the furniture of rich halls may be; he is never allowed to stand in those places where silks rustle and jewels shine; the marbles and the gilded panellings he never saw; the wreaths around the fluted column, the tapestry, and the dais. But he knows of one place he may enter freely; and all his ideas of richness and exuberance therefore are brought from thence. He knows no other imagery. Many of the flowers of the woods he does not know the names of, or perhaps gives them a wrong name, but he knows that they are beautiful; or knows that they speak to his spirit, and hence some of them become companions dearer even

319

than his fellow-men.

Shall I find one other circumstance yet more tending to educate the poetic faculty? It is then here, in the SUPERIOR MOTIVES TO THE RELIGIOUS LIFE; for who does not know how much more potent are the voices of Religion in their appeal to our poorer brethren? Alas! it is true that the earth weans us away from the high incentives to the spiritual and heavenly life. Sorrow is the path that leads to God; and the soul-elevating doctrines of the Christian faith are far more amply felt in the cottage than in the hall. True religion moulds the life of man wonderfully; it sublimes, it spiritualizes the affections; when we really feel that we are not fatherless in the universe, when we trace the footprints of God everywhere around us, when the doctrine of our immortality is conferred to us, when we trace with spiritual eyes a life above us, a life everywhere, probation working out immortal life, when Jesus, the Divine poor man, Saviour, and Cottage Dweller and Teacher, is felt to be related to us, who can doubt that the whole of the being is by thoughts like these elevated and ennobled?

These outlines and hints upon the inspiration of labour and the characteristics of the poet's soul, will not be out of place here, in introducing to the reader a child of genius well known — JOHN CRITCHLEY PRINCE. . . .

Chapter Five

THE DIFFICULTIES OF APPEARING IN PRINT

Limited access to print was, and remained, a central inhibition on the development of self-taught writing in the second half of the nineteenth century. The extent of such limitations in the first half of the century is more open to doubt. The highly developed magazine and periodical based cultural organizations brought into being by the Chartist movement, with well-constructed if often clandestine systems of distribution, did not survive the failures of 1848 or merge easily into less overtly political artisan culture. The continuing encouragement of the liberal literary establishment, described in Chapter 4, in the last analysis proved as inhibiting as it was helpful for the majority of self-taught writers. The London artisan magazines, also described above, were short-lived, and extremely vulnerable to lack of financial backing. In terms of the lack of access to print, the absence of publicity, the failure to develop a professional literary marketplace or wide readerships, it must have seemed inevitable in 1850 that artisan writers would remain peripheral figures in late Victorian literary culture, not primarily because of the failure of their poetic talent, but largely because of the nature of Victorian publishing. The way in which literary relationships affected self-taught writers has recently been explored in Chapter 4 of Nigel Cross's *The Common Writer* (Cambridge 1985). Literary relationships, which had changed so much for the increasingly professional metropolitan writer through the development of a mass readership, the growth of the periodical press, the extension of the public library system, the emancipation of the publisher from the printer, and the beginnings of copyright legislation, still seemed designed to enable the middle classes alone to articulate their attitudes and ideologies while preventing the working populace from appearing in print. These differences between the increasingly professional and commercially orientated literary relationships of established writers in Victorian England and the experiences of the self-taught artisan writers are movingly suggested in the following passages. But before approaching these catalogues of indignity and hardship, it is worth looking briefly at the systems for getting into print which were available to self-taught writers who lived beyond even the Victorian Grub Street described by Cross.

The first publishing relationship open to a self-taught provincial poet derived from the traditional bardic model which had attracted the attention of Wordsworth and Coleridge. The poet was seen to possess a widely recognized skill or talent. He was accordingly encouraged to develop that skill as a social duty with the support of the community, and in return offered his poetic output to the community on the agreed social occasions for poetry. Often the bard was not a professional writer, despite his evident skill, but rather developed his poetic interests as a leisure activity. With a number of complications, the idea of bardic community remained strongly embedded in nineteenth century industrial towns, even when those towns expanded into vast cities. B. E. Maidment's essay 'Class and Cultural Production in the Industrial City: Poetry in Victorian Manchester' in *City, Class, and Culture* (Kidd and Roberts eds, Manchester, 1985) is an attempt to explain this transition in more detail. With the move from the village to the city, the occasions for verse altered from the group gathering into a less personal, oral discourse conducted through local newspapers and magazines, but still the sense of communal obligation and recognition remained a mainspring of the poetic activity. Much evidence of this continuing tradition can be identified, ranging from the local bardic literary clubs which met informally in pubs (M. Vicinus describes the Manchester 'Sun Inn Group' in an essay in *The Victorian City*, Dyos and Wolff eds, 1973) to the extraordinary number of dedicatory poems which self-taught writers wrote to each other; from the production of group anthologies like the *Manchester Festive Wreath* (ed. J. B. Rogerson, 1843) to the continued use of pseudonymous bardic titles. The main characteristics of the bardic world, then, might be described as a belief that poetry had a social function in binding a community together through expressing the simplest commonly held values, an assertion that the poet had a duty to that community, and a further belief that that duty would be acknowledged by the community by according the poet a high status, and by recognizing his (or just occasionally her) specialness. In addition, bardic writing was largely unpaid, largely ephemeral or topical, appearing in newspapers or journals, rather than in books, or even existing solely as oral productions. Despite growing awareness, and rapid exploitation, of new markets, despite new systems of production and distribution, despite increasing literacy and rises in the general standard of living, a great deal of Victorian self-taught writing never gained more than a localized bardic circulation. Dialect culture in particular sustained the bardic relationship, long after social change had made the bard an anachronistic figure in a society dominated by mass production and the cash nexus.

The second literary relationship available to self-taught writers was that of patronage. Patronage is largely thought of as an eighteenth-century system of literary production which was quickly destroyed in the early nineteenth century by the commercial success of Byron and Scott, by the expansion of the literary market, and by the increasingly heavy capitalization and professionalism of the publishing industry. Yet for writers without access to the new professional markets, patronage remained an essential factor in getting into print. That such a continuing dependence on the patronage system was damaging to the development of authentic working class self-expression is hardly open to dispute. There were, however, important changes in the nature of such patronage in the middle of the century, when literary sponsorship became less a matter of finance and more a matter of literary know-how and advice, moving from the aristocracy to the literary middle classes in the process. Another trend, clearly identified by Nigel Cross in *The Common Writer*, is from individual to institutional support through pension funds and literary charities.

The underlying basis of patronage is a sense of obligation on the poet's part. The patron, too, is confirmed in a social duty, that of encouraging and maintaining respectful cultural activity, but with an insistence on the gratitude, and hence, conformity, of the author. Thus beyond the damage caused by any sense of financial and social obligation, the poet was frequently forced to make concessions in the writing itself — concessions in poetic form and language, in social attitudes expressed in the poetry, and even in the kinds of poems produced. One further crucial effect of patronage was that it encouraged the belief that poetry had no financial value. Poetry, under patronage, becomes a matter of obligation and social duty, in which the market value of literature is concealed, even denied, by the intervention of the wealthy patron. Patronage insists that as poetry has no financial value, and hence no widespread market, it must be subsidised as an act of social duty. The poet is constantly reminded that he has no commercial readership at all, and that his skills are not marketable, only existing as a result of the patron's kindliness and belief in culture. Poetry, in other words, has a value which is entirely cultural and social, and is to be separated out from those other forms of cultural production which insist on their place in the open market.

Thus the vigorous continuance of the patronage system in the publication of regional self-taught poetry had contradictory effects. Without patronage many local self-taught writers would never have been published at all. At the same time, the existence of a patronage system meant that the development of a potential market for self-taught writers was severely delayed. The readership available to self-taught poets, too, was under patronage made up of relatively wealthy and educated subscribers, even though the poets themselves may have wished to reach a socially less privileged stratum of readers. The result was the characteristically uncertain or double address found frequently in poems by working-class authors. Prince's Prefaces to *Hours With The Muses*, printed in this chapter, show a poet despairingly grappling with these contradictions and obligations. Patronage doubtless did have an underlying and generous wish to foster artisan cultural development, but the results were far more inhibiting than the intention, and even the intention was often the product of undisguised class interest. One other aspect of patronage is worth mentioning. By soliciting a wide list of patrons, many provincial writers were brought into contact with a readership which was not entirely local in character. Patrons tended to be not only from a different class than authors but also more metropolitan or even cosmopolitan. Accordingly, the pursuit of patrons was one aspect of the self-taught writer's endeavour to transcend the local, and to enter the world of literary London.

The foregoing account of the patronage system implicitly opposes it to the idea of professionalism, where the writer exploits an available range of outlets for his literary productions, all of which have established readerships and established literary genres and conventions. It is fair to say that professionalism was on the whole a totally unrealistic aim for most self-taught writers, however talented. Very few self-taught writers sustained themselves by their writing alone, and the history of self-taught literature is studded with examples of failure, poverty, and neglect. Yet in several important ways self-taught writers did begin to glimpse the opportunities and, indeed, the inconsistencies of the prevailing literary systems. One important piece of knowledge, usually gained through hard experience, was that the patronage system tended to conceal society's true evaluation of the worth of poetry. Patronage suggests that the patron, representing society as a whole, thinks that poetry is important enough to be subsidized in its production despite the knowledge that he can expect no financial reward. The implication is that poetry is so vital that it must be sustained, in spite of its lack of commercial potential, as a potent *moral* force within society. But, and this still seems to be the case, individual and state patronage, although sanctioned by society, in fact conceals a relatively low interest in poetry as an art form. Despite constant protestations of the value of poetry, and hence its high cultural status, society at large is very unwilling to buy poetry or even to believe that it has any real cultural or social effect. As I have already suggested, the interest shown by the middle classes in self-taught writers was rather an interest in cultural and class development than an interest in literature itself. Self-taught writers, for a number of reasons which should already be clear, believed very deeply in poetry as a social and moral force. Their careers often provide tragic testimony to the concealed indifference of society to their literary products except as an aspect of class development.

Another factor which caused the over-estimation of the financial and commercial possibilities of professional literature as a career for self-taught writers was the extent and generosity of the encouragement which they were offered by the liberal literary figures, which has been discussed in detail in Chapter 4. Much of this encouragement took the form of advice rather than financial subsidy — advice about how to market poems, about stylistic and technical refinements, and about how to write to please various readerships. Often such advice was merely confusing or damaging. Rossetti's attempts to help the Tyneside pit-poet Joseph Skipsey resulted in the writer losing his sense of community and the established adviser feeling resentful and insulted. (See R. B. Watson, *Joseph Skipsey — His Life and Work*, 1909.) Similarly, Dickens's attempts to help John Critchley Prince resulted only in disastrous financial and social consequences.

A third aspect of the notion of professionalism among self-taught writers derives from their extremely elevated and ambitious conception of the value of poetry as a moral and social force, a perception described in Chapter 3. Taking the most extreme statements of Wordsworth and Shelley as their texts, self-taught poets often attempted the most serious and ambitious poetic modes, partly to show off their own hard-won poetic skill, but also to demonstrate their extremely high claims for the power of poetry over the moral welfare of the nation, a necessary claim in justifying their own devotion to literary endeavour. As a result, there was an inevitable, if often submerged, connection in the minds of self-taught poets between their severe and demanding apprenticeship to poetic craft and their right to financial reward. Their devotion to learning their poetic craft was inevitably a metaphor for other forms of industrial production, and the poems themselves must have often seemed a product like any other commodity. In short, many self-taught writers began to feel that poetry should have a proper commercial value. It must have been galling for immensely serious self-taught writers to realize that there was a readier market for trivial lyrics than for painstaking philosophical epics. All these perceptions confused the issue of the value of poetry, and whether any equation could be made between cultural value and financial reward. Many of the following passages covertly approach these issues of the 'value' of poetry without ever being able to resolve the issue in any absolute or helpful way.

A final model for the social relationships of self-taught writing has usefully, if inelegantly, been called *artisanal* in Raymond Williams's *Culture* (1981). What this term reveals is really a commercially sophisticated version of the bardic, in which the 'artisan' produces the writing and then markets his own handiwork through a careful use of the available local outlets. Thus the poet avoids patrons and social forms of obligation, and accepts market forces as part of his constraints and opportunities. Such a poet, however, renounces all metropolitan pretentions, and instead works in an area defined by his own limited, but precise, knowledge. The attractions of performing the whole literary process — production, distribution, sales, and promotion — by oneself were obvious to many writers, as this system offers an alternative to the impersonal forces of the national marketplace without denying the cash nexus as a key factor in literary production. Yet the difficulties of the task were prodigious. The moving accounts of John Clare's attempts to market his own works in Martin's biography (F. Martin, *The Life of John Clare*,

1865, 216–7 in particular) provide a warning example of the desperate nature of such a system as a means of making a living. Yet the model remained an attractive one — local, self-reliant, independent, with a close, indeed personal, relationship with every reader. The 'artisanal' mode seemed to offer an 'organic' notion of literary production, free from the obligations of the bard, the deference of patronage, and the prodigious difficulties of professionalism.

It is easy to stress overmuch the difficulties of appearing in print. In his excellent study of working-class autobiography, *Bread, Knowledge, and Freedom* (1981), David Vincent argues that 'in the first half of the nineteenth century access to literary self-expression was not only dramatically greater than it had been in the preceding century, but in many respects was more open than it was later to become, as all forms of publishing became more capital intensive'. Vincent is right to stress the literary opportunity presented in early Victorian England, and the argument about the strength and diversity of his chosen genre, autobiography, can also be applied to poetry. Yet, in spite of the generally acknowledged changes in publishing and book production, it has been hard to find much discussion of the difficulties of publishing from self-taught writers themselves. Detailed accounts of publication are often included in the prefatory material to books of poems, yet the dominant tone and attitude is deferential. Apart from Clare's interesting stray comments, the pieces reprinted here are all from the mid-century or later. I cannot claim that these pieces are necessarily representative, but they do give some idea of the formidable difficulties which needed to be overcome in getting into print. Of course, the difficulties of appearing in print are essentially aspects of wider difficulties in the development of working-class consciousness. If access to print grew rapidly in the first half of the nineteenth century, that access still did not match the social, political, and intellectual development of the working classes in the same period.

John Clare
JOURNALS (1824–5)

Clare's *Journals* offer occasional insights into the problems which beset the publication of self-taught poetry. By virtue of the quality of his writing, the area he lived in, and his relationship with the pastoral tradition, Clare is difficult to place in this anthology. While exhibiting many of the characteristics of a self-taught writer, he is an exception in many ways to available generalisations. I have included only these three short *Journal* extracts in this anthology. The first points to self-taught writers' constant awareness of the injustice of the literary marketplace, while the second offers pungent (and entirely understandable) comment on the way in which editors and publishers altered the texts of self-taught writers, often mistaking powerfully expressive writing for weak syntax or imperfect versification. The third extract suggests the rapidity with which self-taught writing became a phenomenon between 1820 and 1845. The text followed is that of Anne Tibble's edition of *The Journals and Essays* (Manchester, 1980).

Sun. 28 Nov. 1824   A gentleman came to see me today whose whole talk was of Bloomfield & Booksellers he told me to put no faith in them & and when I told him that all my faith & M.S.S. likewise was in their hands already he shook his head & declared with a solemn bend of his body 'Then you are done by G—d — they will never print them but dally you on with well managed excuses to the grave & then boast that they were your friends when you were not able to contradict it as they have done to Bloomfield' he then desired me to get my M.S.S. back by all means & sell them at a markets price at what they would fetch he said that Bloomfield had not £100 a year to maintain 5 or 6 in the family why I have not £50 to maintain 8 with this is a hungry difference

Sat. 30 April 1825   either way Editors are troubled with nice amendings & if Doctors were as fond of amputation as they are of altering & correcting the world woud have nothing but cripples

Tues. 19 Oct 1824   Lookd over a New vol of provincial poems by a neighbouring poet Bantum — Excursions of Fancy & poor fancys I find them There is not a new thought in them 4 years ago a poet was not to be heard of within a century of Helpstone & now there is a swarm Roses Early Muse Wilkinsons Percy both of Peterbro Messing's Rural Walks of Exton — Adcock 'Cottage Poems' of Oakham — Bantums Excursions of fancy of Teigh — Strattons Poems — of Abbots Ripton &c &c all of a kin wanting in natural images &c

330

Charles Fleming
THE DIFFICULTIES OF APPEARING IN PRINT

Published in *The Working Man's Friend and Family Instructor* (Cassell,
April 1850) supplementary number devoted to contributions from
the working classes, 24–6.

Any doubts about the capacity of self-taught writers to express
themselves clearly and lucidly must have been widely dispelled by
such essays as Fleming's unsolicited contribution to *The Working
Man's Friend*. Fleming (1804–1857) was a Paisley hand-loom weaver,
the son of a highly respected trade union activist of moderate progressive views. A gentle, earnest man, Fleming rejected his father's
political activism for a literary and scholarly life, and became part of a
local group of self-taught writers. His collected *Poems, Songs, and
Essays* were published in 1878 edited by a local squire on behalf of the
Paisley Burns Club. Most of Fleming's work suffers from the usual
weaknesses of concessionary self-taught writing, but this early essay,
in the breadth of its argument, the impersonal assurance of its tone,
and in the accuracy of its analysis, offers one of the most sustained and
intelligent comments on the nature of Victorian publishing and its
inhibiting effect on artisan culture.

If a foreigner were to arrive in this country . . . he could not fail to
come rapidly to the conclusion that we were a reading people, and
that everything amongst us was *put into print*, from the view taken
on the mountain's top, to the culinary operations of the kitchen.

We are a reading people. . . . We are the better for having the
wisdom and discernment of the talented placed before us. But who
can endure the languid twaddle of effeminate refinement, that is too
often recorded of those whose intellectual status may be fairly
comprehended under the equivocal term *rank*.

Yet extensive as the publishing trade is, and innumerable as are
the volumes issued by it on almost every branch of knowledge, it is
really a very difficult matter, except to a privileged class, *to appear in
print*. The difficulty vanishes like a shadow before the man of
wealth, influence, or rank; but to the one of lowly degree it is almost
insuperable. Can any good thing come out of Nazareth? is a prejudice
that has spread far beyond the region of Galilee; and we find that
many of our respectable booksellers deem it utterly impossible that a
man standing before them in the habiliments of industry can have
anything new to offer at the shrine of the muses, or any addition to

make to the more sober literature of his country. Such an individual, they think, should lay no claim to authorship; it is entirely beyond his sphere of thought and action. If, therefore, he feels any aspirations after giving the lesson that instructs, improves, and ennobles, or the verse that inspires, with a thrilling enchantment, even the rough and untutored soul, he is told to repress such ebullitions of fancy, and make himself thoroughly acquainted with the particular calling with which he is identified. If he be an artisan, he must make himself conversant with the first principles and latest improvements in his art! If a mechanic, he must comprehend fully the powers of machinery and the adjustment of its parts! Thus is established, at once, a line of distinction between the class who are to write, and the class who are to read — the order who are to become deacons to those around them, and the other order who are to plod on through unrequited toil, and at last be carried to the deep darkness of the tomb, without even leaving the wreck of a name behind.

The diffusion of knowledge through our country, and the correct principles that have been introduced into the method of teaching the arts and speaking and reading in the very remotest nooks of our land, have, in many instances, given birth to the desire of appearing in print — a desire, under ordinary circumstances, indicative of a high-toned morality, and which ought to receive a warm and generous encouragement. But what is often the fate of the pale-faced child of study, whose hours have been devoted to the life-consuming midnight lamp? Perhaps he might have followed Swift, and reproved the follies and corruptions of his age, by exposing the arrogance of aristocratic pretension, and elevating the unobtrusive mass of suffering humanity; or it may be he did not possess the caustic humour apparent in the history of John Bull, but his satire partook of the classical refinement of Juvenal himself. Yet what of all this, when he is told by a bustling man of the world behind a counter, that his work, if published, would only facilitate the process of trunk making, or make good enough envelopes for rolls of tobacco? In fact, if an individual in humble life can obtain even a perusal of his papers, he has certainly gained a conquest; for, although the 'Journal of a lady who made an overland journey to India' will be paid for most handsomely, or 'the Voyage of a war-brig to California' will cause its author to rank as a man of letters, yet a single glance at the pages of a working man will cause them to be pronounced 'too vulgar for publication'.

Another difficulty which attends appearing in print, is the suspicion that, if the author be not of the privileged classes, he has something dangerous in view — something that will have a tendency to uproot established institutions, and sap the foundations of public morality. This is a prejudice of a baneful kind, and has been the means of preventing the publication of treatises of a useful and salutary description. Error must first be seen before it can be exposed and confuted; and whoever dreads the publication of opinions on the grounds that they are different from what is already known to the world, if he be not regarded as the friend of ignorance, should at least be designated an enemy to improvement. Mankind suffers little from those errors which carry along with them their own antidote; and should errors of a virulent kind prevail, there are grounds to conclude that there is a relaxation of duty on the part of those who have obtained the pre-eminence of teaching and guiding the public mind.

But we have a suspicion, notwithstanding all our boasting about the republic of letters — a suspicion that will require much evidence to remove — that the conductors of the periodical and standard literature of our country wish to have nothing to do with that large section of the community who have to toil, but in the shape of purchasers. The snarling answer of newspaper editors to their correspondents may be adduced as proof. How often does it appear that ingenuity has been stretched to find phrases that may aggravate and enrage, and lucky indeed is the individual who escapes betimes under the deep silence of sovereign contempt, and that, too, by journals that profess the most catholic spirit, that pretend to scorn everything selfish and sectarian, and which were called into existence to defend the many from the tyranny, contempt, and arrogance of the few. 'Not accepted', 'declined', 'rather unequal' are refined negatives, and always remind us of the look of a coy maiden, not actually pert, but well calculated to inform a lover of ordinary shrewdness that his addresses are not desired.

The desire of appearing in print is replete with difficulties to the candid and ardent mind. Repulsed on all hands, and sometimes treated as a dreaming enthusiast, he has often to explain the stanzas of a poem to a careless patron, or, it may be, show the sections of an essay to the gratification of idle curiosity, with the view of honeying down a name to a subscription list. This alternative must be gall and bitterness to a sensitive temperament. The walks of genius are often strange and eccentric to the eye of the world. It must be so. Beings that are so constituted that every sigh of the wind, every rustle of the forest, every glance of sunshine, produces a train of sensation altogether unknown to the sneering though successful worldling; — such beings must feel terribly the effects of disappointment, and the bitterness of reproach. No wonder, then, that suffering from these evils, they have sometimes adopted consolations, false in their nature, and having a tendency to render them ridiculous in the estimation of those who regulate their conduct by the more frigid and severe rules of morality.

If we were to continue our remarks on the subject, we might quote the earlier history of Burns, of the Ettrick Shepherd, and a host of others, who have 'Piped the tender notes of love'. They overcame difficulties of no common kind, and their experience shows to the world how hard it is to climb the heights that lead to fame. Some circumstances, it must be acknowledged, are favourable to appearing in print, and ought not to be overlooked. A political crisis may produce a pamphlet — a ludicrous rencontre in rural life may give birth to a satire; but he who has not friends, no influence, and no patronage, must, to appear in print, have great talents, prudence, and address!

Charles Kingsley
ALTON LOCKE (1850)

The importance of the self-taught poet as an image for various processes of class definition in mid-Victorian Britain was quickly apparent to the observant eye of Charles Kingsley, and his novel *Alton Locke* appeared anonymously in 1850 (2 vols.) with a revealing sub-title 'Tailor and Poet'. The use of the self-taught, thoughtful artisan as a centre of fictional consciousness was central to the genre of socially concerned fiction — Felix Holt and Jude Fawley come instantly to mind. *Alton Locke* was Kingsley's first novel, and cannot be called a fictional success. It does, however, contain many passages of indignant power which show an extraordinarily perceptive and sympathetic grasp of the social difficulties of educated artisans. In the following passage, which is strikingly similar to Fleming's essay, Kingsley demonstrates that 'movement of sympathy' which was so central to Victorian literary intentions. The first person narrative gives added bite to Kingsley's brilliant recognition of the way in which bourgeois values impinge on artisan literary aspirations.

(from chapter IX)

. . . and such with me were the two years that followed. I thought — I talked poetry to myself all day long. I wrote nightly on my return from work. I am astonished, on looking back, at the variety and quantity of my productions during that short time. My subjects were intentionally and professedly cockney ones. . . . I had made up my mind, that if I had any poetic power, I must do my duty therewith in that station of life to which it had pleased God to call me, and look at everything simply and faithfully as a London artisan. To this, I suppose, is to be attributed the little geniality and originality for which the public have kindly praised my verses — a geniality which sprung, not from the atmosphere whence I drew, but from the honesty and single-mindedness with which, I hope, I laboured . . .

. . . However, *aestro percitus*, I wrote on; and in about two years and a half had got together 'Songs of the Highways' enough to fill a small octavo volume, the circumstances of whose birth shall be given hereafter. Whether I ever attained to anything like the original style, readers must judge for themselves — the readers of the same volume I mean, for I have inserted none of those poems in this my autobiography; first, because it seems too like puffing my own works; and next, because I do not want to injure the as yet not over great sale of the same. . . .

(from chapter XVIII)

. . . He (the Dean) had heard from his publisher, and read his letter to me. 'The poems were on the whole much liked. The most satisfactory method of publishing for all parties, would be by procuring so many subscribers, each agreeing to take so many copies. In consideration of the Dean's known literary judgement and great influence, the publisher would, as a private favour, not object to take the risk of any further expenses.'

So far everything sounded charming. The method was not a very independent one, but it was the only one; and I should actually have the delight of having published a volume. But, alas! 'he thought that the sale of the book might be greatly facilitated, if certain passages of a strong political tendency were omitted. He did not wish personally

335

to object to them as statements of facts, or to the pictorial vigour with which they were expressed; but he thought that they were somewhat too strong for the present state of the public taste; and though he should be the last to allow any private considerations to influence his weak patronage of rising talent, yet, considering his present connection, he should hardly wish to take on himself the responsibility of publishing such passages, unless with great modifications.'

'You see,' said the good old man, 'the opinion of respectable practical men, who know the world, exactly coincides with mine. I did not like to tell you that I could not help in the publication of your MSS. in their present state; but I am sure from the modesty and gentleness which I have remarked in you, your readiness to listen to reason, and your pleasing freedom from all violence and coarseness in expressing your opinion, that you will not object to so exceedingly reasonable a request, which, after all, is only for your good. Ah! young man,' he went on, in a more feeling tone than I had yet heard from him, 'if you were once embroiled in that political world, of which you know so little, you would soon be crying like David, "Oh that I had wings like a dove, then I would flee away and be at rest!" Do you fancy that you can alter a fallen world? What it is, it always has been, and will be to the end. Every age has its political and social nostrums, my dear young man, and fancies them infallible; and the next generation arises to curse them as failures in practice, and superstitious in theory, and try some new nostrum of its own.'

. . . 'Or, if you must be a poet, why not sing of nature, and leave those to sing of political squabbles, who have no eye for the beauty of her repose? How few great poets have been politicians!'

I gently suggested Milton.

'Ay! he became a great poet only when he had deserted politics, because they had deserted him. In blindness and poverty, in the utter failure of all his national theories, he wrote the works which have made him immortal. Was Shakespeare a politician? or any one of the great poets who have arisen during the last thirty years? Have they all not seemed to consider it a sacred duty to keep themselves, as far as they could, out of the party strife?'

I quoted Southey, Shelley, and Burns, as instances to the contrary; but his induction was completed already, to his own satisfaction.

'Poor dear Southey was a great verse-maker, rather than a great poet; I always consider that his party-prejudice and party-writing narrowed and harshened a mind which ought to have been flowing forth freely and lovingly towards all forms of life. And as for Shelley and Burns, their politics dictated to them at once the worst portions of their poetry and of their practice. Shelley, what little I have read of him, only seems himself when he forgets radicalism for nature; and you would not set Burns's life or death, either, as a model for imitation in any class. Now, do you know, I must ask you to leave me a little. I am somewhat fatigued with this long discussion' (in which, certainly, I had borne no great share) 'and I am sure, that after all I have said, you will see the propriety of acceding to the publisher's advice. Go and think over it, and let me have your answer by post time.'

I did go and think it over — too long for my good. If I had acted on the first impulse I should have been safe. These passages were the very pith and marrow of the poems. They were the very words which I had felt it my duty, my glory, to utter. I, who had been a working man, who had experienced all their sorrows and temptations — I, who seemed called by every circumstance of my life to preach their cause, to expose their wrongs — I, to squash my convictions, to stultify my book for the sake of popularity, money, patronage . . . In short, between 'perhaps' and 'mights' I fell — a very deep, real, damnable fall, and consented to emasculate my poems, and become a flunkey and a dastard.

Elijah Ridings
THE POET'S DREAM (1853)

Elijah Ridings's curious little book might more accurately be called 'The Artisan Poet's Nightmare'. A Manchester imitation of Dickens's Christmas books, and originally written for the Sun Inn group of poets, Ridings replaces Scrooge's redeeming nightmares with a young self-taught writer's dream of lack of recognition, rejection, and hardship. At the end of the book, the writer awakes to find all is well, but the main aim of the book is to provide an appalling compendium of literary hazards which lie in wait for unsuccessful writers.

At this moment a knock was heard at the door, which the mother hastened to answer.

337

'Does one Mr Heatherden live here, ma'am?' asked a man in a very gruff voice.

'I ken he does, my man,' replied the poor woman. 'What's your will?'

'A parcel from Messrs Collins and Cross. No answer, ma'am.'

Mrs Heatherden took the parcel with a sigh, guessing well at once its meaning, and handed it to her son.

Robert, who had raised himself on the bed on hearing the enquiry, now sat upright, and seizing the packet with avidity, hastily broke it open, and taking a letter from the interior, hurriedly perused it; then turning frantically to his parent, asked her, as the letter fell from his grasp —

'Mother, am I "presumptive"? But they say I am, and therefore I must be. They tell me my lines "want strength, and are too rugged and unpolished". The fools!'

'Rob!' exclaimed Mrs Heatherden, in a reproving tone.

'Mother, I have no patience to see Ignorance hold up its head in judgment; for that it is so, here is the key to criticism,' snatching up the letter. 'They tell me, as I "am too poor to publish my poems on my own account, they would recommend me to try someone else, or see if they could not be done by commission, or otherwise obtain for them a list sufficient to guarantee them from loss." Oh the miserable serpents! that would fatten on a poor soul like me! But I must away — try someone else I will!'

John Critchley Prince
PREFACES AND LETTERS (1841–57)

The Lancashire reed-maker John Critchley Prince is an interesting writer largely because of the intense typicality of his career: his life and works provide almost a paradigm for the conflicting aims and pressures in self-taught writing. His career went through a number of phrases — membership of a local bardic group, recipient of generous patronage, professional writer with metropolitan connections, and finally a desperate struggle to sustain himself by local sales and the charity of neighbours. Prince clearly over-rated both his own talent and the financial value of his poetry, although his illusions were sustained by the encouragement of others. The following documents offer glimpses of Prince's literary career and its social relationships.

A. suggests the pressure put on a poet by dependence on patronage. B. shows the overt encouragement, but privately-held low regard, which often typified metropolitan responses to artisan writing. C. suggests Prince partially rejecting his hard-won metropolitan connections in an attempt to re-establish his local loyalties, while D. points to Prince's tragic incapacity to turn his poetry into a saleable commodity, even through a return to eighteenth-century modes of literary production and distribution.

A. Preface to the Second Edition of *Hours With The Muses* (1841)

The publication of a *Second Edition* of 'Hours With the Muses' affords the Author an opportunity to tender, in a more formal and express manner than he has been hitherto enabled to adopt, his grateful acknowledgements for the extraordinary interest which has been manifested, and the efforts which have been made, on his behalf, since the appearance of the first edition of his Poems. That this gratifying circumstance is, in any material degree, attributable to the merits of the Poems themselves, the Author certainly has not the vanity to imagine: rather he ascribes it — as being more consonant with his feelings — to the design which he trusts is obvious in the principal Poems, — that of advocating the rights, and elevating the tastes and pursuits, of his labouring fellow countrymen; and to a generous desire, on the part of the public, to aid the Author in these struggles with poverty and its many attendant evils, which have so far been his portion through life. . . .

Having now discharged, though imperfectly, a most pleasing debt of gratitude, the Author begs to refer briefly to the circumstances of the publication. Fearful of incurring a responsibility which he was by no means able to bear, and not having the slightest anticipation of the success with which his efforts have — owing to the causes already alluded to — since been attended, he limited the impression of the first edition to almost the precise number of subscribers which was obtained at the time the first sheets were put to the press. By the efforts of kind friends, however, such a further addition of subscribers was obtained in the course of the printing of the volume, that upon its issue, the impression was found to fall short of the subscription list, by upwards of *three hundred copies*. The list was further increased after the publication to such an extent, that the Author was soon placed in a position to require another and much larger edition; and, further, was as speedily relieved, by the generous zeal of friends, from the anxiety attendant upon a speculation so far beyond his own pecuniary means.

A careful perusal of the Poems in print, (after the excitement of their composition was over), and the suggestions of friends, soon made the Author aware that there were some passages therein, in which the forms of expression adopted might warrant an interpretation far different from that which he intended. These passages have been strictly revised, so as to obviate the objections to which they were fairly liable. Several stanzas have been added to 'The Poet's Sabbath'; and many additional Poems, including some of the longest in the collection, appear in this edition . . .

With these remarks and a renewal of his grateful acknowledgements, the Author respectfully takes his leave. It may be many years ere he meets his kind friends again in the character of an Author; but however his future lot be cast, he can never revert to the circumstances upon which he has now been dwelling without feelings of the most heartfelt gratitude.

B. Charles Dickens to J. C. Prince, 2 November 1843

The Pilgrim Edition of *The Letters of Charles Dickens* (ed. M. House, G. Storey, and K. Tillotson, Oxford, 1974), III, 592.

Dear Sir,

I regret too, I assure you, that we had not the pleasure of a longer conversation when we became known to each other at Manchester.

I should say that the chances of your being able to connect yourself with a London Magazine as a paid contributor, were very good. I would recommend you to send one or two pieces, with a short note, to the Editor of Blackwood's Magazine; and one or two to Mr. Ainsworth for insertion in *his* Magazine. That gentleman is a native of Manchester, and very likely, I think to be interested in you. If Blackwoods say No, try if Tait will say Yes.

My Dear Sir / Faithfully Yours
Charles Dickens

P.S. I have no connection with any magazine myself, or I would gladly assist you.

C. Preface to the Fourth Edition of *Hours With the Muses*, 1847
(People's Edition, London, Simpkin Marshall;
Ashton-under-Lyne, Williamson)

In the year 1841 this little work was put forth by the Author with fear and trembling, with uncertainty as to its fitness for the public eye. It is gratifying to remember, that its appearance attracted immediate attention in the neighbourhood of its publication. Warmly commended by a few generous and intellectual friends, and encouragingly noticed by the public journals, both in this country and in America, it gained a popularity which far exceeded its Author's expectations. Not the least flattering of its results, are, the kindly aid and goodwill which have been extended to him, by gentlemen whose rank, benevolence, and genius, have given them an elevated and influential position in society. A combination of these favourable circumstances, perhaps, rather than any commanding merit in the Author's effusions, has brought the work to a *Fourth Edition*.

Nearly all the poems contained in the volume were written for, and addressed to, the humble and industrious classes: but the price of the former impressions being beyond their means of purchase, a neat edition for the people has been projected and ventured upon at a large cost, and at the smallest remunerative price, in the hope and desire that it may be widely diffused among that class to which the Author belongs, that peaceful order of workers and readers, whose wishes prompt them to solace and cultivate their minds by such productions as win by their truthfulness, yet endanger not by their harshness of language, or their violence of thought.

The work has been carefully and conscientiously revised, and for some verses of a trifling and unimportant character, most of them the Author's boyish efforts, have been substituted poems never before published, which, it is hoped will be found an acceptable feature in the edition.

In conclusion; that the ensuing pages, read by the evening fire of the industrious artisan, to a friend, to a wife, a child, may have some effect in awakening thought in the thoughtless, arousing the listless to useful action, steadying the restless, reforming the rude, solacing the sad, inspiring with hope and endeavour the desponding, or in any way dropping a flower, or shedding a gleam of light, on the poor man's heart and hearth, is the sincere wish of their friend and brother,

The Author

Henry Square, Ashton–Under–Lyne
    January 1, 1847.

D. Unpublished Letters between J. C. Prince and G. Booth, printer, Ashton–Under–Lyne (now in the possession of Surridge Dawson Ltd, Manchester).

4 Jan. [1857]

I have had very bad luck these few weeks past. Some difficulties have come suddenly upon me, and I have not been able to send for any books, or I could have removed some of the difficulties.

If you could let me have 20 more copies to make a start with I might manage shortly to make all things satisfactory both to you and myself. Is there any thing I can write for you for those 20 copies? Please drop me a line.

I send you another poem. I hope you found the other.

7 Jan. [1857]

I really cannot part with the copyright of 'Autumn Leaves' at present. I have lost all command over the other, and I must have something out of this, by hook or by crook. Please to give my daughter 6 copies, for which she will pay you. I decidedly think that they ought to be something less a copy, being not gilt, and worse bound than the other. They ought to be only 1/- a copy.

I will send you a small sum shortly towards the debt.

22 Jan. [1857]

I will part with the entire copyright of 'Autumn Leaves' on the following terms, and if you agree I will add a new poem or two.

1st Give me 60 copies of 'Autumn Leaves' on signing the agreement.
2nd Let me have the remaining number at ⅓ a copy, as usual, all future editions to be entirely your own.
3rd Let what I owe you be paid by instalments, the first instalment to be paid on Saturday, the last of this month, and so on weekly till the whole be paid. If you will agree to this, please draw up a paper, and I will send for it tomorrow forenoon (Friday) will sign it, and send it

back in the evening, when you will send the books by the bearer. I cannot leave the house; I am in a difficulty.
The engraver of my portrait has not caught the correct expression at all.

26 Jan. [1857]
I propose to pay Mr. George Booth, of Hyde, the debt I owe him, by instalments of 5/- a week (and more if possible), weekly and every week, till the whole is discharged, commencing on the 7th March 1857
When I get work, which I expect will be soon, I will make a point of paying 10/- a week.

3 Feb. 1857
I beg you will let me have a few books to go on with, say 7 copies, and deduct them when I receive the others. I am quite fast for necessities.
If the stamped paper is ready send it, and I will sign and return it. I cannot come over myself, as my shoes are worn out, and I have no means of getting them mended. I will muster up what notices of my books I can, and send them along with the agreement.
Do not refuse me a few copies I beseech you
['Lent 6' is added in ink]

25 Feb. 1857
Received from Mr. George Booth printer and bookseller, Hyde, 240 copies of Autumn Leaves as payment for all and every parts of the copyrights and privileges of the 4 books entitled Hours With the Muses, Dreams and Realities, Poetic Rosary, and Autumn Leaves, as witness my hand
John Critchley Prince.

Charles Street,
Ashton, 9 April [1857]
Dear Sir
I want you to do me a favour, which if you will grant I will not ask another. I wish you to let me have 10 copies of 'Autumn Leaves', which I will pay you for on or before Saturday week, April 18th. You shall certainly be paid for them on or before that time. Please to send them to my mother's at Hyde; for I shall be there by tomorrow

at noon. Do please send them, never mind its being Good Friday. Do me this favour and I will return the kindness in any way I can.

I am not yet in work, I fancy I see a brighter prospect before me. A gentleman of this town has taken me under his wing. He has considerable influence, and I doubt not, that with prudence on my part, good will soon result to me. I have written a poetical address for him and his party, and it will be read at a Tea Party on Easter Monday. The Bishop of Manchester is expected to be in the chair. I am also requested to be present, which I intend. Please to let this be private and confidential between you and me, as I want to try my best to bring about a good result.

Please not to fail sending the parcel to my mother's as soon as you have read this note. I trust to be able to pay off all arrears within a short time. Enclose a copy of your Herald. I will write something original for it.

Yours respectfully,
J. C. Prince

William Heaton
A SKETCH OF THE AUTHOR'S LIFE
Written at the request of a number of his friends

Preface to *The Old Soldier* (London, 1857)

The study of working-class autobiography has been an essential element in the recent historiography of early Victorian culture and class development. It is not my intention to use a great deal of the autobiographical material found as Prefaces, Introductory Essays, or integral elements of volumes of poetry in this anthology, except where it offers particular insight into the nature of literary production. None the less, as the previous chapter has illustrated, the perception by contemporaries of self-taught writers could never separate out their lifes, and what they meant as evidence of cultural change and class development, from their actual writings. A clear discussion of William Heaton, a handloom weaver from Luddenden Foot who later worked in a Halifax carpet factory, can be found in David Vincent's study of working-class autobiographies (*Bread, Knowledge, and Freedom*, 1981) which also provides a detailed bibliography including the autobiographies of many self-taught poets. Heaton's

account of his literary life, by turns rueful and assertive, offers a
compendious version of many other similar prefatory essays, and
offers an interesting comparison with Thomas Ince's essay in a similar
genre which appears on p. 271.

On the 26th September, 1837, I married Elizabeth, the widow of
John Gaukrodger, my present wife. Soon after my marriage, I sold
all my specimens of natural history, and began to write poetry with
redoubled energy. Poem after poem was written and placed with the
old ones; but never thinking of them being printed. At length I was
requested to send one to the *Halifax Guardian*, which I did, but
without success. It is true, it was mentioned in the 'Notice to
Correspondents,' but nothing more. I sent one soon after to the
Leeds Times, but with no better success; still, in this manner I sent
upwards of thirty poems to different papers, and received nothing in
return but abuse.

My wife, one day, when about to clean the house, asked me
where she must put my roll of poems; I told her to put them on the
fire, which she did. Thus perished all my early productions, and I
resolved never to write another verse. This resolution, I kept,
however, but a short time; something seemed to urge me to try
again so repeatedly that I thought I would. Accordingly, in 1842, I
wrote the 'Widow and her Child;' besides several other pieces; and a
little previous to Whitsuntide, 1844, I wrote 'Lines of Ancient
Forestry,' which I had printed, and of which I sold upwards of 500
copies in less than four weeks. I then wrote to different papers, but
with no better success than before. I met with nothing but rebuffs
and ungentlemanly conduct from the hirelings of the press. At last, I
wrote to the editor of the *Leeds Times*, who sent me a lengthy letter,
abusing me for my ignorance of grammar, a science I never had the
opportunity of studying. This so discouraged me, that I was about
to give it all up again, but it was of no use, the magic words, 'Try
again,' kept sounding in my ears, and on the 24th of May, 1845, my
first poem, with the exception of 'Lines on Ancient Forestry,'
appeared in print, in the *Leeds Intelligencer*, entitled 'I Love to Walk in
the Twilight Grey'. How often and eagerly have I examined the
papers, after I had sent one for insertion, but to no purpose. Judge
then of my delight, the first time I was so gratified. I read it, rubbed
my eyes and read it again, as if afraid there might be some delusion in
it; but, no! it was there, together with my name and place of abode.

In a few weeks I had had six pieces inserted in that paper, for which I shall ever feel grateful. These were mostly transferred to other periodicals, thus attracting the attention of the Rev. James Nelson, Incumbent of Luddenden, and other influential gentlemen in the neighbourhood, who, on looking over the manuscripts in my possession, wished me to publish a volume by subscription, which I at last agreed to do. I wrote to Lord Morpeth, now Earl of Carlisle, who sent me his name for four copies, and also to George Lane Fox, Esq., of Bramham Park, (since deceased) who kindly sent me his name for eight copies.

Thus encouraged, I set about getting more subscribers, and completing pieces that were partly written; and in the month of December, 1847, I published the 'Flowers of Calderdale'. (A few copies still remain on hand, and may be had of the Author, 37, Green Lane, Halifax. Price 2s.) When I came to deliver them I found ninety-five of the subscribers, on whom I had relied, declined taking the copies, which caused me to have a number left on my hands. This made me rather regret that I had written them, but it was no use. As soon as I had finished one piece another was begun, till at length my friends wished me to publish another volume which I now present to the public.

Often, when all around me have been asleep, have I invoked my muse, till my pen has fallen from my powerless hand, and tired nature has found refuge in balmy sleep.

Many of the short pieces in this work have been carefully examined by a gentleman, in every way qualified to understand them . . .

My products have found their way to distant lands; and some have been pleased with their simple and melodious strains; yet it has not added one comfort to my fireside, nor put one guinea in my pocket; but I have climbed to the top of the Parnassian Mountains, and have gazed in rapture on the wonderful, the sublime, and the beautiful, until, wrapped in deep meditation, I have sung my feeble and unadulterated strains to tunes of my own composition. This has not been achieved by college learning, for I have had none; nor yet by my own acquirements, but by the gift of Him who says that a sparrow shall not fall to the ground without His knowledge; if it was not so, why should I have more exalted tastes than those around me of my own station, or why should I feel a pleasure in spending every leisure hour away from the gay thoughtless world, who dance away their short life among the glittering sunbeams of pleasure? And

346

when they have closed their earthly career, leave not a single stone to tell of their departure. Surely, this dower was given me for some wise and good purpose, over which I have no control, urges me onward, and points me to joys which to sordid minds are unknown. . . .

If these my humble endeavours should gratify my friends, or tend to raise the class to which I belong, I shall be well repaid; if not, I have toiled in vain, and have lived till my fifty-third year, without a shilling to call my own, or a strip of land to rest my weary foot on.

W. Dearden
ADVERTISEMENT to the Fourth Edition of The Poems of John Nicholson

London and Bingley, 1859.

The difficulties of appearing in print often had to do with the well-meaning attention of literary sponsors from the middle classes, who were prone to tidying, refining, and rewriting the texts of the authors that they were bringing to public attention. Often such attention resulted in a loss in distinctiveness or verbal energy in the poems concerned, although there can be little doubt that on many other occasions self-taught poets needed all the technical help they could get. The following passage by the editor of Nicholson's poems reveals many of these tensions. The process of editorial control is clearly laid out, as well as the assumptions on which such 'polite refinements' were undertaken. Dearden's vocabulary — 'benevolent', 'refined', 'respectable', and 'polished' — deadens where it should celebrate, so that the reader is left wondering whether Nicholson's poems are worth this editorial effort at all.

A poet from among the ranks of the people, to gain 'a fit audience' at the present day, must possess higher qualifications than were expected from one of his grade some twenty or thirty years ago, — so refined, since then, has become the taste of all lovers of poetic literature. He must not only possess the soul of poetry, but, as his name implies, he must be able to *create* for it a form of expression through which it may 'breathe and burn'. That John Nicholson had the poetic element in no ordinary degree, few will deny; but that he did not always

347

embody his thoughts in the most coherent and intelligible diction, every reader of discernment will be free to acknowledge. This fault, which a benevolent criticism might attribute to defective education, would, on that score, have been venial, were it not asserted by those who knew him best, that he was deaf to any suggested improvements in his lines, from whatever quarter they might emanate. 'What I have written I have written, and it shall stand' he was wont to say with the air of one who understood the divine right of kings. This conduct, to say the least of it, was very unwise; and it has necessitated a revision of his poems, in which, where practicable, such emendations have been made, and such only, as would render the ideas more intelligible and agreeable to readers of refined taste. It is but right to state, that the three leading poems in this collection had passed through the press before the writer of this article undertook the responsibility of revision.

To endeavour to anticipate criticism by making alterations in a work that has long been in the hands of the public, by whom its excellencies and its defects have been more or less canvassed, would be a perilous undertaking. Few readers like to see a poem or a story changed into a form different from that in which it originally won their attention and regard, merely to gratify a critical taste. No such liberties have been taken with Nicholson's productions. The reader will find every incident with which he has been familiar, and the vraisemblance of every idea, faithfully preserved. In short, he will meet with the poet, in this edition, identically the same as he has met with him before, though somewhat, perhaps, more respectable in appearance, and more polished in address.

Thomas Ince
INTRODUCTORY PREFACE

to *Beggar Manuscripts* (Blackburn, 1888)

Ince's spirited Preface, with its direct attack on the public attitude towards poets from humble backgrounds, makes an interesting contrast with the wry and self-conscious assertions of Heaton or the self-abasement of Prince. The confidence of Ince's challenge is not, unfortunately, sustained by his poetic skills, but even if his appeal to

posthumous fame is not relevant in his case, his forthright sense of
public indifference still carries some of its original sting.

In presenting this work to the reader, I venture to avail myself of the
liberty of offering a few remarks which to my mind appear very
applicable in this connection. I refer to the extreme difficulty which
bars the way to success against any humble aspirant to literary fame,
who may have had, like myself, to fight against adversity from his
youth up. I make no pretentions above my deserts, but I cannot
refrain from thinking that the subscribers to this volume attach
some little merit to my endeavours, and in justice to them I feel
called upon to protect against the principle which prevents many
capable but indigent writers from receiving encouragement for
meritorious work. I know my own shortcomings too well — a
neglected education and unfortunate surroundings have turned me
out as I am, in truth, an unfinished article; but there have been, and
are still, many worthier devotees to what was and is to them — and
to myself — a noble attainment and a labour of love. The converting
of genius or talent, by any process whatsoever, into hackneyed
effort, is disastrous to a people's well-being; but when instances of
this kind are continually occurring the blighted hopes and broken
hearts are peculiar spoils of genius, then, I say, that the charge is an
unfounded one. All that is truest and best in our national instincts —
all that is dearest and most refined in our private sentiments — are
embodied in the lives of those unlucky beings, whose hearts have
warmed with the honest fervour of literary ambition, but have been
in the very budding of their genius ruthlessly despoiled by cynical,
cold, and cutting neglect. Amongst local writers who have suffered
in this respect may be mentioned Wilton, Nicholson, and Prince. I
care nothing for the note of admiration for life services when the
author has departed hence, and gone beyond all worldly needs; for
nothing can compare creditably one tittle with the evidence of the
hand and brain of departed worth. Poets and writers there have also
been of immortal fame, who during life had to battle with the pangs
of hunger and remorse, aided considerably by the neglect of a selfish
world, but whose life-work has since been used as foundations for
the upraising of immense fortunes to speculators and strangers to
the family. My simple, earnest wish, is then, to infuse, if possible,
by my humble efforts, something more of love into the relationships
of humankind. The harshness of tutelage may occasion grief — the

venom of jealousy may beget ill-will — the spleen of rivalry may encourage strife — but my desire is to inspire friendship. In the Spirit of Love I offer the Book, free from egotism I yield it, contented to abide by your verdict. If, when that verdict be given, I shall have succeeded in inspiring a truer manliness of feeling for others who choose to tread the better track of literature, then I know that I shall feel over a thousand times repaid for any infliction which follows. The more than tinge of melancholy which pervades many of the selections, will, I trust, be excused to a certain extent, for I may in extenuation plead that a man can scarcely be expected to smile whose heart is torn and bleeding.

UNPUBLISHED LETTERS TO EDWIN WAUGH

From the papers of the Lancashire Dialect Society, now in
Manchester Public Library.

Viewed from literary London, Edwin Waugh must have seemed a marginally successful regional writer who had slowly built a market in his own region. Yet if Waugh seemed small enough beer, the following letters show how avidly he was looked up to by even more obscure figures whose literary ambition outstripped their capacity to publish or market their work. Writers like the Barons and 'Aston Clair' speak from the most localized and hopeless corners of literary endeavour. Yet both the Barons did manage to publish volumes and even to enjoy some kind of local literary reputation extensive enough to ensure their place in George Hull's *Poets and Poetry of Blackburn* (Blackburn, 1908). Hull's anthology is typical of many such local celebrations of regional literary life. The irony of these appeals to Waugh, as a local literary lion, is that at the end of his own career Waugh was forced back on pensions and donations. Even his impressive ability to work his copyrights on the local literary market place and to sustain interest in his work through readings, recitals, and lectures, could not ensure that he maintained an adequate income throughout his career.

Manchester, Aug. 28th 1885

Sir,
    Being an utter stranger to you, & without the slightest claim on your sympathy save such as the general spirit of your writings might

warrant me advancing, I trust, as a Manchester man, I take no undue liberty in allowing myself to send a copy of my maiden venture in poetry to one to whom Manchester deservedly points as her representative poet.

I need scarcely say that it is the work of youth, and as such will doubtless discover many instances of immature and extravagant thought to one of your experience: nevertheless I would fain believe my motive for writing is something more than a mere 'Cacoethes scribendi' and that the fear I so often entertain of falling short of the mark I seek to attain, or debasing the noble art to which I would gladly devote my life, are to some little extent groundless. 'Deliver me from my friends and myself' is my daily prayer.

Should I meet with favour at your hands I should feel deeply bounden to you: should it, on the contrary, encroach in any manner upon your time or otherwise be inconvenient, kindly accept the apologies of

Yours very respectfully,
Aston Clair

N.B. My real name is John McClair Boraston but as my volume has already cost me one situation on account of my name having been divulged to my employer I need hardly say I would wish it kept quiet. Please address Hampton Terrace Steven St. Edge Lane Stretford.

1 Edgeware Road, Blackburn, 22 November 1888

Dear Mr Waugh,

I send you by this post the 'Blackburn Pieces' for the last four weeks commencing the first 4 instalments of my 'Blegburn Dick-Shonary' — Perhaps you will let me have your opinion of it, and if you think a 'Lankysher Dickshonary' on same principle would take, with a little philology thrown in. . . . . In the papers I send you you will observe some 'Dialect Rhymes' by Jack O' Arms: he is brother to William Baron (Bill o' Jacks) & is at present out of work. He has written about 110 poems in consecutive weeks, and for *decent* remuneration he would write much better. Can you do anything for him in the way of a letter of introduction to a Manchester paper. If so I shall be very glad — and especially if you could shove me in as well.

Perhaps you have seen notice of me in 'North Country Poets' for this month; if I got on a good paper I could write verse or prose, stories or humorous. You have spoken of several of my poems &c very highly and urged me to try to get on good magazines, but I find that a shove is wanted. Will you do your best to give me and my friend a 'leg up'? Perhaps a little word from a man of your position will do great good — Trusting to hear from you soon, & that your scotch tour did you good.

believe me
Yours faithfully
Jos. Baron

68 Griffin Street, Blackburn, March 2nd, 1889
Dear Sir,

Accept my heartiest & most cordial thanks for your kindness in sending the portrait of your dear self with which I am indeed pleased. Rest assured it will always be treasured for its giver's sake. Your remarks on 'Art and Song' are very encouraging, & I will endeavour to carry out your advice. I could send you a batch of my printed verses for perusal but refrain from boring you with them, unless you desire me. All my rhymic work was done in the scanty leisure that is mine after heavy and laborious work in an iron foundry. My younger brother ('Bill o' Jacks') honoured himself & our town by dedicating his 'Bits o' Broad Lancashire' to you, which dedication you so kindly accepted.

Rumour whispers that you are now engaged upon a new volume of poems. Is it true? I hope so. When will they probably appear? Anything from your pen is highly relished by 'gradely Lancashire' foak and ther greedy; for when they getten a good feeast, ther nod content, especially if its o' thy mekken but like Oliver Twist, ther o agin axin for mooar!

Hoping that your health is all that you desire & with best wishes & renewed thanks

I remain yours sincerely
John T. Baron

Chapter Six

THE DEFENCE OF THE DIALECT

A child handloom weaver

Martha Vicinus called her chapter on dialect writing in *The Industrial Muse* 'An Appropriate Voice', and, even if an implicit question mark is added to this title, the chapter conveys a deliberate sense of dialect writing as the most important literary context in which the working classes talked to each other and reflected back their own concerns and ideologies. The other main recent critical work on dialect writing in the industrial cities, Brian Hollingworth's *Songs of the People* (Manchester, 1977), also stresses both the link between dialect writing and the working classes and the traditional and oral nature of much dialect writing. The major critical orthodoxy in the study of nineteenth century working class literature seems to be that of the 'authenticity' of dialect as an accurate representation of the values and insights of working-class communities: that is, it is widely viewed as a direct expressive medium for industrial working class culture. While there is some substance in this view, I think that there is a need for considerable caution in accepting the view of dialect writing as an authentic and representative working-class discourse.

Dialect writing quickly became a literary convention. To be sure much dialect writing was intended to re-create the speech rhythms, inflections, and narrative methods of the speech of ordinary people, but even in the ballads and folk narratives, the development of consistent and widely used conventions in dialect writing was immediately apparent. Dialect writing came early to print, and the work of the mid-eighteenth-century writer John Collier ('Tim Bobbin') had quickly passed into communal awareness. Collier had only incidentally been a poet, but he had pioneered the notation of dialect as a literary language, and he had also established a number of stereotyped characters as dialect literary personae. By the 1830s and 1840s there was an acknowledged method of annotating dialect speech, used as confidently by Mrs Gaskell as by Edwin Waugh or Joshua Ramsbottom, a development which suggests the self-conscious nature of much dialect writing. Most dialect writers had in fact two languages — standard English and the dialect — and often moved between the two in the course of a single story. While such bi-lingualism had certain advantages, it increasingly led to the association of dialect with certain genres and literary modes (especially comic ones) and occasions. Although dialect, it can be argued, was pre-eminently an *oral* mode up to the 1860s at least, it also had a written circulation from a very early date, a circulation which attempted to exploit its oral characteristics. By 1860, however, the printed culture had largely ousted the oral one, and with the development of universal education and the growth of national mass communications, the oral vigour of dialect speech, if it had ever existed, became a literary and cultural myth, widely exploited by the growth of a local market for dialect writing and entertainment in the industrial cities. In the works of Edwin Waugh and Ben Brierley, the two great Lancashire entrepreneurs of dialect writing, the dialect became inextricably associated with a mythic version of the old 'organic' rural hand-loom weaving communities of the Pennines. Clearly, the relationship between dialect as 'real speech' and dialect as a literary convention is a complex one, and all I want to do here is to remind readers that the authenticity of dialect writing as direct expression of working class values has to be evaluated in terms of the literary conventions and traditions through which it is mediated.

One way in which the 'literariness' of dialect writing is apparent is obvious from the defences of dialect offered by such writers as Ramsbottom and Brierley. Such polemics always include references to standard English authors who wrote in dialect. Burns, Dickens, and Tennyson are persistently invoked as a justification for literary endeavours in the Northern dialects. Such a comparison shows the anxiety of dialect writers — there was no reason why dialect should not have a value of its own — but it also suggests the extent to which the literariness of dialect was a constant element in its perception by Northern writers. Dickens, Burns, and Tennyson all used dialect in a very self-conscious and deliberate way — in Tennyson's case more for rhythmic and musical purposes than for any intellectual or propagandist reason — and for specific literary effects. The whole point of the sophisticated literary use of dialect was to create an implicit or explicit contrast between standard English and dialect as expressive mediums. The aim of local and self-taught dialect writing was far more serious: to use dialect as a way of articulating values, concepts, and ideologies which were not available in standard English. The constant comparison of local dialect writing with

356

Burns in particular ultimately damaged the case for local writing, as it showed only the parochialism and unself-consciousness of much Lancashire and Yorkshire writing.

A further impulse towards literariness and away from orality in dialect writing was created by the middle class antiquarian interest in dialect. It was only late in the nineteenth century that the work of linguists like Max Müller gave theoretical justification for treating dialect as expressive and complex language on a par with standard English, hence making a previously antiquarian impulse to study dialect intellectually respectable. Indeed, the discovery of the evolution of languages, with its inevitable implicit assault on Greek and Latin as ideal languages, was almost as much of a shock to the Victorian mind as the evolutionary hypotheses of Darwin and others. The careful historical placing of dialect in the evolutionary processes of language, and the new high status given to variation and deviation in language as indication of growth, were not applied widely until the 1870s and 1880s, and were significant only to Barnes and Hopkins among the major Victorian poets. For the rest, medievalism and Italianate ornamentation remained the ideal, and dialect was only important for its picturesque variety and quaint inversions. The market for much dialect writing remained middle class and scholarly, among those squires and clergymen who were not afraid to admit an interest in vernacular culture and who maintained close ties with their local community. Evidence of the nature of the readership for dialect can be found in the various editions of the *Lancashire Songs* of Edwin Waugh. Widely circulated in penny pamphlets, sixpenny booklets, and reprinted in local papers, Waugh's work was also produced in an elaborate volume designed and printed at the leading London commercial printing house and available on subscription only. Harland's *Lancashire Lyrics — Modern*, too, was available in both a small and large paper edition, the latter limited to a hundred copies, and both were aimed at the libraries of local scholars and mill owners as a representative sample of local cultural progress. Of course it is not true to say that dialect writing had no popular readership, but it is important to stress that some of the factors which permitted the development of local dialect writing depended on a knowledge of literature and literary traditions outside the merely local or provincial. Dialect writing was in some respects

357

an aspect of literary trends and fashions throughout Britain as a whole. The market was a mixed one, and the literary conventions of dialect writing were closely related to bourgeois taste as well as to the oral and popular traditions of the industrial North.

At this point, one is entering a discussion of dialect writing and class. In many ways both dialect speech and dialect writing cut across specific class allegiances. Mill owners and navvies from the same area shared some similarities of speech and expression. I am not enough of a linguist to pursue this extremely important issue, but I think it necessary to note that dialect writing does reflect both this shared regional culture and the anxieties caused when regional allegiances cut across the wider issues raised by developing class consciousness. The movement between standard English and dialect characteristic of so many local writers reflects the contrary impulses of wanting to belong to a national culture without sacrificing local identity illustrated elsewhere in this anthology. The use, for example, of literary personae derived on the one hand from local myth and story and on the other from the European literary picaresque tradition shows the cultural ambiguity of dialect writing. Accordingly, even the most contentious critical issue concerning dialect writing — its apparent lack of political, radical, or oppositional social perspective — is not straightforward in its resolution. A certain populist idealism among contemporary scholars has led to many attempts to recognize the true voice of working-class opinion in dialect writing but the difficulty has always been to reconcile a belief in a radical, self-reliant, articulate proletariat with the quietist, domestic, and humorous modes of most dialect writing. Equally, the explanation of the nature of dialect writing which argues that the middle class controlled access to print with a thoroughness which precluded radical expression seems too simple an answer given the way in which the market for dialect literature developed. Dialect literature clearly does show the difficulties of locating ideologies through literary expression. Dialect writing is compounded out of a variety of social and literary traditions each of which is itself in complex relationship to ideas of class, and a proper study of the literary modes, language, and values of dialect writing has still to be undertaken.

It is not only for these reasons that I have chosen to exclude dialect poetry from this anthology as a distinct category. Many dialect poems will be found in their appropriate place among the more orthodox standard English writing in earlier chapters. Clearly, some dialect writing does exemplify aspects of 'self-taught' culture which are not well illustrated in standard English writing. None the less, I have retained standard English as an important defining characteristic of the writing I have chosen to discuss in this book, and I have assumed, crudely, but with the qualifications explained in chapter 3, that the aspiration towards standard English was one of the central endeavours of self-taught writers, in early Victorian England at least. Yet I have retained this section, which comprises extracts which illustrate how dialect was understood and discussed as a literary and cultural formation in the period between 1840 and 1900. The aim is to suggest the variety of approach, perhaps even confusion, which informed the defences of the dialect in the nineteenth century. It is interesting that contemporary criticism seems equally confused about the same issue.

Elizabeth Gaskell
NORTH AND SOUTH

London, 1854–55. Serialized in Charles Dickens's weekly
periodical *Household Words*. From chapter XXIX.

The following defence of dialect in terms of its expressivity in areas where standard English is inappropriate is an important foreshadowing of later, more extended, defences. Mrs Gaskell's refutation, through the narrative voice of Margaret Hale, of the charge of 'vulgarity' is part of the wider strategy of the novel in defining industrial culture not as worse than, but as different from, metropolitan society. Elsewhere, especially in *Mary Barton* (1848), Elizabeth Gaskell uses dialect speech and popular song to give authenticity to the surface texture of her accounts of working-class life in Manchester, drawing heavily on the scholarly interests of her husband William in the history and structure of the local dialects in Manchester.

'As you please. As Dixon pleases. But, Margaret, don't get to use these horrid Milton words. "Slack of work": it is a provincialism. What will Aunt Shaw say if she hears you use it on her return?'

'Oh, mamma! don't try and make a bugbear of Aunt Shaw,' said Margaret, laughing. 'Edith picked up all sorts of military slang from Captain Lennox, and Aunt Shaw never took any notice of it.'

'But yours is factory slang.'

'And if I live in a factory town, I must speak factory language when I want it. Why, mamma, I could astonish you with a great many words you never heard in your life. I don't believe you know what a knobstick is.'

'Not I, child. I only know it has a very vulgar sound; and I don't want to hear you using it.'

'Very well, dearest mother, I won't. Only I shall have to use a whole explanatory sentence instead . . .

'Mamma is accusing me of having picked up a great deal of vulgarity since we came to Milton.'

The 'vulgarity' Margaret spoke of referred purely to the use of local words, and the expression arose out of the conversation they had just been holding. But Mr Thornton's brow darkened; and Margaret suddenly felt how her speech might be understood by him; so, in the natural sweet desire to avoid giving unnecessary pain, she forced herself to go forwards with a little greeting, and continue what she was saying, addressing herself to him expressly.

'Now, Mr Thornton, though 'knobstick' has not a very pretty sound, is it not expressive? Could I do without it, in speaking of the thing it represents? If using local words is vulgar, I was very vulgar in the Forest — was I not, mamma?'

Ab O' th' Yate (Ben Brierley)
GOOSEGRAVE PENNY READINGS

c. 1865. First published in Manchester as a penny pamphlet and then widely reprinted in magazine and book form.

Ben Brierley (1825–1896) and Edwin Waugh (1817–1890) were the two most popular dialect authors of the late nineteenth century. Both turned from periodical and pamphlet writing to professional careers as lecturers and public entertainers in an attempt to exploit the orality and communality of dialect culture in Lancashire. Unfortunately, by 1860 print had already seriously weakened the strength of the dialect tradition, and dialect writing had in general become a homely and conventional expression of respectable working-class values. None the less, the strength of dialect writing lay in humour, and Brierley retained the ability to ridicule the pious hypocrisies of middle-class society. In this passage, basically in standard English, Brierley wittily attacks the cultural aspirations of Lancashire worthies towards a snobbish imitation of metropolitan culture. Brierley also offers an interesting description of the 'penny reading' as a form of social control.

It was time to commence proceedings. Rising like a tilted cask from his chair, the civic dignitary said —

'Ladies and Gentlemen, — On the occasion of inaugerating oor third session of penny readings, I wish it to be understood that waur gaun to be mair classical in oor selections of readings and music than we hae bin on either of the twa privous occasions. It has been remarked by many people that I hae met, that on the twa privous occasions we have had ower muckle o' the Lancashire dialect. Noo I must just tell ye that I am apoosed to a' dialucts, an mair especially the Lancasheere: an' by my ain adveighs the committee hae resoalved to have nae mair dialuctal readings given on this platform. Iverything must be in proaper Henglish, sic as is written by oor Scoatts, oor Burnses, an oor Shakspeares; mair parteclarly the first twa. The same spirit shall gueide us in the selection of the music, — nae 'Cam hame to thy childer an a'; nae 'The deil's i' this bonnet sae braw'; nor ither Lancasheere sangs o' the same ilk; but we'll hae sic classical sangs as —

> Doon i' the glen by the lown o' the trees
> Lies a weel-thecket bield, like a bike for the bees.

and

> I coft a stane o' haselock woo'
> To mak' a coat for John o' t.

(A voice — 'Dun yo' co that English?')

'We'll hae nae interrooption. The sangs are British classics an' every Briton ought to understand his ain language. (Another voice — 'Talk gradely, an' then we con understand yo'.') Weel, noo let this be understid, that if there be any mair interrooption the parties will be turned oot, as they deserve to be. D'ye understand me noo? The first part of the programme is an overture by Miss Macsarkin — the Edinbro' Quadrilles.'

His worship hereupon sat down amidst the applause of some, and strong expressions of disapprobation from others . . .

. . . It was all over. Nobody would sit on the platform after that ebullition of merriment, and we had 'God Save The Queen' at least an hour earlier than usual; but not before the rector had made the announcement that, through the behaviour of the cheaper portion of the audience, that would be the last penny reading that would ever be permitted to take place in the National School of 'Goosegrave-cum-Bumblethorpe'.

Thus was a cheap and wholesome kind of pastime brought to a close by the overweening priggishness of a class of people who refuse to attend popular entertainments, and by their non-support of such give up to the mercenary and licentious the charge of providing amusements for the multitude.

Joseph Ramsbottom
WRITING IN THE DIALECT

From *Country Words* (Manchester periodical) 15 December 1866, 104–105.

Like the Darwinian theories of biological evolution, Victorian study of language had important repercussions on intellectual life. The discovery of the Indo-European common root for many European languages gave status to what had previously been insignificant languages with negligible literary traditions. The recognition that languages 'evolved' also rendered spoken English — and hence dialect — central to the language. Defences of the dialect as a literary medium, especially among ordinary people, were thus given a new status furthered by the continuing interest of such poets as Hogg, Scott, Tennyson, Hardy, and Barnes. Celebration of the dialect as part of the English literary heritage began to appear widely in the periodical literature of the 1860s and 1870s — a typical example is J. W. Hales's 'English Dialects' in *Good Words* (1 August 1867, 557-561). Ramsbottom's cogent article is especially interesting as the author was himself an accomplished dialect writer whose volume *Phases of Distress* (Manchester 1864) had offered a working class perspective on the Cotton Famine. *Country Words* addressed both middle- and working-class readers and published, as well as Ramsbottom's verse, other articles on the evolution of dialect by 'Jonathan Oldbuck' (John Harland). Ramsbottom's defence of the dialect here is not in terms of its historical authenticity, however, but rather through its cultural value as an expressive medium for ordinary people.

There is a strong feeling, freely expressed, amongst a great body of educated people about us, that dialectal writing ought to be discountenanced. It is contended that all *good* things can be as well said, and with better effect, in pure English; that where it is most fitly introduced, it gives prominence chiefly to low tastes and worse desires, and, therefore, it is a waste of time to read it . . . we submit that there may be and are cases in which the dialect is an appropriate, if not the best form of language an author can use to say what he has got to say effectively. . . .

In almost every village there is a stock of well-known songs and stories in dialect, of various qualities, the best of which have seldom risen to the dignity of being printed, even on a broadsheet; yet they maintain their hold on the minds and in the hearts of our villagers, by whom the songs of our greatest singers are altogether uncared for, and almost unknown; and with whom even the popular street lyrics of our large towns obtain only a transient resting place before they pass away into obscurity. But our dialectal songs and stories present themselves in the old form, full of reminiscences of the olden time. The old expressions get ready access to the feelings, and find a permanent place in the heart and memory, with the cherished ones already existing. We do not know either, as someone has said, 'it is better to write the songs of the people than make the laws;' but we are strong believers in the power of songs for good and evil. And we have little doubt that the singer has greatest influence, and is most loved by the people, who, avoiding all elaborate forms of expression and high flights of sentiment, comes to them in their own simple way, and, with their own homely phrases, weaves his songs, as it were, with a musical thread into portions of their everyday life.

. . . None but those who have lived it, or lived with it, and are able to describe that which they have seen, can show us the life of an honest, striving poor man, with a large family and an aspiring soul. Among other things, this has yet to be done; and the dialect should enter largely into the means of doing it, in order that our poor brethren may feel its full force, and draw the encouragement they so much need from the contemplation of commendable examples of silent heroism.

The over-anxiety of our friends for the purity, strength, and beauty of the English language makes them unjust. For when they are frowning down the dialect; when they are attacking its use by open speech or covert sneer, or in any other way, they are literally 'stoning the prophets'. The custom of writing in local dialects is an old one; and the reason, perhaps, that we have more of it today than hitherto, is that there is more to be said of, and for, our country populations; that they have more to say for themselves; that the great and hitherto dumb portion of our brethren has found a voice; and, rude and uncouth though it be, it is better, rather than attempt to stifle that we should try to understand it. . . .

In conclusion let us say, that though we are at variance with our friends on this matter, we honour them for their love of the English tongue. Yet we regard it as no sickly nursling, requiring summer weather and tender care at their hands; but rather in the condition of rough, robust, and vigorous youth, fond of forcing its own way, and capable of fighting its own battles. Therefore is their immoderate zeal uncalled for. By its own innate strength it is spreading itself all over the earth, striking, as it were, deep root in every land. It will, doubtless, become the speech of millions to whom the existence of our dialects will never be known. Yet these dialects will continue to be written so long as they are spoken; and while their homely phrases are the substances of our children's songs, the echoes of our mothers' voices, shall they be welcomed to our lowly hearth.

Ben Brierley
THE LANCASHIRE DIALECT

From an editorial in *Ben Brierley's Journal* (Manchester), December 1871, 308.

The passages already cited from Brierley and Ramsbottom have touched upon the association in the middle-class mind between dialect culture and vulgarity. Such moral and social censure of local speech is met head on by Brierley in his own magazine, which was the most long-lasting and successful of the magazines published in Victorian Manchester. But in spite of his earlier attacks on the unjustified moral censure of dialect entertainments, and the dignity and good sense of Ramsbottom's article, Brierley here concedes the partial justice of such attacks, and chooses to defend the dialect as a morally refining force within local culture. The result is rather half-hearted, and Brierley, himself writing in standard English of editorial purity and refinement, seems anxiously uncertain of his readers' expectations and affiliations.

A correspondent has called our attention to an article which recently appeared in a local weekly contemporary, and which contains some rather severe strictures on what the writer is pleased to call the 'Lancashire Dialect'. As the circulation of the journal alluded to may not be such . . . as to carry its influence in quarters where it ought to be felt, we take the opportunity of giving a portion of the article . . .

In our opinion it behoves all classes in this great and important county to do all that they possibly can, both by example and precept, towards the abolition of a dialect as boorish and uncouth as can well be imagined. We have heard of, but have never been able to discover, an alleged beauty and rhythm about true 'Lancashire' which may indeed be perceptible to the native though it may be far beyond the ken of the uninitiated. There can be no good object to serve in thus keeping alive a mere relic of barbarism which sooner or later must disappear. They who use or encourage the use of Lancashire dialect are doing all in their power to perpetuate a system at variance with social, moral and political progress, though happily their opposition to the march of intellect is as futile in effect as it is mischievous in purpose. We hope yet to see the day when the 'Lancashire Dialect' will be a thing of the past, and when pure and refined English shall alone be spoken in the County Palatine.

We readily accord our concurrence in these remarks; and if the writer had watched the progress of the Journal, and understood the secret of its mission, he would have seen that we were quite alive to the necessities of the age. Since our commencement we have been gradually refining the tone of what some people choose to call the dialect, but which is simply the language in which a humble Lancashire operative would speak when endeavouring to express his thoughts and feelings in the most natural and forcible manner. In adopting this course we have only been imitating, in our own humble way, the example set by many writers who have gone before. Neither

Burns, Scott, Ramsay, Dickens, Lover, nor even Tennyson (we could name a host of others) ever thought of putting into the mouths of their humbler characters the language spoken by a Cambridge scholar. They made them speak in their natural language, which may be called either a dialect or English very much broken up and ground down. And yet who dislikes these creations, or finds fault with their creators for their being such? . . .

Our object in making use of the humnbler method of speech has been to get at a stratum of society to which no other class of journal can carry so potent an influence, and by degrees lift our readers out of their present 'barbarism' and lead them to the pursuit of a higher class of literature. When we have succeeded in that we shall have accomplished a greater good than if we had merely entered upon the occupation of a literary yard-dog, or addressed ourselves to the fashionable novel-reading public.

George Milner

INTRODUCTORY ESSAY ON THE DIALECT OF LANCASHIRE CONSIDERED AS A VEHICLE FOR POETRY

From *Poems and Songs* by Edwin Waugh (Manchester, John Heywood, c. 1895).

Milner's essay is a sophisticated late synthesis of previous arguments about the vernacular as an expressive medium, bringing together an antiquarian interest in philology with a strong local pride. Milner's stress on the scholarly and literary respectability of dialect reveals the persistent anxiety of its defence.

In the biographical and critical Introduction prefixed to the first volume of this edition of Waugh's Works, I have briefly alluded to the widely prevalent idea that there is some innate vulgarity in a dialectal word, and also to the equally erroneous impression that the Lancashire dialect is not capable of expressing poetic conceptions with delicacy or force. It may not be thought inappropriate, in connection with the publication of a volume which depends for much of its attraction upon the poetic use of dialect, to consider

366

more fully what is the real nature of folk speech, and how far the particular dialect of Lancashire, for instance, lends itself to the expression of such ideas as are usually associated with the forms of verse.

Of late years, no doubt, some change has taken place in the popular view. Formerly the great majority, both of readers and of critics, were in the habit of regarding all the dialects, except the Scottish, as beneath their attention; literature, to have any influence with them, must be what was called 'polite'; all folk-speech was uncouth and vulgar — a thing to be got rid of, by the aid of the schoolmaster, with as little delay as possible — and even those who ventured, or vouchsafed, as the case might be, to use a dialect, only took it up as an instrument for the production of grotesque effects, or to cloak the poverty, perhaps the grossness, of their ideas. These opinions, however, are no longer held by educated persons. The true nature and importance of dialects having been apprehended, they have become the objects of investigation to many of the ripest scholars of our time. To study philology in a scientific spirit was to be forced back, as a necessity, upon the examination of dialects, because in them were so frequently to be found the very roots and springs of the modern literary language.

Probably most people have not realized how large an element dialectal speech is found to be in the total sum of language. . . .

We may now ask ourselves the question — What is a dialect, and how does it differ from the ordinary current speech? It will be found to consist mainly of such English words as are not of classical origin. Of course, each dialect will not contain the whole of these terms; but a person writing in any one of them would find that he could use nearly all words of Anglo-Saxon derivation without offending against the genius of provincial speech. These words may be thus sub-divided — First, those whose pronunciation does not differ from that which is usual; second, those which are pronounced in an archaic or provincial manner; third, provincial words which are common to most English dialects though differing occasionally in form; fourth, words peculiar to a particular district, and these, contrary to the general impression, will be found to be but few in number; fifth, idioms and phrases, and in these last will probably be discovered, more than elsewhere, the distinction and the Doric flavour of each dialect.

If this be a true statement of the nature of dialects it will be clear that there can be no reason why they should not be used for the purposes of poetry. At least three poets of eminence have indeed so used them — Spenser, Burns, and Tennyson . . . The reason of this is obvious. The truest poetry requires for its expression only the simplest words; and in poetical composition the nearer we are to the roots of the language the safer we are from jarring notes and false associations. For poetry we need a *clear* medium far oftener than we require a *complex* one. . . .

Let us now, however, turn to the particular dialect of Lancashire. Has it, in the first place, a vocabulary adapted for poetical expression? I believe that it has. Look over any list of words which form the Saxon, Scandinavian, or Celtic element in English, and it will be found that there is not one word in a hundred which could not, either with slight change of pronunciation or without it, be naturalized and used in the dialect of Lancashire . . . By some curious and, as yet, only half-defined, but quite natural canon, the poet finds himself rejecting a multitude of words which in prose would be eminently the best. And these are usually the words which are not native to us — words which are foreign and complex in their nature and derivation — the very words, in fact, which a dialect, by a self-imposed law, casts out from itself as being alien to its spirit and purpose. . . .

It will be perceived that I am making large claims for the dialect. I am asking the reader to believe, not only that it offers a fair vehicle for the conveyance of essentially poetical ideas; but that it also actually exerts, in a certain direction, a restraining and purifying influence — compels the poet, in short, to choose, little as he may know it, the preferable word.

Joseph Cronshaw
LOST IN LONDON or
THE DIALECT IN DISTRESS

From *Dingle Cottage — Poems and Sketches* (Manchester, 1908), 147–155.

Joseph Cronshaw was a self-made working man who became a large merchant despite humble beginnings as a barrow boy. He continued to live in the Manchester suburb of Ancoats, and wrote for his own pleasure in local papers and magazines, mostly in dialect. 'Lost in London' is however a standard English poem, which takes the form of a dialogue between a Lancashire author and one of his dialect books, which the author finds on a barrow in London. The following section, in which the book addresses its author, gives an interesting if sentimental account of the unifying force of dialect for a wide range of working class gatherings. Thus the orality and vigour of the dialect are stressed against the imposed Board School English. When reading this poem, it is as well to remember that Cronshaw begins another poem in *Dingle Cottage* with the line 'Am I a poet? I rather think not'.

I remember when you wrote me, with anxious thoughts and fears,
I've heard your merry ringing laugh, and seen your honest tears;
Oh, how your neighbours praised you for your genius and skill —
I remember, too, a jolly row about a printer's bill.

With what rapture I was hailed when first I left the press:
I was quoted, read, recited, oftimes in evening dress;
At bands of hope and festivals I've often taken part,
For juveniles, and elders, too, recited me by heart.

In family circles I was read when nights were dark and long;
What tears of pity I have seen at some pathetic song;
And I have heard their merry laugh at some humorous joke;
Ah, that was up in Lancashire where the dialect was spoke.

But at last came Mr Board School, who said that it was wrong
To read or write, sing or recite, in our own mother tongue;
And teaching in the Board School now was rather circumspect,
And they had made a solemn vow to kill the dialect.

My owner then grew furious; he loved my rural song,
He gloried in the dialect, he loved his mother tongue;
He oft would take and read me when journeying by rail,
While others thought me out of date, and said that I was stale . . .

Suggested Further Reading

The Social History of Artisan Culture

R. D. Altick	*The English Common Reader* (1957)
J. F. C. Harrison	*Learning and Living* (1961)
T. R. Tholfsen	*Working Class Radicalism in Mid-Victorian England* (1976)
D. Vincent	*Bread, Knowledge, and Freedom* (1981)
E. P. Thompson	*The Making of the English Working Class* (1968)
R. K. Webb	*The British Working Class Reader* (1955)
B. E. Maidment	'Magazines of Popular Progress and the Artisans' in *Victorian Periodicals Review* (Fall 1984), 82–94

General Studies of working class literary and cultural achievements, and of early Victorian popular literature

M. Vicinus	*The Industrial Muse* (1974)
Louis James	*Fiction for the Working Man* (1963) Especially Afterword on working class poetry
F. Klingender	*Art and the Industrial Revolution* (1947, revised ed. 1968)
R. Elbourne	*Music and Tradition in Early Industrial Lancashire* (1980)
ed. J. Dyos and M. Wolff	*The Victorian City — Images and Realities* (2 vols., 1973). Especially the essays by M. Vicinus and V. Neuburg

Chartist and Radical Writing

| Y. Kovalev | *An Anthology of Chartist Writing* (Moscow 1956) |

P. M. Ashraf   *An Introduction to Working Class Literature in Great Britain* (East Berlin Part I Poetry 1978 Part 2 Prose 1979)

F. B. Smith   *Radical Artisan* (Manchester 1973)

Parnassian Writing

N. Cross   *The Common Writer* (1985) especially chap. 4
K. Chandler   Unpublished C.N.A.A. M.Phil. thesis on Ebenezer Elliott, Sheffield Polytechnic, 1984
B. E. Maidment   'Essayists and Artisans — the making of Victorian self-taught poets' in *Literature and History*, vol. 9, no. 1 (1983)

Local Bards and Homely Rhymers

B. Hollingworth   *Songs of the People* (Manchester, 1977)
B. E. Maidment   'Poetry in Victorian Manchester' in ed. Kidd and Roberts *City, Class, and Culture* (Manchester) 1985)

Associated Ballad Literature

R. Palmer   *A Touch on the Times* (1974)
R. Colls   *The Collier's Rant* (1977)
J. Raven   *Victoria's Inferno* (1978)

Index of Authors Represented